Princeton University

THE LOUIS CLARK VANUXEM FOUNDATION
LECTURES FOR 1920

THE LOUIS CLARK VANUXEM FOUNDATION
OF PRINCETON UNIVERSITY

was established in 1912 with a bequest of $25,000 under the will of Louis Clark Vanuxem, of the Class of 1879. By direction of the executors of Mr. Vanuxem's estate, the income of the Foundation is to be used for a series of public lectures delivered in Princeton annually, at least one half of which shall be on subjects of current scientific interest. The lectures are to be published and distributed among schools and libraries generally.

The following lectures have been published:

The Theory of Permutable Functions, by Vito Volterra.

Lectures delivered in connection with the dedication of the Graduate College of Princeton University, by Emile Boutroux, Alois Riehl, A. D. Godley, and Arthur Shipley.

Romance, by Sir Walter Raleigh.

A Critique of the Theory of Evolution, by Thomas Hunt Morgan.

Platonism, by Paul Elmer More.

Human Efficiency and Levels of Intelligence, by Henry Herbert Goddard.

The Defective Delinquent and Insane, by Henry A. Cotton.

Louis Clark Vanuxem Foundation

PHILOSOPHY AND CIVILIZATION IN THE MIDDLE AGES

BY

MAURICE DeWULF

Professor of Philosophy in the University of Louvain and in Harvard University; Member of the Academies of Brussels and of Madrid

PRINCETON UNIVERSITY PRESS
PRINCETON
LONDON: HUMPHREY MILFORD
OXFORD UNIVERSITY PRESS
1922

Copyright, 1922
Princeton University Press

Published 1922
Printed in the United States of America

189
W961g

PREFACE

The material of these lectures, which I had the honor of delivering at Princeton University, on the Vanuxem Foundation, was prepared, during the War, at the Universities of Harvard, Poitiers, and Toronto. Certain portions of the work, relatively few, have already appeared in the form of articles, viz.: part of Chapter I in the *Revue de Métaphysique et de Morale,* July, 1918; Chapter IV, ii, in the *Philosophical Review,* July, 1918; Chapter V, iii, in the *International Journal of Ethics,* January, 1919; Chapter III, ii, and Chapter VII, i-v, in the *Harvard Theological Review,* October, 1918. These now take their place as integral parts of what may be regarded as a supplement to my *History of Mediaeval Philosophy.*

The purpose of the study as here presented is to approach the Middle Ages from a new point of view, by showing how the thought of the period, metaphysics included, is intimately connected with the whole round of Western civilization to which it belongs. My work represents simply an attempt to open the way; it makes no pretense to exhaustive treatment of any of the innumerable problems involved in so vast a subject.

I desire to express my cordial thanks to the

friends who have aided me in translating these lectures, in particular to Mr. Daniel Sargent, of Harvard University. And it is a special duty and pleasure to acknowledge my obligations to Professor Horace C. Longwell, of Princeton University, who has offered many valuable suggestions while assisting in the revision of the manuscript and in the task of seeing the work through the press.

Harvard University
   January, 1922

ANALYTICAL TABLE OF CONTENTS

PREFACE

CHAPTER ONE

INTRODUCTION

i. Relational aspects of philosophy in the Middle Ages. ii. Methods. iii. The importance of the twelfth century and of the thirteenth century in mediaeval civilization. iv. Survey of these centuries.

CHAPTER TWO

SURVEY OF CIVILIZATION IN THE TWELFTH CENTURY

i. Feudal Europe. ii. Catholic influences: Cluny, Citeaux, the bishops, the Pope. iii. A new spirit: the value and dignity of the individual man. iv. New forms of art. v. The twelfth century one of French influences.

CHAPTER THREE

THE CIVILIZATION AS REFLECTED IN PHILOSOPHY

i. Location of philosophical schools; invasion of French schools by foreigners. ii. Delimitation of the several sciences; philosophy distinct from the seven liberal arts and from theology. iii. Harmony of the feudal sense of personal worth with the philosophical doctrine that the individual alone exists. iv. The feudal civilization and the anti-realistic solution of the problem of universals.

CHAPTER FOUR

THE GREAT AWAKENING OF PHILOSOPHY IN THE THIRTEENTH CENTURY

i. The causes: The acquired momentum. ii. The rise of the Universities (Paris and Oxford). iii. The establishment of the mendicant orders (Dominicans and Franciscans). iv. The acquaintance with new philosophical works; translations. v. General result: among the numerous systems the scholastic philosophy issues as dominant. vi. The comprehensive classification of knowledge.

CONTENTS

CHAPTER FIVE
UNIFYING AND COSMOPOLITAN TENDENCIES
i. Need of universality; the "law of parsimony." ii. Excess resulting from the felt need of simplifying without limit; the geocentric system and the anthropocentric conception. iii. The society of mankind (*"universitas humana"*) in its theoretical and practical forms. iv. Cosmopolitan tendencies.

CHAPTER SIX
OPTIMISM AND IMPERSONALITY
i. Optimism in philosophy, in art, in religion. ii. Impersonality. iii. History of philosophy and literary attribution. iv. Perenniality.

CHAPTER SEVEN
SCHOLASTIC PHILOSOPHY AND THE RELIGIOUS SPIRIT
i. Common definition of scholastic philosophy as a religious philosophy. ii. Reflective analysis of the distinction between philosophy and theology. iii. The religious spirit of the epoch. iv. Connections of philosophy with religion not affecting the integrity of the former. v. Subordination of philosophy to Catholic theology in the light of this analysis. vi. Solution and adjustment of the problem. vii. Influences of philosophy in other fields. Conclusion.

CHAPTER EIGHT
INTELLECTUALISM
i. Intellectualism in ideology. ii. In epistemology. iii. In Psychology (free volition). iv. More generally (psychology, logic, metaphysics, ethics, aesthetics). v. In other forms of culture.

CHAPTER NINE
A PLURALISTIC CONCEPTION OF THE WORLD
i. What metaphysics is. ii. Static aspects of reality. iii. Dynamic aspects; the central doctrine of act and potency. iv. Application to substance and accident; to matter and form. v. The problem of individuation. vi. Human personality. vii. God: as pure existence.

CONTENTS ix

CHAPTER TEN
INDIVIDUALISM AND SOCIAL PHILOSOPHY

i. Social theory the last addition to scholastic philosophy. ii. Fundamental principle: the group exists for its members, and not conversely. iii. Ethical foundation of this principle. iv. The idea of the group in the teaching of canonists and jurists. v. Metaphysical basis: the group not an entity outside of its members. vi. Comparison of the group with the human body. vii. Conclusion.

CHAPTER ELEVEN
THE THEORY OF THE STATE

i. Sovereignty from God. ii. It is a function; morality of governors not different from that of the governed; what the function implies. iii. Sovereignty resides in the people who delegate it. iv. The best form of government according to the philosophy of Thomas Aquinas. v. Making of laws the essential attribute of sovereignty: natural law and human law. vi. This form of government compared with the European states of the thirteenth century; with the modern nationalities; with the theories of preceding centuries.

CHAPTER TWELVE
THE CONCEPTION OF HUMAN PROGRESS

i. The constant and the permanent. ii. Progress in science, in morals, in social and political justice, in civilization.

CHAPTER THIRTEEN
PHILOSOPHY AND NATIONAL TEMPERAMENT IN THE THIRTEENTH CENTURY

i. Scholastic philosophy reflected in the temperament of the peoples who created it. ii. Three main doctrines: the value of the individual; intellectualism; moderation. iii. Scholastic philosophy the product of Neo-Latin and Anglo-Celtic minds; Germanic contribution virtually negligible. iv. Latin Averroism in the thirteenth century. v. The lure of Neo-Platonism to the German. vi. The chief doctrines opposed to the scholastic tendencies: lack of clearness; inclination to pantheism; deductive method à outrance; absence of moderation.

CHAPTER FOURTEEN

EPILOGUE
　i. Influence of thirteenth century philosophical systems on later thought in the West. ii. Pedagogical value of scholasticism for the history of modern philosophy.

SELECTED BIBLIOGRAPHY

INDEX OF NAMES

PHILOSOPHY AND CIVILIZATION IN THE MIDDLE AGES

CHAPTER ONE

INTRODUCTION

i. Relational aspects of philosophy in the Middle Ages. ii. Methods. iii. The importance of the twelfth century and of the thirteenth century in mediaeval civilization. iv. Survey of these centuries.

I

The study of mediaeval philosophy has undergone considerable change in recent years, and the developments in this field of research have been important. On all sides the soil has been turned, and just as in archaeological excavation, as at Pompei or at Timgad, here too discoveries unexpectedly rich are rewarding our search. For such men as John Scotus Eriugena, Anselm of Canterbury, Abaelard, Hugo of St. Victor, John of Salisbury, Alexander of Hales, Bonaventure, Albert the Great, Thomas Aquinas, Duns Scotus, Siger of Brabant, Thierry of Freiburg, Roger Bacon, William of Occam,—these are truly thinkers of the first order, and their labours are worthy of the notable studies now increasingly made of them.

There is, further, a host of other philosophers whose thought has been unveiled, and whose significance will become the more clear as historical research progresses.

The study of mediaeval philosophy, however, has heretofore contented itself chiefly with establishing actual doctrines, and with indicating their development or the connection between one philosopher and another, while little attention has been given to the historical setting of these doctrines in the mediaeval civilization itself. But in the throbbing vitality of a civilization there is an interdependence of the numerous and complex elements constituting it; such, for example, are the economic well-being, the family and social institutions, the political and juridical systems, the moral and religious and aesthetic aspirations, the scientific and philosophical conceptions, the feeling for progress in human development. The interdependence of these various momenta is perhaps more readily apparent in the realms of economics and politics and art, but it is to be found also in the operation of the intellectual and moral factors.

It might seem at first sight that philosophy would enjoy a certain immunity from the vicissitudes of temporal change, because of the problems with which it deals; but closer view reveals that it too is caught inevitably within the meshes of the temporal net. For the work of Plato or of Aristotle, this is admitted as a commonplace by the historians of philosophy; the thought of these philosophers reflects the conditions of the Athenian society of their day. Similarly, no one pretends to arrive at a proper understanding of such thinkers as Francis Bacon and Hobbes except in the light of the political and economic and the broadly cultural conditions of their age. Just so in our study of mediaeval philosophy, we may not properly consider Anselm, or Thomas Aquinas, or William of Occam as men whose thoughts float free without anchorage. They too are the sons of their age. Nay more, there is a certain philosophical atmosphere which is created by the collective thought of numerous thinkers; and this is subject to influences issuing from the spirit of the age, in its economic, political, social, moral, religious and artistic aspects. Moreover, while philosophical thought is thus affected from without, it also exerts its own influence in turn upon the general culture with which it is organically connected.

For the thought of the Middle Ages the time has come when we must take account of this mutual dependence. Indeed we may even regard with advantage the example of natural history, whose museums no longer exhibit their specimens as so many lifeless objects in a bare cage,—on the contrary, they are represented as if they were still alive in their native jungle.

The point of view, therefore, which we choose for our treatment in these lectures, is that of the relational aspects in mediaeval philosophy—a study which relates the philosophy to the other factors in that civilization taken as an organic whole. We shall be concerned therefore less with isolated personalities than with the general philosophical mind of the age, its way of conceiving life and reality.

II

Before indicating the chronological limits and the general outline of our study, it is of paramount importance to examine a question of method which confronts us at the outset, the right solution of which is of great consequence:—Just how may we *understand* the mediaeval civilization in order to *judge* it aright?

To *understand* the mediaeval civilization,—to penetrate into its very spirit—we must first of all avoid forcing parallels with the mentality and customs of our own age. Many a study has been marred because its author was unable to resist this temptation. Mediaeval civilization is not the same as that of our own age. Its factors have a different meaning; they were made for men of a different age. Charlemagne's famous sword can now be wielded only with great difficulty, and the heavy armor of the iron-mailed knights no longer suits the needs of our twentieth century soldiers. Nor is it otherwise with the mediaeval civilization considered as a whole; it is not fitted to our own conditions.

Further, in order to understand the Middle Ages, we must think directly after their manner of thinking. When a beginner commences the study of a foreign language, he is invariably advised to think directly in that language, instead of painfully translating words and phrases from his native tongue. Just so a right study of the civilization of the Middle Ages must take it in and for itself, in its internal elements and structure; it must be understood from within. To this end each factor must be separately considered and defined,—in itself and also with due regard to the particular significance attaching to it at any given epoch.

Furthermore, the several factors that make up a civilization should be collectively examined and viewed as a coherent whole; for only so is its unique harmony revealed. Such a harmony varies from one period to another. Therefore, we should violate the most elementary principles of historical criticism, if we were to predicate of the fifteenth century truths which apply only to the twelfth and the thirteenth centuries; or to attribute to formative periods such as the tenth and the eleventh centuries what is evidenced only in the central period of the Middle Ages.

If the above principles of internal criticism are necessary in discerning the spirit of mediaeval civilization, they are no less indispensable for arriving at a *just estimate* of that spirit. While this civilization is different from our own, it is not to be judged as either worse or better. To determine its worth we must not compare its institutions with those of to-day. It is positively distressing to see historians, under the spell of special sympathies, proclaim the thirteenth century the best of all centuries of human history and prefer its institutions to our own. Such *laudatores temporis acti* really injure the cause which they intend to serve. But it is equally distressing to see others, more numerous, decry thirteenth century civilization, and strenuously declaim against the imprudent dreamer who would carry certain of its ideas and customs into our modern world. To go back to the Middle Ages is out of the question; retrogression is impossible, for the past will ever be the past. To prefer to our railways, for instance, the long and perilous horseback rides of that age is of course absurd; but in the same way, to depreciate the Middle Ages by contrasting them at all with our modern ways of living, thinking, or feeling seems to me meaningless.

This would be tantamount to reviving the errors of the Renaissance, which was infatuated with its own world and disdained everything mediaeval.[1] This error has been strangely persistent, and it merits examination because of the lessons entailed. Disdain for the past begot ignorance, ignorance begot injustice, injustice begot prejudice. Being unable or unwilling to go back to thirteenth century

---

[1] The very name "*Middle* Ages" was disparaging; it implied an intermediary stage, parenthetical, with no value saving that of connection between antiquity and modern times.

documents, the critics of the fifteenth and sixteenth centuries judged the whole period by reference to late and decadent scholasticism; the golden age was thus involved in the condemnation deserved only by the age of decadence. The historians of the eighteenth century, and of the beginning of the nineteenth century, inherited the estimate thus erroneously made by the men of the Renaissance and the Reformation; they accepted it uncritically and passed on the error unchanged. That, in brief, is the story of the perpetuation of the reproach attaching to the Middle Ages.[2]

A singular instance of the loss involved in thus failing to appreciate the merits of the past is the contempt which was professed for the "Gothic" architecture,—both because of its mediaeval origin and because the term came to be synonymous with "barbaric." One can understand, to be sure, how through ignorance or routine or education cultured minds in the Renaissance period might refuse to open dusty manuscripts and bulky folios; their preference for humanistic works,—such as those of Vives or of Agricola or of Nizolius or of others even more superficial—to the dry subtleties of the contemporary "terminists" is perfectly intelligible. But it is inconceivable to us how the great cathedrals of Paris, Rheims, Amiens, Chartres, Cologne, and Strasbourg failed to find favor with men of cultivated taste, and how they could have been in-

[2] *Cf.* my *Histoire de la Philosophie Médiévale*, Louvain, 1912, p. 106.

cluded in the general condemnation of things mediaeval. For, those wonders in stone were not hidden in the recesses of library cases. On the contrary, they raised high above the cities their spires, their arches, their silhouettes,—and, indeed, as an heroic protest against the injustice of men. That a revival of Greek architecture might have aroused enthusiasm is easily intelligible; but it is hard to understand how Montesquieu, Fénelon, Goethe, who passed daily such Gothic cathedrals, could turn away from them and speak of them disparagingly and even refuse to cross their thresholds,—being, as they said, the remnants of a decadent age. Goethe's confession on this point is significant indeed. He tells us how at the beginning of his stay at Strasbourg, he was wont to pass the cathedral with indifference; but one day he entered, and as he did so his eyes were fascinated with a beauty which he had not before seen; thereafter, not only did he give up his prejudices against Gothic art, but he became enamoured of the beautiful cathedral that raises its red-brown spires above the plains of Alsace. "Educated among the detractors of Gothic architecture," he writes, "I nourished my antipathy against these overloaded, complicated ornaments, which gave the effect of gloomy religion by their very oddity. . . . But here I seemed suddenly to see a new revelation; what had been objectionable appeared admirable, and the reverse,—the perception of beauty in all its attractiveness, was impressed on my soul."³

The discredit in which mediaeval art was held has now definitely yielded to a more just estimate. Romanesque and Gothic architecture are now universally acknowledged to be things of beauty in and for themselves; certainly, in any case, without reference to the architecture of the twentieth century. Again, we acknowledge the merit of Giotto's frescoes, of the translucent stained glass of Chartres, without estimating them by modern standards of painting.

Similarly, no one today would commit himself to the prejudice, also not so old, that before Rousseau nature was not understood and that the thirteenth century was ignorant of its beauty. All of those who are familiar with the sculpture of the cathedrals and with illuminated manuscripts, or who have read the *Divine Comedy* of Dante and the poems of St. Francis, know how unjust that reproach is; and they never compare the thirteenth century interpretation of nature with that of our modern writers.

This marked contrast, between our appreciation of mediaeval art and the condemnation of it in the sixteenth and seventeenth centuries, indicates the canons to which we should adhere in reaching a just judgment of the past. Plainly, in order to understand the value of things mediaeval, we must have

³ Goethe, *Dichtung und Wahrheit*, Buch IX, Teil 2.

recourse to a standard other than that set by the conditions of our own time. For, what is true of art is also true of all other factors in a civilization.

If, then, we are to estimate aright the civilization of the thirteenth century, we must refer it to a fixed norm: *the dignity and the worth of human nature.* This will be readily granted by all who believe that human nature remains essentially the same, in spite of historical changes; and of course this was the common mediaeval doctrine.[4] By this standard a civilization stands high when it achieves its own intense and coordinated expression of the essential aspirations of the individual and the collective life; when it realizes, in addition, an adequate degree of material welfare; when it rests also on a rational organization of the family, the state, and other groups; when it allows, further, for full development in philosophy, science and art; and when its morality and its religion foster their ideals on a basis of noble sentiments and refined emotions. In this sense the civilization of the thirteenth century must be counted among those that have succeeded in attaining to a high degree of perfection; for, certain unique functions and aspirations of humanity are therein revealed, and indeed in rare and striking form. Hence it furnishes us with documents of the first importance for our understanding of humanity; and for this reason it may instruct our present generation as it surely can all

[4] See ch. XII, i.

those to come. *Homo sum, nil humani a me alienum puto.*

From this point of view, and from this alone, may we properly call good or bad—let us not say better or worse—certain elements in our heritage from the Middle Ages. The praise or the blame which may be given to things mediaeval in these lectures will not proceed from a comparison of mediaeval conditions *with those of our own age,* but rather by reference to their harmony, or lack of it, with the *essential nobility of human nature.* We may speak then of things good and beautiful achieved by the Middle Ages; for they are human realities, even though they are enveloped within the historical past. The *Fioretti* of St. Francis, the *Divine Comedy* of Dante, the cathedrals, the feudal virtues, these are all sparks of the human soul, *scintillae animae,* whose lustre cannot be obscured; they have their message for all of humanity. And if certain doctrines in scholastic philosophy have maintained their value, as have certain doctrines of Plato, Aristotle, Augustine, Descartes, Leibnitz, and others, this must be because they have a deeply human meaning which remains everlastingly true.

Within these limits it would be neither proper nor possible to abstain from praise and criticism. For, the historian is no mere registering machine, unmoved by love and hatred. On the contrary, he cannot be indifferent to good and evil, to progress and decline, to lofty aspirations and social evils;

therefore, he cannot refrain from approving and condemning.

III

This method of historical reconstruction and appreciation is especially necessary in studying the twelfth and the thirteenth centuries,—perhaps more so than for any other mediaeval period. To this period, as the very heart of the Middle Ages, we shall limit our study, and for certain reasons which we may now consider.

First of all, this is the period when mediaeval civilization assumes definite form, with outlines and features that characterize a unique age in the life of humanity.

Before the end of the eleventh century, the mediaeval temperament is not yet formed; it is only in process of elaboration. The new races, Celts and Teutons[5] (the Teutons including more especially Angles, Danes, Saxons, Francs, Germans, and Normans) had passively received something of the culture of the Graeco-Roman world, certain elements of organization, juridical and political, and some fragmentary scientific and philosophical ideas. During the ninth, tenth, and eleventh centuries, these new races react upon what they have received and subject everything to an elaboration of their own. They apply themselves to it, with their vir-

[5] The terms Teuton and German are sometimes employed in the inverse sense; but I prefer the usage above indicated.

tues and their defects; and the outcome begets the
new order of things. Christianity directs the whole
work,—and it is not a light task to soften the rough
mentality of the barbarians. The work is nearly
completed at the dawn of the twelfth century, and
the period of groping is over. Thus there are
three factors in the process of forming the mediaeval civilization: the heritage from the ancient
world, the reactive response of the new races, and
the directing guidance of Christianity.

With the twelfth century the results of this long
and gradual process of formation begin to appear.
This is the springtime period. And just as the
springtime of nature excludes no plant from her
call to life, so the springtime of civilization buds
forth in every branch of human activity; political,
economic, family and social regime, morals, religion, fine arts, sciences, philosophy,—all of those
sublime emanations of the human soul which form
a civilization, and determine its progress, now reveal their abounding vitality and burst forth in
bloom. Of these factors, the political organization
ripens first, very naturally, while philosophy comes
to its maturity the last of all. The former is, as it
were, the body; the latter belongs to the complex psychic life. And since civilization is essentially the expression of psychic forces, the real
mediaeval man must be sought for in his religious
feelings, his moral aspirations, his artistic work,
his philosophical and scientific activities.

With the thirteenth century we reach definitely the climax of the development,—that is, the period of maturity. At this stage the total complex of the mediaeval civilization reveals its striking and compelling features.

A second reason exists for concentrating our attention upon the twelfth and thirteenth centuries. These are also the centuries in which the philosophical temperament of the Occident is definitely formed.

All historians agree in ascribing to the French genius the leadership of the world during this period. It was in France that the feudal mind was formed. A moral, artistic, and religious tradition began to appear on the soil of French provinces. Chivalry, feudalism, the Benedictine organization, monastic and religious reforms, Romanesque and Gothic art are just so many products born of the French temperament; and these spread throughout the whole western world by virtue of the current travel and trade, the Crusades and the migrations of religious orders. From France the ideas of the new civilization spread over the neighboring countries, like sparks from a blazing fire. The twelfth and the thirteenth centuries were centuries of French thought; and this leadership of France was retained until the Hundred Years War. Naturally, therefore, the same leadership was maintained in the field of philosophy, as we shall see.

Moreover, the thirteenth century is the period

when both the Neo-Latin and the Anglo-Celtic minds distinguished themselves clearly from the Germanic type. If one seeks the origin of the difference in mentality found in the nations of the West, one is forced inevitably back to the thirteenth century. This century witnessed the formation of the great European nations, the dawn of a more definite conception of *patria,* the decisive outlining of the ethnical features of the peoples who were henceforth to fill history with their alliances and rivalries. The thirteenth century is characterized by unifying and cosmopolitan tendencies; but, at the same time, it constitutes a great plateau whence are beginning to issue the various channels which will later run as mighty rivers in different and even opposite directions. Many peculiarities in the mediaeval way of conceiving individual and social life and many of their philosophical conceptions of the world have entered into the modern views; and, indeed, many doctrines which are now opposed to each other can be traced to their origin in the thirteenth century.

IV

We may now outline broadly the plan of these lectures. From the general point of view, the twelfth century is perhaps of more decisive importance. But from the philosophical standpoint the thirteenth century is supreme, and therefore it will demand more of our time and attention. This difference is due to the fact that civilization always develops more rapidly than philosophy, the latter being a tender fruit which thrives tardily and only when the general growth has been attained.

The twelfth century is a creative and constructive era, and the development of thought and of life is extraordinarily rapid in all directions. All the forces are in ebullition, as in a crucible. The heritage from the Graeco-Roman world, the reaction of the new races, the direction of Christianity: these three factors in the making of mediaeval civilization are now in process of compounding, and the result is a conception of life, individual and social, which is *sui generis*. A new spirit pervades the policy of kings. The particularism of the local lords comes into diverse conflict with the aspirations of the central power, whilst the rural classes welcome the dawn of liberty and the townsfolk awake to the possibilities of vast commercial enterprises. Men are seeking governmental forms in which all classes of society can find their place and play their part. The Crusades, once begun, recur at brief intervals and bring the various peoples together and direct their attention to the Orient; at the same time they foster in a manner hitherto unparalleled the ideal of a great human brotherhood, resting upon the Christian religion. The Church pervades all circles, through her monks, her clerics, her bishops. The Papacy, which has been central since the days of Gregory VII, assumes international significance and gradually organizes itself into a theocratic government. The customs of feudalism and of chivalry arise, as characteristic of the age. The early mediaeval man is developing; he may go to excess in his virtues and his vices, but beneath his rough exterior he cherishes a Christian ideal, and often at the cost of his life. A new form of art arises which finds its most ardent promoters in Churchmen. Other Churchmen give themselves to the cultivation of science and letters, and thus are laid the foundations of that imposing philosophical monument, scholasticism, which is to guide and direct the thought of centuries. Thus philosophy is only one of the elements in this new civilization. In reality it receives more than it gives. Some of the influences which operated upon it from the surrounding environment we shall outline in due time.[6] But first we shall make a rapid survey of French mediaeval society and of the type of mentality which passed over from it to the intellectual circles of the West.[7] Concluding the present chapter, let us consider briefly the thirteenth century.

In the thirteenth century mediaeval civilization brings forth its full fruit. The feudal monarchy receives into its organic being all those social forces which make for national life. Material welfare increases and the relations between nations grow apace. Art speeds on its triumphal way. Gothic

[6] See ch. III.
[7] See ch. II.

architecture springs up beside the Romanesque; painting comes into existence; and literature begins to take wing in a flight which issues in Humanism. Religion contributes more than ever to unity; it enters into all the sentiments and the life of the age. The Papacy reaches the apex of its power; and, supreme over kings and emperors, it dominates every aspect of social activity. Everywhere a sort of stable equilibrium prevails. Men are proud of the way in which they have organized human existence. Philosophical ideas and systems appear in abundance, exhibiting a luxuriance unequalled since the Hellenistic age.[8] Among these numerous systems scholasticism is most in harmony with the age, and as its completest expression becomes the reigning philosophy. Its roots are to be found everywhere in the civilization of the thirteenth century. First, because it exhibits those relational aspects which unite it with all the other spheres of activity.[9] Second, because many of its doctrines bear the stamp of characteristically mediaeval ideas, both social and moral.[10] Third, because scholasticism is above all, the philosophy of those people who are at the head of the cultural movement in the thirteenth century.[11] In what follows we shall endeavour to substantiate these statements.

[8] See ch. IV.
[9] See chs. V-VII.
[10] See chs. VIII-XII.
[11] See ch. XIII.

CHAPTER TWO

SURVEY OF CIVILIZATION IN THE TWELFTH CENTURY

i. Feudal Europe. ii. Catholic influences: Cluny, Cîteaux, the bishops, the Pope. iii. A new spirit: the value and dignity of the individual man. iv. New forms of art. v. The twelfth century one of French influences.

I

To understand how the civilization of the twelfth century is reflected in its philosophy, we must view in a general way the elements of that civilization which are most intimately connected with intellectual life,—namely, political institutions, moral and social ideals, standards of art, and religious beliefs.

These several elements operate in various ways in the different countries of Europe; but in our general survey we shall consider rather the resemblances, without meaning thereby to deny or to belittle the differences. Since it is in France that this civilization produces its choicest fruits, it is there especially that we must seek its most original and coherent forms.

In the political and social orders feudalism had become general. Barons, dukes, earls, and lords lived independently in their own castles and usurped more or less of the sovereign right. Not only did relations of personal loyalty exist between them, but obligations founded upon a free contract bound one man to another, according to some privilege or some land given and received. The one, the vassal, was bound to render service; the other, the lord, was equally bound to protect and defend.

In France, where the new organization appears in its purest form, nothing is more complicated than the scheme of feudalistic relations. At the head, theoretically, but not always practically, stood the king. The greatest lords were vassals of other lords. Were not the feudal relations of Henry II of England and Louis VII of France the starting point for all their wars and quarrels? For, the first became the vassal of the second on the very day he married Eleanor of Aquitaine, whose duchy was granted by the French king to the English monarch. The particular and local lords were forced to fight against the centralizing tendencies of the kings, and the antagonism of the vassals and the king, their suzerain, was the main feature of French policy in the twelfth century.[1] Particularism remained, but it was on the decline, and the following century witnessed the triumph of the centralizing principle.

A similar development occurred in England.

[1] A. Luchaire, "Louis VII, Philippe Auguste, Louis VIII," *Histoire de France*, pub. par Lavisse, 1902, vol. III.

For, that country was so closely connected with France that their combined territories may be called the common soil of the mediaeval civilization. English society, as a whole, had its origin in French soil; at any rate, the seeds were planted in 1066 by William the Conqueror and his French barons, Kings of French blood, who came from Normandy and from Anjou, ruled over the British Isles; but much of their time was spent in their French provinces. French was the court-language; they made provision for burial in the Norman abbey of Caen or the Angevine abbey of Fontevrault; they drew their counsellors from France and favoured the establishment of French clergy and French monks in England. The English King Henry II, the first of the Plantagenet dynasty, was one of the most thorough-going organizers of the age; indeed one might well take him for a contemporary of Philip the Fair of France.[2] Is it then surprising that we find England too being divided into feudal domains, and the royal policy exhibiting the same centralizing tendency?

But while monarchy and feudalism were so closely akin in France and in England, they presented quite a different aspect in Germany. The reason was that at the very time when the king's power was weakening in France, the Saxon dynasty of the Ottos had established in Germany an autocratic

[2] A. Luchaire, *op. cit.*, p. 49. Henry II, 1133-1189; Philip the Fair, 1269-1314.

régime, patterned after that of Charlemagne. The German kings, who had been crowned Emperors of the West, held the nobles in a sort of military servitude; they appointed bishops and abbots and bound them to military service. However, little by little, the principalities asserted their rights; the fast developing towns gained more freedom. We shall see[3] how the monks of Cluny contributed to this change. Thus, by a process of decentralization, Germany gradually assumed in the twelfth century a more feudal aspect, while France and England were developing toward centralization.

During the eleventh and twelfth centuries, the destiny of Italy is intimately connected with that of Germany. The reason for this was that the German imperial ambitions involved the seizure of Italy, a great country which was also divided into various principalities. The emperors were successful for a time; but much opposition developed. Hence their long struggle against the Lombard cities, which were true municipal republics; against the Papacy, which was to triumph finally; against the great southern realm of the Sicilies, which had been founded by Norman knights and was a centre of French feudal ideas, being governed by French princes.

As for Spain, situated as it was on the confines of the western and the Arabian civilizations, it presents a unique aspect. The Christian kingdoms of

[3] See ch. II, ii.

Castille, of Leon, of Navarre, of Aragon, had undertaken to "reconquer" the Peninsula from the Mussulman, and they were organized on French feudal principles. On the other hand, the South remained in the hands of the Infidels, and the infiltration of Arabian civilization was to have its part in the philosophical awakening of the thirteenth century, as we shall see.[4]

Hence, when we consider the outstanding features of the political and social situation, feudal divisions are found everywhere. France, which seems to be the starting point for the system, England after the Conquest, some parts of Italy and of Spain, and also Germany—the whole of western Europe, in fact, presents the appearance of a checkerboard.

II

The Catholic Church was intimately connected with this feudal system, through her bishops, who were lords both temporal and spiritual, and more especially through the abbots of her monasteries. The twelfth century is the golden age of the abbeys. In no period of history has any institution had a closer contact with both religious and social background than had the abbeys of Cluny and Citeaux. These were the two great branches of the Benedictine stem, the two mother-houses whose daughters were scattered throughout France and Europe.

[4] See ch. IV, iv.

The ninth century had witnessed a disastrous relaxation of religious discipline, and it was Cluny which first returned to the faithful observance of the rule of St. Benedict. The monastery was founded in Burgundy in 910 by a feudal lord, Duke William of Aquitaine. And just here we meet with a peculiar phenomenon, which shows how the religious spirit had become the great moral force of that period. "The abbeys built in the ninth and the tenth centuries," says Reynaud,[5] "to restore the ancient rule of St. Benedict, were all, or nearly all, the work of the military class." After a life of adventure and war, or after a stormy youth, these proud feudal lords often shut themselves up in cloisters, to do penance. They renounced the world, and henceforth their austerities were performed with the same ardour which they had formerly exhibited in their exploits of war. Thus, Poppo of Stavelot was affianced to a wealthy heiress, when one evening, on his way home after visiting her, a bright light suddenly shone about him; whereupon he was terrified, and in remorse for his past life he donned the Benedictine cowl. Examples of such conversions are numerous.

The monks of Cluny not only instilled a new religious zeal within their own cloister, not only did they restore discipline and vows and piety, not only did they sustain and augment the fervid faith of the

[5] L. Reynaud, *Les origines de l'influence française en Allemagne*, Paris, 1913, p. 43.

people depending on them; they also awakened the same spirit in a great many other monasteries. This was effected through a far reaching reform: *the federation of monasteries.* For, up to that time, the Benedictine monasteries had been independent. But Cluny organized these groups and placed itself at the head of a strongly centralized régime. It became a mother-house whose daughters spread rapidly abroad throughout all France and England and Germany and Northern Spain and Hungary and Poland. At the beginning of the twelfth century, two thousand Benedictine houses were dependent on the Cluny system; and today dozens of French villages still bear the name of St. Benedict, in memory of one or another of those Benedictine monasteries. All western Christendom was enmeshed in a great network of monastic institutions, of which Cluny was the soul and the inspiration; and thus one mind and one polity permeated the whole system.

In this process of federalization the abbey of Cluny was successfully modelled after the feudal system; but it then in turn proceeded to impregnate that same feudalism with its own spirit. Thus, the feudal conception appears in the vow of devotion which attached a monk to his monastery as a vassal to his lord, and which he might not break without his superior's consent; in the sovereignty of the abbot; in his visits as chief to his subordinates; in the contributions of the affiliated monasteries to the mother-house; and in the graded series of federated groups. But, by its far reaching influence, so mighty a power could successfully combat the forces of evil in contemporary society, and it could also turn current ideas to the service of Christianity. Cluny christianized feudalism. This influence is revealed to us in four main aspects, which we shall now consider.

First, the monks treated their serfs with justice and kindness; those fellow human beings who were born on their land and who worked with them in forest and field. And this was done at a time when the lay barons considered their serfs as slaves and mere instruments. "We exercise the same authority as the seigneurs," writes Peter the Venerable, abbot of Cluny at the beginning of the twelfth century, "but we make a different use of it. . . . Our serfs are regarded as brothers and sisters. *Servos et ancillas, non ut servos et ancillas, sed ut fratres et sorores habent."*[6]

Second, and most important, the monks introduced Christian ideals into the minds of feudal barons. By the sublime morality of Christ, compounded of gentleness and love, they tempered all that was brutal in the ways of those developing Gallo-Franks and Anglo-Celts, whose blood was eager for war and for combat and for cruelty. Cluny imposed on them the *Peace and Truce of God,* wherein we find something of those rights of

[6] *Epist.* 28, Migne, Patr. lat. vol. 189, col. 146.

humanity that exist for all time. Once the *Truce of God* is established, so runs the enactment, all clerks, peasants, merchants, and non-combatants in general, shall be entitled to relief from the violence of the warriors. Even animals must be respected. Religious edifices and public buildings are to be safeguarded. Furthermore, hostilities shall be suspended between Wednesday evening and Monday morning during all of Advent and Lent and the Emberdays, as well as on all principal holidays. When any community of human beings exhibits consciousness of such duties, it has already emerged from barbarism; and, whatever its structure in detail may be, it must be counted among those societies of mankind that are destined to a high civilization.

Moreover, in the third place, Cluny moulded the moral sense of chivalry, transformed its ideals, and introduced religion into its ceremonies. Once the knight came in contact with Christian morality, he was no longer an egotistic, ambitious, and brutal warrior; he learned to be loyal and generous; he became the born-defender of the Church, the champion of the weak, the opponent of violence. Whenever conferences were called to discuss peace, the monks urged charity and forgiveness upon the nobles, who frequently repented in tears; or, indeed, the very men who had pillaged on the previous day would forthwith set out on long pilgrimages to St. James of Compostella or to Rome or to Jerusalem, to expiate their crimes. And so the monks of Cluny galvanized into life the nascent virtues of the race. The word "Frank," originally the name of a people inhabiting Gaul, came to be synonymous with "loyal."[7] It is under this aspect that chivalry is represented in the numerous twelfth century romances, in the *Chansons de Geste* of which the *Chanson de Roland* furnishes the most beautiful example. The union of the martial spirit with the religious, and the alliance between feudal system and Church became indissoluble. When the time came to preach the Crusades, Cluny could call with confidence upon the nobles to carry their arms into the Holy Land. The First Crusade was in fact a strictly Cluniac enterprise, and Pope Urban II, who proclaimed it at the famous council of Clermont, had been himself a monk of Cluny. And where, indeed, does the influence of the monastic ideal, as a social force, appear more clearly than in those epics of audacity, those distant journeys on which so many young nobles lost their lives?

But the abbots of Cluny performed a fourth social service; they undertook the reform of the secular clergy, both priests and bishops. They condemned the scandalous abuses of married bishops, who lived like feudal barons, wholly given over to feasting and war. They also worked to free the bishops from the patronage of the great feudal

[7] Reynaud, *op. cit.*, p. 339.

lords, who sold the episcopal offices, and they proclaimed aloud that the bishops ought to be elected by the people and by the clerics,—in the famous investiture strife. The abuse, however, exercised its most baneful influence in Germany, where the dukes and abbots and bishops were, as we have seen, mere creatures of the Emperor.[8] Moreover, the Pope himself had served as a German functionary ever since Otto I had conquered Italy and placed upon his own head the crown of Charlemagne. It was the great abbey of Cluny which altered this state of affairs. It was Cluny that by one of its daughter-houses, the abbey of Hirschau in the Black Forest, introduced the ideas of the French feudal system along with its monastic reform. The French influence of Cluny not only softened the barbaric habits of the German feudal lords, but it also put an end to that dangerous privilege of naming the Pope, which the German Emperors had appropriated to their own advantage; and thus it delivered the Papacy from that humiliating yoke. The famous Hildebrand had been formerly a monk of Cluny; and, as Pope Gregory VII, he waged the famous investiture strife against the Emperor, Henry IV. This duel issued in the defeat of the Emperor at Canossa. In that dramatic scene, which concluded the struggle, were symbolized with early mediaeval harshness the humiliation of the Emperor and the triumph of the Cluniac ideas.

[8] See above, p. 22.

Henry IV was forced to cross, in midwinter and without escort, the snow covered Alps, and for three days to await audience with the Pope. Hugh, the abbot of Cluny, was witness of the Emperor's humiliation. For the first time, French ideas had triumphed over the power of Germany,[9] and these French ideas were the ideas of Cluny. It was because of such widespread and profound influence, exercised on the mentality of the Middle Ages by the celebrated monastery, that in 1910, at the millennial congress which reunited at Cluny learned men from everywhere, one of them could say, "We are come to Cluny to sing a hymn to civilization."[10]

But the very prosperity of Cluny, especially with its extraordinary wealth, became one of the chief causes of its declining influence. At the beginning of the twelfth century its monastic life had become more lax, and henceforth its influence as a social force waned.

But, after the order of Cluny had performed its great service, there was established another Benedictine congregation, which renewed that famous rule: the order of Citeaux in Burgundy, which immediately spread throughout all France, and Europe generally, in the twelfth century. This new order, commonly called Cistercian, was also a federation of Benedictine houses, although each of them was more independent than was the case in the

[9] *Cf.* Lamprecht, *Deutsche Geschichte,* III, pp. 192 and 193.
[10] *Millenaire de Cluny,* Academie de Mâcon, 1910, vol. XV, p. lxxiv.

system of Cluny. The congregation of Citeaux continued the work of reformation, moral and religious, with which Cluny had occupied itself; but it attached more importance to that part of the rule which called for manual labour,—and, indeed, by undertaking works of public utility, such as draining swamps and clearing vast expanses of territory, the Cistercians changed the agricultural map of Europe. At the same time, they did much to abolish serfdom.

The religious and social spirit of Citeaux is most apparent in the authoritative and energetic figure of St. Bernard, who dominated the whole twelfth century. Abbot of Clairvaux — a monastery founded by him and a dependent of Citeaux—this extraordinary monk was not only saint, and ascetic, but he was surprisingly man of action as well. He was a leader, an eloquent orator whose sermons moved multitudes, and he dared to reprove the great and the humble alike. Thus, he criticizes the monks of Cluny as men "whose cowl is cut from the same piece of cloth as the dress of the knight," and whose churches are decorated with useless luxury. He criticizes the abuses of the Roman court, and he has no eye for the successor of Peter adorned with silk and borne upon a white palfrey and escorted by clamorous ministers. He criticizes the abuses in the lives of the clerics, and he cries out to their teachers: "Woe betide you who hold the keys not only of knowledge but also of power." He dares to correct the most renowned professors, like Abaelard and Gilbert de la Porrée, and summons them to ecclesiastical councils. He urges men and women alike to crowd into the monasteries; he promotes the Second Crusade; he encourages the rising order of the Templars, that military order whose members were at once monks and warriors, and who added to the vows of religion those of defending the Holy Land and the pilgrims; he takes interest in the founding of the order of the Carthusians, in 1132, and of the Premonstratensians, in 1120; he dreams of moulding all society after the plan of an ascetic ideal. His own ideal was even more lofty than that of his age; and when he died, in 1153, mediaeval society had already achieved the height of its monastic ideal.[11]

But our picture of the mentality of the period would be incomplete if we rested simply with the activities of the Benedictine orders; in addition we must point out briefly the activities of bishops and Pope.

The bishops were involved more intimately in the working of the feudal machinery than were the monasteries; for they were temporal princes within the limits of their fiefs and prelates in their dioceses. They owed to their overlords support in time of war, and such bishops as Hugh of Noyers, at Auxerre, or Mathew of Lorraine, at Toul, were warriors of a rough and primitive type. Others, like

[11] See Vacandard, *Vie de S. Bernard,* 2 vol. Paris, 1902.

Etienne of Tournai, Peter of Corbeil, William of Champagne, were humanists and men of letters. Maurice of Sully, elected bishop of Paris in 1160, was a model administrator in the days of the great changes in studies effected at Paris. The bishops of Chartres, of Laon and of Tournai play no less important a part in the domain of letters.

Finally, we could not understand the political and social spirit of Europe, in the twelfth century, without taking into account the growing prestige of the Papacy. After having been freed, by the action of Cluny, from the humiliation of the German Emperor, the way was open to the Papacy of becoming the greatest moral force in the world. During the twelfth century it was in process of organizing the theocracy, which was to reach its zenith in the following century, under Innocent III. On those pious Christian kings of France, the action of the Papacy exerted always a powerful political influence. "In the Middle Ages, the French crown and the Papacy could be near to falling out with each other, but they were never separated."[12]

[12] Luchaire, *op. cit.*, p. 149. The bourgeoisie of the towns, or communes, should be mentioned also in this connection. The towns first rose, in Italy and elsewhere, at the beginning of the eleventh century, and during the twelfth century they became real factors in the general progress. The bourgeoisie, or body of merchants, assumed organized form, and it adapted itself to feudalism. *"L'air de la ville donne la liberté,"* since a serf who lived in a town for a year and a day secured thereby his freedom and retained it. In the

III

We have now seen how a new spirit was in process of formation. What then constitutes the essence of this spirit—the spirit which arose from the depths of the mediaeval soul, and which became impregnated with Christianity, and which, from England and France, penetrated the whole of western Europe?

The feudal sentiment *par excellence*, which is still so deeply embedded in our modern conscience, is *the sentiment of the value and dignity of the individual man*. The feudal man lived as a free man; he was master in his own house; he sought his end in himself; he was—and this is a scholastic expression—*propter seipsum existens;* all feudal obligations were founded upon respect for personality and the given word. The scrupulous observance of feudal contract engendered the reciprocal loyalty of vassal and lord; fraternal feelings and self-sacrifice among men belong also to this class.

Under the influence of Cluny, this feudal sentiment became Christian in character, because Christianity placed upon each soul purchased by Christ's sacrifice an inestimable worth, and it furnished the poor and the rich and the great and the small with the same standard of value. The scrupulous observance of the feudal contract engendered *loyalty*.

thirteenth century the nouveaux riches of the merchant class laid the foundations of a "patriarcat urbain" which was destined to rival the nobility in wealth.

When loyalty became a Christian virtue, it increased respect for women and probity in the poor,—that probity which St. Louis IX said was like sweet honey to his lips. Honour became the pass-word of *chivalry*—a sort of moral institution superimposed on *feudalism*. The social habits of educated laymen were made gentler by the warm contact of chivalry, and courteous manners spread far and wide.

IV

But the twelfth century gave birth also to entirely new forms of art,—and, indeed, in a marvelous way. All branches on the tree of art began quickly to flower under the grateful zephyrs of the new spring that was come: *chansons de geste,* or romances invented by the troubadours; the letters of Abaelard and Heloise, which, however restrained, reveal all the fervour of human love; those hymns of purest Latin writen by men like St. Bernard,—whose flow suggests now the murmuring of a brook and anon the roaring of a river in flood—or those stanzas penned by Adam of St. Victor, that wonderful poet who, in the silence of his cloister at Paris, sang the festivals of divine love in most perfect Latin form.[13]

But, above all, there were built at that time those magnificent Romanesque abbeys and

---

[13] *Cf.* Henry Adams, *Mont St. Michel and Chartres,* ch. XV: "The Mystics."

churches with their varied new forms,—such as barreled vaults, towers, doorways, cruciform ground-plan, choirs with surrounding ambulatories and radiating chapels. In these forms the functions of the Church shine forth with marvelous clarity, and yet in them the virile power of the period is harmoniously revealed. Local schools of architecture appeared, such as those of Normandy, of Auvergne, of Poitou, of Burgundy; and the Benedictine abbots were promoters of the new standard of architecture. They did not adopt a uniform Romanesque style; rather they took over and developed the architecture of the region in which they happened to be. At the same time, they pressed into the service of architecture all the devices of ornamentation. The bare pillars were clothed with life, their capitals were covered with flowerings in stone; the portals were peopled with statues; painted glass was put in the windows of the sanctuaries; frescoes or mural paintings covered the walls and concealed the nakedness of the stone: the whole church was covered with a mantle of beauty. Artist-monks were trained in sculpturing columns and statues and they travelled from one workshop to another, while yet others opened schools of painting, as in St. Savin near Poitiers where the twelfth century frescoes still retain their bright colouring.[14]

[14] In these frescoes the "courtesy" of the time is very striking, especially in the bearing of ladies and knights, so full of elegance.

V

It is generally admitted that the feudal customs and the manifestations of art born in France spread thence into other countries,—and the Benedictines of Cluny and of Citeaux were the principal agency in this diffusion. In England the infiltration of feudal customs is easily explained by the close relations existing between the two countries; and the orders of Cluny and Citeaux swarmed thither like bees from a hive. The abbey churches of St. Albans and Malmesbury and Fountains Abbey were built upon principles brought over from Normandy. But for all their borrowing, whatever it may have been, they certainly possess the charm of originality. Epic literature, however, which attained such a high degree of perfection in Chaucer, shows still the influence of the French *fabliaux*. For, in the twelfth and in the thirteenth centuries "France, if not Paris, was in reality the eye and brain of Europe, the place of origin of almost every literary form, the place of finishing and polishing, even for those forms which she did not originate."[15]

German historians, such as Lamprecht and Steinhausen, recognize the same hegemony of French ideas in Germany.[16] The Cistercians, who poured forth from France, undertook in Germany

[15] Saintsbury, *The Flourishing of Romance and the Rise of Allegory*, London, 1897, p. 266.

[16] Steinhausen, *Geschichte der deutschen Kultur*, Bd. I, 1913, p. 312: "Frankreich wird das kulturell-führende Land."

and Bohemia and Hungary the work of clearing the forests—which so changed the economic face of Central Europe. But it was also Frenchmen who introduced at the Swabian court the habits of courtesy,—from the manner of greeting and the way of comporting oneself at table to the habit of control and moderation in all things. The monks of Cluny carried Romanesque architecture along the Rhine, while the Cistercian monks became later the propagators of Gothic architecture.

Finally, Romanesque architecture borne on the wings of French influence was carried, together with chivalry, across the Alps. They crossed the Pyrenees as well, and the Moorish genius imparted its smile to the severer forms of Occidental art.

So, turn where we will, the twelfth century is a constructive one; great forces are in the making, though their action is not yet a combined one. The local spirit, which splits France, England, and the other countries into small feudal municipalities, and is revealed even in the separate workshops of the artists, appears in every detail of the organized social and religious life.

CHAPTER THREE

THE CIVILIZATION AS REFLECTED IN PHILOSOPHY

i. Location of philosophical schools; invasion of French schools by foreigners. ii. Delimitation of the several sciences; philosophy distinct from the seven liberal arts and from theology. iii. Harmony of the feudal sense of personal worth with the philosophical doctrine that the individual alone exists. iv. The feudal civilization and the anti-realistic solution of the problem of universals.

I

Such a civilization was ripe for the things of the spirit. And so it came about that culture, both intellectual and philosophical, burst into bloom in this flowering season of things mediaeval. As a plant of rare nature, it shot up in the midst of an exuberant garden. We shall limit ourselves to a threefold consideration of the reflection of civilization in philosophy during the twelfth century: namely, the localization of schools; the definite distinction of the several branches of learning; the affirmation in philosophical terms of the worth of human personality.

First, it was quite natural that *philosophical life* should be subjected to the confinement of that same local spirit which appeared everywhere.

All over France numerous independent schools were gathered about the cathedrals and the abbeys. Each was a child of liberty, a literary republic, depending only on bishop or abbot; for in the twelfth and thirteenth centuries there was no government control of education. Each school sought to outrival the others by increasing its library, by attracting professors of renown, and by drawing students to its intellectual tournaments.

This educational régime was salutary, for it promoted the study of the sciences and raised a legion of remarkable humanists, theologians, lawyers, and philosophers. We need but cite the schools of Cluny and Citeaux in Burgundy; of Bec in Normandy; of Aurillac and of St. Martin at Tours; of Lobbes; of St. Omer; the cathedral schools of Laon, of Chartres, of Rheims, of Paris; and many others. All of them developed in the midst of feudal principalities, in spite of the fact that the overlords were generally at war. This was possible at that time because war interested only the professional fighting men, and did not affect the living conditions of any country as a whole. Among the most famous teachers of the twelfth century were Anselm of Laon, William of Champeaux, Abaelard, Hugo and Richard of St. Victor, Adelard of Bath, Alan of Lille, and the scholars of Chartres; but there were many others, whose names will appear as we proceed. They liked to go from one place to another, and we see a certain system of exchange professors in vogue. William of Champeaux taught philosophy successfully in the cathedral schools of Laon and of Paris, and in the abbey of St. Victor in Paris; Theodoric of Chartres was professor at Chartres, and also at Paris; William of Conches and Gilbert de la Porrée went to Chartres and to Paris; Adelard of Bath was at Paris and at Laon; Peter Abaelard—the knight-errant of dialectics, who summoned to the tourney of syllogisms as others of his family summoned to the tourney of arms—lectured in Melun, in Corbeil, in his private school at the Paraclete, and he returned several times to the cathedral schools in Paris.

In the time of Abaelard, the invasion of the French schools by foreigners had reached its height. Above all, the influx of English students was ever increasing. This was due to the close relations existing between both countries and to the lack of educational centres in the British Isles. More than one remained to teach where he himself was taught. For example, there was Adelard of Bath, who speaks of the *Gallicarum sententiarum constantia*, and who left his nephew at Laon to master the *Gallica studia* while he himself travelled in Spain;[1]

[1] "Meministi nepos, quod septennio jam transacto, cum te in gallicis studiis pene parvum juxta Laudisdunum una cum ceteris auditoribus in eis dimiserim, id inter nos convenisse, ut arabum studia ego pro posse meo scrutarer, gallicarum sententiarum constantiam non minus adquireres." *Adelardi Batensis de quibusdam naturalibus quaestionibus*, Man. lat. Escorial, O III, 2, fol. 74 R^a. *Cf.* P. G. Antolin, Catalogo de los codices latinos de la real Bibl. del Escorial,

also there was the Scotchman Richard of St. Victor in the mystic cloister of St. Victor in Paris; and there was Isaac of Stella, also an Englishman, in the abbey of Stella close to Poitiers; and the most famous of all was John of Salisbury, who became bishop of Chartres after having taught in its cathedral school. Others settled in their native country, after having studied at Paris, such as Walter Map and Alexander Neckham. Meanwhile, French scholars also went to England and settled there; such were, for example, Peter of Blois and Richard Dover.[2] All of these men agree in recognizing the importance of the training afforded by the French schools.

As for Germany, the attraction of French learning was no less irresistible. Even in the tenth century the German Emperors recognized this superiority, and summoned to their court French

vol. III, p. 226. I have not succeeded in finding a copy of the incunabel edition of this interesting treatise.

With the above compare the expression: "Franci(a)e magistri," in an unpublished thirteenth century manuscript, in connection with the difficulty of translating Aristotle's *Posterior Analytics* (C. H. Haskins, "Mediaeval Versions of the Posterior Analytics." *Harvard Studies in Classical Philology,* 1914, vol. XXV, p. 94.) "Nam translatio Boecii apud nos integra non invenitur, et id ipsum quod de ea reperitur vitio corruptionis obfuscatur. Translationem vero Jacobi obscuritatis tenebris involvi silentio suo peribent *Francie magistri,* qui quamvis illam translacionem et commentarios ab eodem Jacobo translatos habeant, tamen noticiam illius libri non audent profiteri."

[2] J. E. Sandys, "English Scholars of Paris and Franciscans in Oxford," in *The Cambridge History of English Literature,* vol. I, pp. 199 ff.

masters. Thus, the Emperor Otto III wrote a letter to the famous Gerbert, professor in Rheims and who later became Pope Sylvester II, in which he said: "We heartily desire your presence here, distinguished man, that you may relieve me of my Saxon rusticity, *Saxonica rusticitas.*"³ Otto was successful in creating an interesting intellectual movement within the confines of his country. But this renaissance of learning was not of long duration; and from the eleventh century on the schools of Fulda and Reichenau and St. Gall fell into decline and decay. In the twelfth century the same fate befell the schools at Liége, which were dependent on the Empire.⁴ The German clerics also went to French schools,—to Rheims, Chartres, Laon, Paris, Le Bec—and the young barons considered it a privilege to be educated at the court of Louis VII. Otloh of St. Emmeram, Otto of Freisingen, Manegold of Lautenbach, Hugo of St. Victor, in fact all German theologians and philosophers and humanists of repute in that century, were educated in French schools. Paris is the source of all science, writes Cesaire of Heisterbach;⁵ scientists, adds Otto of Freising, have emigrated to France,—and both chronicles merely reëcho the saying of the time: "To Italy the

³ *Lettres de Gerbert (983-997)*, ed. Havet, Paris, 1889, p. 172.

⁴ *Cf.* my *Histoire de la Philosophie en Belgique*, Louvain, 1910, pp. 18-22.

⁵ Steinhausen, *op. cit.*, p. 355.

Papacy, to Germany the Empire, and to France learning."

Italy also sent men in no small numbers. In the eleventh century the monk Lanfranc, a type of wandering professor, serves as an example. From Pavia and from Bologna he went to the abbey of Bec, and there was joined by another Italian, the Piedmontese Anselm of Aosta. In the twelfth century, Peter Lombard and Peter of Capua, and Praepositinus of Cremona all taught at Paris. Rolando Bandinelli, the future Pope Alexander III, pursued his studies under Abaelard; and he who was to become Innocent III learned his theology and his grammar at Paris. It must be said, however, that in Italy more than in England and in Germany, there were independent centres of intellectual life. Suffice it to mention the schools of Bologna, whence arose a university as ancient and as influential as that of Paris, and the Benedictine schools of Monte Cassino, where in the eleventh century Constantine of Carthage established one of the first Occidental contacts with the world of Arabian learning, and where later on Thomas Aquinas received his early education.

But not all French schools enjoyed equal celebrity; they were rated according to the fame of their professors, just as today a school's reputation and its worth depend upon the excellence of its teaching staff. Hence, we can understand the change in the fame of the schools. Thus, for example, with the opening of the twelfth century, the cathedral schools of Tournai (Odon of Tournai), of Rheims (Alberic of Rheims and Gauthier of Mortagne), of Laon (Anselm of Laon), had shed their last splendor. For they were eclipsed by the cathedral schools of Chartres, founded by Fulbert, at which there developed during the first half of the twelfth century a humanist movement, which devoted itself to achieving a Latin style of rare elegance, a perfect knowledge of the classics, and an acquaintance with the complete *Organon* of Aristotle. Bernard of Chartres, in 1117, became the first of a line of famous masters; and Thierry of Chartres, about 1141, wrote his celebrated treatise on the liberal arts, the *Heptateuchon,*—written just as the south portal of the cathedral was receiving its ornamentation, with its detail of sculptured figures which represent the *trivium* and *quadrivium.*

But even before this Paris had been in position to assert the superiority of her schools. The fame of Abaelard at the schools of the cathedral and of St. Genevieve drew a host of students and masters to Paris; the monastery of St. Victor, where William of Champeaux founded a chair of theology, became a centre of mystical studies; and the university was all but born.

The localism of these schools did not, however, prevent a certain uniformity in method of teaching and in curriculum and in scholarly practise; and this uniformity helped to pave the way for the cosmopolitan character of the teaching of philosophy in the universities. The localism and the centralizing tendency commingled,—very much as the autonomy of the feudal barons and the unifying policy of the kings did in the political realm.

Studying and teaching were monopolized by one social class, the clergy. The international hierarchy of the Church, and the universal use of Latin as the scientific language established a natural union among the masters of the West; the frequent migration of students and scholars, from school to school, facilitated the spread of every innovation in method, program, and vocabulary.

II

The twelfth century remained faithful to the traditional program of the *seven liberal arts,* but the frame was enlarged in every direction. This brings us to a second group of ideas connected with the spirit of the civilization, and which I call the *demarcation of boundaries between the sciences.* In the early centuries of the Middle Ages, the program of studies included grammar-rhetoric-dialectic (logic), which comprised the *trivium,* and arithmetic-geometry-astronomy-music, which comprised the *quadrivium;* in this program one readily recognizes the beginnings of our modern secondary education.

Grammar included not only the study of the ancient and mediaeval grammarians (Donatus,

Priscian, and Remi of Auxerre), but also a study of the classics themselves,—such as Virgil, Seneca, Horace, and others. Cicero and Quintilian and Marius Victorinus are mentioned as among the authors preferred for instruction in rhetoric.[6] For a long time law was also regarded as a branch of rhetoric; and it was not until the time of Irnerius of Bologna that law was taught as a branch distinct from the liberal arts course.[6a] About the middle of the twelfth century the study of dialectics included all the *Organon* of Aristotle. As for the teaching of the *quadrivium,* it always lagged behind that of the *trivium.* Euclid is the master in mathematics. The study of astronomy was given a certain impulse by Adelard of Bath, who was initiated into the Arabian science in Spain about the middle of the twelfth century.

But such a program was felt to be too narrow in the twelfth century, and philosophy notably received a definite place outside the liberal arts,— which it leaves below, with theology above.

It has been long supposed, and people still say, that philosophy in the Middle Ages was confused with dialectics (one of the three branches of the *trivium* above described); that it reduced to a handful of arid disputes quarrels on the syllogism and

[6] Clerval, *Les écoles de Chartres du moyen âge du V'e au XVI'e siècles,* pp. 221 ff.

[6a] Be it observed, however, that the study of Roman law had never been wholly abandoned in Western Europe.

on sophisms. This thesis has a seeming foundation, thanks to certain dialectical acrobats who, in the eleventh and twelfth centuries, emptied philosophy of all ideas and rendered it bloodless and barren (*"exsanguis et sterilis,"* are John of Salisbury's words). But the truth is quite otherwise. These "virtuosi," with their play on words and verbal discussions, were strongly combated; and the men of real worth—such as Anselm of Canterbury, Abaelard, Thierry of Chartres, John of Salisbury, and others—not only practiced dialectics or formal logic with sobriety and applied it in accordance with doctrine, but they created a place for philosophy separate from and beyond the liberal arts, and consequently beyond dialectics. Their writings treat of the problems of metaphysics and psychology, which is matter quite different from formal dialectics.

While it hardly exists in the "glosses" of the Carlovingian schools, philosophy rapidly progresses towards the end of the eleventh century, and in the middle of the twelfth century consists of a considerable body of doctrine, which the following centuries were to make fruitful.

Now when philosophy had gained its distinct position, the propaedeutic character of the liberal arts became evident: they serve as initiation to higher studies. Men of the twelfth century take them into consideration, and the first who are engaged with the classification of the sciences express themselves clearly on this subject. Speaking of the liberal arts, *"Sunt tanquam septem viae,"* says a codex of Bamberg; they are, so to speak, the seven ways that lead to the other sciences—physics (part of philosophy), theology, and the science of law.[7] Hugo of St. Victor and others speak in the same sense. At the end of the twelfth century, the iconography of the cathedrals, the sculptures, and the medallions in the glass windows, as well as the miniatures in manuscripts, confirm this thesis. The philosophy which inspired artists is represented as existing apart from and by the side of the liberal arts; for instance, at Laon and at Sens, and much more so in the window at Auxerre placed above the choir. The copy, still preserved at Paris, of the *Hortus Deliciarum* by Herrad of Landsberg (the original at Strasburg was burnt during the bombardment in 1870) places philosophy in the centre of a rose with seven lobes disposed around it,[8] and in the mosaic pavement of the cathedral of Ivrea, philosophy is seated in the middle of the seven arts.[9]

[7] "Ad istas tres scientias (phisica, theologia, scientia legum) paratae sunt tanquam viae septem liberales artes que in trivio et quadrivio continentur." Cod. Q. VI, 30. Grabmann. *Die Geschichte der scholastichen Methode.*, 1909, Bd. II, p. 39.

[8] E. Mâle, *L'art religieux du XIIIe siècle en France. Etude sur l'iconographie et sur ses sources d'inspiration.* Paris, 1910, pp. 112 ff. Cf. L. Bréhier, *L'art chrétien. Son développement iconographique des origines à nos jours.* Paris, 1918.

[9] A. K. Porter, *Lombard Architecture*, New Haven, 1907, vol. I, p. 347.

But the twelfth century did more than clearly distinguish the liberal arts from philosophy; it also inaugurated a completer separation between philosophy and theology. And the establishment of this doctrine of scientific methodology is of the highest importance in the study in which we are engaged. The question of the existence of philosophy as distinct from theology is, for philosophy, a matter of life or death; and it is now definitely answered, we may say unhesitatingly. But here also there are historical stages, and their study is illuminating and suggestive. The Middle Ages, in the beginning, took up the Neo-Platonic and Augustinian idea of the entire identification of philosophy with theology. Thus it is that John Scotus Eriugena wrote in the ninth century: *"Quid est aliud de philosophia tractare nisi verae religionis, qua summa et principalis omnium rerum causa Deus et humiliter colitur et rationabiliter investigatur, regulas exponere."*[10] But at the end of the eleventh century, and especially after St. Anselm had given his solution of the problem of the relation between faith and reason, the distinction between the two sciences was practically accepted; and it is easy to see that St. Anselm, for example, speaks sometimes as a philosopher and sometimes as a theologian. The twelfth century advances a step further, and the distinction between philosophy and theology becomes one of its characteristic

[10] *De divina praedestinatione*, I, 1 (Patr. lat. vol. 122, c. 357-358).

declarations. A codex of Regensburg of the twelfth century clearly distinguishes philosophers, *"humanae videlicet sapientiae amatores,"* from theologians, *"divinae scripturae doctores."*[11]

I am of course aware that besides these texts there are others in which philosophy is abused or misunderstood; that reactionary minds, narrow theologians or disdainful mystics, condemned profane knowledge as useless, or if they admitted philosophy, they reduced it to the rank of a vassal and a serf of theology. In the eleventh century Otloh of St. Emmeram forbade monks the study of it; they, he said, having renounced the world, must occupy themselves only with divine things. Peter Damien wrote concerning dialectics, that even though sometimes (*quando*), by way of exception, it is allowed to occupy itself with theological matters and with mysteries of divine power (*mysteria divinae virtutis*), it should nevertheless renounce all spirit of independence (for that would be arrogance), and like a servant place itself at the service of its mistress, theology: *Velut ancilla dominae quodam famulatus obsequio subservire.*[12]

Here for the first time this famous phrase appears. It is repeated in the twelfth century by a united group of so-called "rigorist theologians"— Peter of Blois, Stephen of Tournai, Michael of Corbeil, and many others. The lofty mystics of the

[11] Grabmann, *op. cit.*, I, 191. cod. Clm. No. 14401.
[12] *De divina omnipotentia*, c. 5 Patr. lat. vol. 14, c. 603.

convent of St. Victor at Paris—Walter and Absalon of St. Victor—went so far as to say that philosophy is the devil's art, and that certain theologians who used it were "the labyrinths" of France.

But one must not forget that these detractors of philosophy were a minority, just as the quibbling dialecticians formed an exceptional class also, and that already in the eleventh and the twelfth century the best minds rejected the unhappy phrase of Damien. St. Anselm had disavowed it. The Chartrains, John of Salisbury, Alan of Lille, either expressly oppose it or show by their writings that they reject it. Moreover, the speculative theologians who appeared at the beginning of the twelfth century and almost immediately formed three great schools—Abaelard, Gilbert de la Porrée, Hugo of St. Victor—condemned the timidity of the "rigorists," and the apologetic which they created (of which we shall speak further on)[13] is an effectual counterpoise to the tendencies of Damien. Peter Lombard himself, in spite of his practical point of view, protests against such excessive pretensions. The formula is condemned by the majority of intellectual philosophers and theologians. Hence it is very unfair to judge the philosophers of the Middle Ages by the doctrines of a minority—and that in the twelfth century—against which the best openly rebel. To make clear the origin of the formula, that philosophy is the handmaiden of the-

[13] See ch. VII, iv.

ology, should suffice to do justice in the matter. This consideration should relieve the philosophy of the Middle Ages of that grave contempt which has weighed upon it so long,—a contempt resting upon the belief that it had no *raison d'être,* no proper method, no independence!

To say that philosophy, by the twelfth century, had become clearly distinguished from the liberal arts on the one hand and from theology on the other hand, is to recognize that its limits were clearly defined and that it had become conscious of itself. Now this great first step in organization had been made simultaneously by other sciences as well, and they were thus all given independence, though in different degrees. For example, there was the development in dogmatic theology, which progressed rapidly, as we have just said, and spread widely in the great schools of Abaelard, of Gilbert de la Porrêe, of Hugo of St. Victor, and of Peter Lombard. It appeared also in the liberal arts, of which one branch or another was more especially studied in this school or that; for example, grammar at Orléans and dialectics at Paris. It was evidenced, moreover, in the appearance of medicine, as a separate discipline, and especially of civil (Roman) and canon law. Thus the important mental disciplines, on which the thirteenth century was to thrive, had asserted their independence and intrinsic worth.

These demarcations, which seem to us so natural

and matter of course, have come at the cost of great effort in every period of history which has attempted their establishment—and necessarily so. Thus the first Greek philosophers encountered the same difficulty in this regard as did the scholastics of the twelfth century. Even today, when classification is so far advanced, discussions arise in fixing the limits of new sciences; witness the example of sociology. But this delimitation of philosophy in the twelfth century was only one aspect of a rapidly developing civilization. Do we not see a similar movement in the political, the social, the religious, and the artistic life? The royal prerogatives, the rights and duties of vassals, the status of the bourgeoisie and of the rural population, the distinction between temporal charge and spiritual function of abbots and prelates, the monastic and episcopal hierarchy, the clear establishment of new artistic standards,—all of these are features of an epoch in process of definition. The chaos and the hesitation of the tenth and the eleventh centuries have disappeared. The new era exhibits throughout a sense of maturing powers.

III

We may now penetrate more deeply, and consider the mass of philosophical doctrines which issued out of the efforts of the twelfth century. As one does this, one cannot help noting how the chief doctrines of the developing metaphysics harmonize with the predominant virtues of the feudal spirit. And this brings us to our third point, and indeed the most interesting one, concerning the reflection of the civilization in the philosophy: namely, *the harmony of the feudal sense of personal worth with the philosophical doctrine of the reality of the individual.*

The feudal man was athirst for independence, his relations with his overlord being determined by free contract; moreover, by a kind of contagion, the desire for a similar independence spread to the townspeople and to the rustic population. This natural disposition took on a Christian tone by virtue of the Church teaching concerning the value of the individual life,—the individual soul bought at a price. It was according to this humanitarian principle that Peter the Venerable called the serfs his brothers and sisters.[14]

Roman civil law and canon law and feudal law— the three forms of jurisprudence which developed so rapidly from the eleventh century onward—had come to remarkable agreement regarding the existence of natural right; and in the name of this right, based on human nature, they had proclaimed the equality of all men. With this beginning, they came to regard all differences of rank as conventional; and slavery and serfdom were declared to be contrary to natural law. If, however, the three forms of law recognized the legitimacy of serfdom,

[14] See above, p. 26.

it was because of the special conditions of the time. Serfdom was considered a social necessity. Under the influence of Christianity, all three systems of law sought to mitigate serfdom; and this was especially true of the civil lawyers and the canonists, who put into effect a series of measures for the benefit of the serf, which guaranteed the indissolubility of his marriage, assured him his right of sanctuary, encouraged his emancipation, and prescribed rules in regard to his ordination and his entry into a monastery. These ideas made headway,—slow, to be sure, but steady—toward that state of society wherein the serf could be set free with the liberty which is due all human beings.[15]

Now the scholastic philosophy of the twelfth century based these juridical declarations upon metaphysical foundations; and they came, after the many centuries of discussion, to this important conclusion—a conclusion no longer doubted—*that the only existing reality is individual reality.* Individuals alone exist; and only individuals ever could exist. The thesis was general in its application. Whether man or animal or plant or chemical body or what not, a being must exist as an individual, incommunicable, and undivided in itself. Similarly, everything that affects an existing being is

[15] For the conceptions of natural right and of serfdom among the feudal theorists of the eleventh and twelfth centuries, see Carlyle, *A History of Mediaeval Political Theory in the West,* vol. III, Part II, ch. I; among the civil lawyers, *ibid.,* vol. II, Part I, ch. IV; among the canonists, *ibid.,* vol. II, Part II, ch. V.

particularized; man's act of thinking, the shape of an animal, the height of a plant, the activity of a chemical molecule,—everything that exists, exists in the condition of particularity. Scholastic philosophy is pluralistic; it regards the real world as a collection of individuals and particulars.[16]

Individuality when applied to a human being is called personality. Throughout the twelfth century the philosophers are unanimous in repeating the words of Boethius: *persona est rationalis naturae individua substantia.*[17]

For a long time, the schools had oscillated between the extreme realism which taught with Plato that universal essences, such as humanity, have a real existence, and the anti-realism which denied the existence of such realities. But by the twelfth century the debate had been closed in favor of anti-realism. Notwithstanding their various shades of difference,[18] the theory of *respectus* advanced by Adelard of Bath in Laon and in Paris, the doctrine of *status* taught by Walter of Mortagne, the so-called "indifference-theory" and the "collection-theory" reëchoed by the anonymous author of the *De Generibus et Speciebus,*—all of these theories, mentioned by John of Salisbury in his *Metalogicus,*[19] agree in maintaining that universal essences

[16] See below, Chapter IX.
[17] Boethius, *De duabus naturis.*
[18] *Cf.* my *Histoire de la Philosophie Mediévale,* pp. 217-221.
[19] II, 17.

could not exist, and that only the individual possesses real existence.

Hence, the human perfection which constitutes *human reality* is of the same kind in each person,— king or subject, seigneur or vassal, master or servant, rich or poor, these all have a similar essence. The reality that constitutes the human person admits of no degrees. According to scholastic philosophy, a being is either man or not man. No one man can be more or less man than another, although each of us possesses more or less powerful faculties which produce more or less perfect acts.[20] In this sense Abaelard and Gilbert de la Porrée, and scores of others, agree with Peter the Venerable and declare in philosophical terms, based on metaphysical principles, that "serfs are no less and no more human beings than are their masters."

But Abaelard went a step further. As has been only recently disclosed by the important discovery of his *Glossulae super Porphyrium*,[21] we can now say definitely, that to Abaelard belongs the great credit of having solved the problem of the universal in the form that was followed throughout the twelfth, the thirteenth, and the fourteenth centuries. Indeed, to the metaphysical doctrine, Abaelard adds

[20] See ch. IX.

[21] By Grabmann and Geyer in the libraries of Milan and Lunel. For the publication of this important text, see Bernhard Geyer, "Peter Abaelards philosophische Schriften. I. Die Logica Ingredientibus. 1. Die Glossen zu Porphyrius," (*Beiträge zur Geschichte der Philosophie des Mittelalters*, Bd. XXI, Heft 1, Münster, 1919).

the psychological, which may be briefly summarized as follows: Although there exist only individual men, although each one is independent of the other in his existence, the mind nevertheless possesses the general notion of humanity which belongs to each of them; but this form of generality is a product of our conceptual activity and does not affect the real existence.[22] Therewith was given in compact form essentially the scholastic solution of the famous problem of the relation between the universal and the particular.

This doctrine had grown up gradually, and its formation runs parallel with that of the feudal sentiment. Even while it is being clearly expressed in the various philosophical works, the feudal feeling of chivalry appears in all its purity and strength in the *Chansons de Geste*. The most ardent defenders of the philosophical solution are the sons of chevaliers,—the impetuous Abaelard, heir of the seigneurs of Pallet; Gilbert de la Porrée, bishop of Poitiers; the aristocratic John of Salisbury, who writes concerning this question: "The

[22] "Illud quoque quod supra meminimus, intellectus scilicet universalium fieri per abstractionem et quomodo eos solos, nudos, puros nec tamen cassos appelemus . . ." Edit. Geyer, pp. 24 ff. The epistemological solution appears clearly in the following text: "Cum enim hunc hominem tantum attendo in natura substantiae vel corporis, non etiam animalis vel hominis vel grammatici, profecto nihil nisi quod in ea est intelligo, sed non omnia quae habet, attendo. Et cum dico me attendere tantum eam in eo quod hoc habet, illud tantum ad attentionem refertur, non ad modum subsistendi, alioquin cassus esset intellectus." *Ibid.*, p. 25.

world has grown old treating of it, and has taken more time for its solution than the Caesars took to conquer and govern the world."[23]

The great scholastics of the thirteenth century will appropriate this doctrine to their purposes, bringing it into harmony with psychology and ethics and social and political theories; and they will incorporate it in that great synthesis which is the most commanding product of the mediaeval mind,—that is, scholasticism.

To sum up. The twelfth century witnesses a new civilization established in a striking form. The struggles of kings with vassals, the coming of the communes, the establishment of citizenship, the freedom of the serfs,—all of these facts are evidence that the balance is being established among social forces. New habits, based upon the dignity and the self-respect of the individual, were born out of feudalism, and the Church impressed upon them the stamp of Christianity. A new art springs into life, and intellectual culture makes noteworthy progress. The spirit of localism, which was the result of split-up feudalism, breaks out in the numerous schools of the West; and herein appears first the reflection of the age in its philosophy. The demarcation of boundaries between philosophy and all other disciplines discloses a further harmony between its philosophy and the general spirit of the age,—an age which constructs in all departments

[23] *Polycraticus,* VII, 12.

and destroys in none. Finally, the fundamental quality of feudalism is reflected in one of the chief doctrines of their metaphysics: the self-sufficiency of the individual, whether thing or person, is proclaimed in the schools of France and of England; and the French and the English have never forgotten this proud declaration of their ancestors, the scholastics of the twelfth century.

CHAPTER FOUR

The Great Awakening of Philosophy in the Thirteenth Century

i. The causes: The acquired momentum. ii. The rise of the Universities (Paris and Oxford). iii. The establishment of the mendicant orders (Dominicans and Franciscans). iv. The acquaintance with new philosophical works; translations. v. General result: among the numerous systems the scholastic philosophy issues as dominant. vi. The comprehensive classification of knowledge.

I

It is now generally agreed, that the thirteenth century marks the climax in the growth of philosophical thought in western Europe during the Middle Ages. With the decade 1210-1220 begins a development of extraordinary vitality which extends over a period of one hundred and fifty years. Let us examine the causes and the results of this movement of thought.

What are the *causes* of this remarkable development of philosophical thought? How does it happen that we see the appearance of so many vigorous systems, as though the seed had been thrown with lavish hand upon the fertile soil of western Europe?

The first cause is what I shall call the acquired momentum. The intellectual labours of the twelfth century gave the initial impulse. We have already observed some of their achievements; for example, their contributions in methodology, by which the limits of each science and discipline were established, and without which no intellectual progress would have been possible. We have noted also the deliberate and unanimous declaration, that the individual alone can be endowed with actual existence and substantiality. To the individual man,—lord or vassal, freeman or serf, clergyman or layman, rich or poor—philosophy spoke these bold words: "Be yourself; your personality belongs only to yourself, your substance is an independent value; keep it; be self-reliant; free contract alone can bind you to another man."

There are many other philosophical theories which the twelfth century contributed to later generations. Among them are the distinction between sense perception and rational knowledge, and the "abstraction" of the latter from the former; the many proofs of the existence of God, the studies in his Infinitude, and the essays in reconciling Providence and human freedom; the relation between essence and existence; the views on the natural equality of men and the divine origin of authority. But these doctrines had not been combined into an integral whole; and therefore the philosophers of the thirteenth century used them as material in the construction of their massive edifice of knowledge.

But not alone in philosophy was the growth extraordinary and the ripening rapid; the same was true of all domains. The constitution of the Magna Charta (1215), the granting of privileges by Philip Augustus to the University of Paris, the birth of St. Louis and of Thomas Aquinas, the death of St. Francis,—these are all events closely coinciding in time; and the height of development in scholastic philosophy followed closely upon the height of development in Gothic architecture.

The best proof, however, of the value of the work already accomplished lies in the very celerity of the development during the thirteenth century; for the succeeding generations of that century took swift advantage of the favourable conditions which had already been created for them. Thus, a few years after these happy conditions obtained, that is about 1226-30, William of Auvergne, bishop of Paris, and the Franciscan Alexander of Hales conceived their great systems of thought; and then almost immediately there appeared such men as Roger Bacon, Bonaventure, Thomas Aquinas, and Raymond Lully. What they did would not have been possible if their age had not been prepared to accept their work,—a preparation already assured in the twelfth century leaven of doctrine, with its promise of growth and of increase.

But there were also external causes which hastened this elaboration of doctrine. Among these there are three to be especially noted. Namely, the rise of the University of Paris; the establishment of the two great religious orders, both of them devoted to learning; and the circulation of a large number of new philosophical works, which were brought from the Orient and which had been unknown to the Occident before that time in the Middle Ages. These three causes coöperated in a unique manner. For, the University of Paris was the centre of learning; the new orders supplied the same University with professors; and the books brought from the Orient made a notable increase in its working library.

II

During the last years of the twelfth century, the French metropolis monopolized, to its advantage, the intellectual activity which previously had been scattered in the various French centers. The University eclipsed the episcopal and monastic schools, and thereby replaced the spirit of localism with that of centralization in study.[1]

Towards the middle of the twelfth century the schools of Paris were divided into three groups: (a) the schools of the cathedral of Notre Dame, under the authority of the chancellor and, through him, of

[1] See Rashdall's excellent work: *The Universities of Europe in the Middle Ages*. Oxford, Clarendon Press, 1895. *Cf.* H. Denifle, *Die Universitäten des Mittelalters bis 1400*, Berlin, 1885.

the bishop of Paris; (b) the schools of the canons of St. Victor, which had become the throbbing centre of mysticism, but where also William of Champeaux had opened a school in which he had been teaching philosophy for some time; (c) the outside schools of the abbey of St. Genevieve. But the schools of Notre Dame occupied the foremost place, and it was from them that the University sprang. It arose not indeed through a decree of the government or a committee of trustees, but as a flower grows from its stem, by a natural convening of masters and pupils; for their number had multiplied as a result of the constant development of studies. Masters and pupils were grouped in four faculties according to their special interests—the University documents compare them to the four rivers of Paradise, just as the iconography of the cathedrals symbolically represents the four evangelists as pouring water from urns toward the four points of the compass. These are the faculties of Theology, of Arts (thus called in memory of the liberal arts of the early Middle Ages), of Law, and of Medicine.

The program of studies in the University is a living and moving thing. It takes form in the second half of the thirteenth century, and at that moment it is revealed in great purity of outline, like something new and fresh, a distinctive and pleasing product of the Middle Ages. If one should take, as it were, a snap-shot of the faculty of arts—

or of philosophy—as it was about 1270, he would find that it is entirely distinct from the other faculties, even from that of theology, as in our own day. But the studies under its control fill a very special place in the University economy, because they are the usual, or even required, preliminary to studies in the other faculties. They have a formative and preparatory character, and for this reason the faculty of arts appears in the documents with the title of inferior faculty, *facultas inferior,* in distinction from the three other faculties which are placed over it and hence are called superior, *facultates superiores.*[2] On this account the student population of the faculty of arts was young and numerous, a population of adolescents—*pueri,* the charters say. They entered at fourteen years; at twenty they might have finished their course in arts and graduated. Then usually they entered another faculty. But they had received the imprint of their masters; and the impressions given by philosophical teaching are indelible, be it remembered. On their side the masters or professors of the faculty of arts, recruited from among the graduates in arts by a curious custom of which we will speak in a moment, also constituted the youthful, and therefore stirring, element in the teaching staff.

It is easy to distinguish in the faculty of arts the two main features which characterize the entire

[2] Denifle et Chatelain, *Chartularium Universitatis Parisiensis,* I, p. 600.

University: the corporate spirit and the extension of instruction. The University as a whole is a corporation, or group of masters and scholars. It is even nothing but that; the word *"universitas"* is taken from the Roman law and means corporation or group; and the mediaeval period applies this term to every kind of grouping, to the city, to the parish, even to the universal Church; while documents name the University proper, a *general centre of studies,—"studium generale."* The corporation idea appears therefore in the organization of faculties, and gives to the faculty of arts or philosophy a characteristic meaning. It includes masters and apprentices. Indeed, the *student* at Paris is an *apprentice-professor,* a candidate for the mastership. His career is normally crowned, not by receiving a diploma—which is simply the recognition of knowledge—but by teaching in the *corporation* of his masters. The studies, too, constitute simply a long apprenticeship for the mastership or the professorship. He becomes a professor by doing the work of a professor, as a blacksmith becomes a blacksmith by forging. Indeed, the whole situation strongly resembles the organization of workmen, of stonecutters and masons, who about this time were building and carving the great cathedrals of France. They, too, had their working-men's syndicates; and professional schools were organized in their midst. The apprenticed workman was subjected to a severe and long initiation, and worked under the direction of a master. To become master in his turn, he must produce a work judged worthy and called a *masterpiece*. The process was none other for the future professors of philosophy at the University of Paris.

During his six years of attendance, the pupil cleared the three stages of baccalaureate (*bacchalaureus*), licentiate (*licentiatus*), and mastership (*magister*). But the tests for the baccalaureate had already included an attempt at public lecture. After the new member had been subjected to some preliminary examinations (*responsiones et examen*), he was required to mount a platform, and invited to defend a systematically prepared thesis— a process which sometimes lasted all through Lent —and to answer the objections of those present. This public defense was called *determinatio*, and the student left it as a bachelor,—a term which was employed by the corporation of workmen in a special sense, the bachelors being "those who have passed as masters in the art but who have not been sworn in." The examination for the baccalaureate is surrounded with the corporate ceremonial so dear to the thirteenth century. The student puts on a special cap. Then, the séance ended, wine is served and a banquet arranged. Youth is everywhere the same—the great days of university life must be gaily celebrated. Between the baccalaureate and licentiate there was a period of variable length, during which the bachelor was at once student and apprentice-professor. As student, he followed the master's lessons and continued to acquire knowledge; as apprentice-professor, he himself explained to others certain books of Aristotle's *Organon*. When his term of six years had rolled around and he had reached his nineteenth or twentieth year, the bachelor could present himself before the chancellor to be admitted to the licentiate. Ceremonies multiply: thus, the new examination to be undergone before some of the professors of the faculty (*temptatores*), and then before the chancellor assisted by four examiners chosen by him and approved by the faculty; the public discussion at *St.-Julien-le-Pauvre* upon a subject left to the choice of the bachelor; and finally, amid great pomp, the conferring of the long-coveted right to teach and to open his own school.

There was still the third step to be taken—the mastership; and here we are taken back to the purest conceptions of the mediaeval corporation. The mastership is the enthroning of the newly licensed member before the faculty or society of masters—that close organization, so jealous of its monopoly, to which one had access only through the agreement of all the members, and after having given a pledge of fidelity to the rector and to the faculty which bound the master for life.

The mastership was in principle a *free profession,* with no rules except the rules applying to the organization as a whole, and with no limit upon the number of the members. In consequence of this arrangement, there was a great increase in the teaching profession. The right to teach could not be withheld from any student who had completed the regular course of studies; and the number of masters of arts incorporated in the faculty was theoretically unlimited. We readily recognize certain characteristic features in this system of university instruction of the thirteenth century: free competition in teaching among all those who have taken their degree; freedom of the students who have become doctors, or "masters," to open schools beside their former masters; and freedom of the students to select their own masters,—the clearest in exposition, the most eloquent in delivery, the most profound in thought—entirely according to choice.

This freedom in the teaching career was reflected in the teaching itself,—in the spirit and action of the masters. There was really great freedom of thought and of speech in the thirteenth century,—notwithstanding what is now commonly believed on this subject. A very striking example may be taken from the end of the century, in the person of the philosopher Godfrey of Fontaines,—who was also a "Doctor in Theology." From the teacher's chair,—and aware of his privilege and responsibility—he directs the severest criticism against his superior, the Bishop of Paris, Simon of Bucy.³ He justifies his audacity by invoking the principle that a Doctor of the University is bound to declare the truth, however his speech may offend the rich and the powerful. "Few there are to be found," he says, "who can be blamed for excess of frankness; but many indeed for their silence." *Pauci inveniuntur qui culpari possunt de excessu in veritate dicenda, plurimi vero de taciturnitate.*⁴ One could cite many more examples of this great freedom of speech among the masters; the University sermons especially are full of it.⁵

Although the University of Paris possessed four faculties, it was especially famous for its teaching of philosophy and theology, just as Bologna, the twin sister of Paris, was famed for its juridical learning. Paris outstripped by far the University of Oxford, which was its only rival in this particular field.⁶ Thus Paris became the philosophical

³ For details see my study of Godfrey of Fontaines; *Etudes sur la vie, les oeuvres et l'influence de Godefroid de Fontaines*, Louvain, 1904.

⁴ *Godefridi de Fontibus Quodlibeta*, XII, q. vi, (fol. 278 Rb), Latin MS. No. 15842, Bibl. Nat. I am editing these Quodlibeta, with the aid of former pupils; three volumes have appeared (in the series: *Les Philosophes Belges*, vols. II and III, Louvain, 1904 and 1914), and two or three more will follow.

⁵ See, for example, C. Langlois: "Sermons parisiens de la premiere moitié du XIII'e s. contenus dans le Ms 691 de la Bibl. d'Arras" (*Journal des Savants*, 1916, pp. 488 and 548).

⁶ Many other universities were established on the model of Paris and Bologna; for instance, Cambridge, Montpellier, Toulouse, Salamanca, Valladolid, Naples,—all of the thirteenth century.

centre of the West, the international "rendez-vous" for all those who were interested in speculative thought,—and their name was legion. By way of glorifying this philosophical speculation at the University, the documents refer to Paris in the most pompous terms: *parens scientiarum,* the *alma mater* of the sciences; *sapientiae fons,* fountain of wisdom, that is, the fountain of philosophy.

Paris drew to itself an endless stream of strangers interested in these subjects. During the thirteenth century all of those who have a name in philosophy or in theology come here, sooner or later, for a more or less prolonged sojourn. Italians such as Bonaventure, Thomas Aquinas, Peter of Tarantaise, Gilles of Rome, James of Viterbo, meet with masters from German provinces such as Albert the Great, Ulric of Strasburg, Thierry of Freiburg. From the region of Flanders or from the Walloon country come Gauthier of Bruges, Siger of Brabant, Henry of Ghent, Godfrey of Fontaines, and they meet Danes, such as Boethius the Dacian, and especially the English masters, such as Stephen Langton, Michael Scot, Alfred Anglicus (of Sereshel), William of Meliton, Alexander of Hales, Richard of Middleton, Roger Bacon, Robert Kilwardby, Walter Burleigh, Duns Scotus and William of Occam. Spain also is represented by notable men, such as Peter of Spain, Cardinal Ximenes of Toledo, and Raymond Lully. Indeed, one can count on one's fingers the philosophers of the thirteenth century who were not trained at Paris, such as the Silesian Witelo or Robert Grosseteste, the organizer of the University of Oxford,—and even the latter was indirectly influenced by Paris. All of these strangers mingle with the masters of French origin, William of Auxerre, Bernard of Auvergne, William of St. Amour, William of Auvergne, bishop of Paris, John of La Rochelle, and Vincent of Beauvais. From their midst are recruited the artificers of that great cosmopolitan philosophy which is to mould the minds of the educated classes.

III

The vigorous growth of the philosophical and theological schools of Paris was singularly quickened by the rise of the two new religious orders,— the Dominicans and the Franciscans—and by their incorporation in the University. This stimulus was so important that it justifies treating these orders as a further cause of the rapid development of philosophy in the thirteenth century.

The Benedictine monasteries had fallen into decline, chiefly through excess of wealth which had finally weakened their austerity. Francis of Assisi and Dominic, who founded the two celebrated orders of Franciscans and Dominicans at about the same time, effected a return to evangelical poverty by forbidding the possession of this world's goods,— not only to each of their disciples, but also to the religious communities themselves. Hence their name of "mendicant" orders; and Francis, called *Il poverino,* spoke of poverty as his bride. It was because they wished to preach to the multitudes and to mingle more intimately in public and social life that the Franciscans and the Dominicans established themselves in the town, whilst the Benedictines and the Carthusians had settled in the country.

At the same time the Dominicans and the Franciscans were not slow in forming an intellectual élite. For both orders, each in its own way, fostered learning in their members; and so they became, almost on the day of their inception, nurseries of philosophers and theologians. It is really very wonderful to follow the intense intellectual life which is developed in the midst of these vast corporations of workers. Hardly are they founded before they establish themselves at Paris, in 1217 and 1219 respectively; they create in the young University centre separate establishments of advanced studies, *"studia generalia,"* for their own members. But at the same time, they are engaged in incorporating themselves in the intellectual life of the University, by obtaining chairs in the faculty of Theology. Fortune favoured the rapid rise of the orders in the University faculty. In 1229 a strike of the secular professors, at the schools of Notre Dame, gave them their initial opportunity. The voice of Parisian learning had become silent, as the documents put it,—*in omni facultate silet Parisien-*

sis vox doctrinae. At this juncture the Dominicans and the Franciscans offered their services to the chancellor, and they were accepted. When later the strike was concluded, the orders succeeded in maintaining themselves in the faculty of Theology, in spite of the opposition from the other members of the faculty. The Dominicans had obtained two chairs (one in 1229 and one in 1231), and at the same time the Franciscans had secured a chair, of which Alexander of Hales was the first incumbent.

The burning fever for work and the need of reconsidering doctrine, in the light of the new philosophies brought from Arabia and Spain and Byzantium, created among the Franciscans and the Dominicans a unique spirit of emulation and served as a spur to zealous discussion. In every branch of their activities and in every country the rivalry between the two great orders breaks out. In religious matters, they discuss the merits of their respective ideals; in matters of art, their best artists glorify the remarkable men of their own orders,—thus, following a capricious impulse intelligible in artists, the Dominican Fra Angelico shows in his pictures of the Last Judgment certain Franciscans tumbling toward hell, while the Dominicans are received into heaven! But nowhere are they more eager to surpass each other than in the realms of philosophy and theology. Those who would hold back are shaken from their torpor; thus, in the vigorous though rude style of the day, Albert the Great speaks of the reactionaries of his order as "stupid animals who blaspheme philosophy without understanding it."[7] In 1284 the Franciscan John Peckham,—who reminds one of Roger Bacon, in his impulsive character and in his tendency to exaggerate—writes to the Chancellor of the University as follows: "Certain brothers of the Dominican order boast that the teaching of truth has a higher place of honor among them than in any other existing order."[8]

On the other hand, a certain blind rivalry persists between the "regulars" (those subjects to Dominican or Franciscan rule), and those who call themselves "secular" teachers (*seculares*). The latter could not conceal their animosity toward their monkish colleagues: and the University writings of the period are full of the quarrels which resulted. Thus, as Dominicans and Franciscans opposed each other on points of doctrine, the seculars reveal their malice by comparing the twin orders to Jacob and Esau who quarreled in the very womb of their mother. However, these twin brothers accomplished great things, and Roger Bacon, the *enfant terrible* of his time, in spite of his quarrels with his fellow friars could not refrain from writing in

[7] "... tanquam bruta animalia blasphemantia in iis quae ignorant," *In Epist. Beati Dionysii Areopagitae,* Epist. VIII, No. 2.

[8] "Quidam fratres ejusdem ordinis praedicatorum ausi sunt se publice jactitari doctrinam veritatis plus in suo ordine quam in alio contemporaneo viguisse." *Epistola ad cancellarium.* Oxon., Decemb., 1284.

1271, with his usual exaggeration, that in forty years no "secular" had written anything of any value either in Philosophy or in Theology.[9]

IV

The extreme fondness for philosophy, however, which appears in the University of Paris during the thirteenth century, is explained only in part by the acquired momentum, the influx of foreigners to Paris, the place given to philosophy and theology in the program of studies, and the feverish activity of the impressive Dominican and Franciscan corporations with their remarkable masters. In addition, and finally, we must consider the introduction of new philosophical texts, which served as food for individual reflection and for discussion and for writing.

It is hard for us adequately to realize what this enrichment must have meant at that time. The great treatises of Aristotle,—his Metaphysics, his Physics, his Treatise on the Soul, works of which doctors had spoken for five hundred years, but which no westerner had read since the days of Boethius—were brought to them from Greece and from Spain. Neo-Platonic works were added to these,—principally the *"Liber de Causis,"* written by a compiler of Proclus, and the *"Elementa Theologiae"* of Proclus himself. Henceforth the West knows the best that Greek thought had produced.

[9] *Compendium Studii*, cap. V, ed. Brewer p. 428.

Nor is that all. Along with these works, the Parisian doctors receive a vast number of commentaries, made by the Arabs of Bagdad and of Spain. Finally, they also come into possession of a large collection of Arabian and Jewish works, having their sources in Alfarabi, Avicenna, Averroes, Avicebron, not to mention others.

All of these riches, in Latin translation, were brought to Paris, to France, to England, to Italy, to Germany; and the study and evaluation of these translations is one of the most difficult and far-reaching problems connected with the history of that age. In the last century, work on this great problem was begun by eminent scholars; nor can we even now say that it is solved. Will it ever be solved? For, it continually enlarges as further insight into it is gained. But results have been obtained; and within recent years specialists of all nationalities have taken the work in hand.[9a]

We get some idea of the difficulties, with which these scholars have to deal, when we recall that the work of translation was accomplished in a century and a half; that the Latin translations were made from Greek works, pseudo-Greek works, and books of the Jews and Arabs; that the Greek works were

[9a] Menendez y Pelayo in Spain, Marchesi in Italy, Vacant in France, Mandonnet in Switzerland, Little in England, Charles Haskins at Harvard, Pelzer in Rome, besides a number of Germans (such as Rose, Wüstenfeld and Grabmann).

nearly all twice translated into Latin and in two different ways, the one including the direct translations from the Greek and the other the translations by a sort of cascade of intermediate languages (Arabic and Hebrew and even the vernacular); and, finally, that it was carried on in three main centres,—in Greece itself, in the Greek speaking countries of southern Italy (The Sicilies), and in Spain. Often the same work was translated many times and at different places; many were anonymous or undated.

Through the three great frontiers raised between West and East—Spain, Byzantium, Sicily—the influence of these ideas is set in motion; but it is especially through Spain that the influx is the greatest. It is at Toledo, indeed, the most advanced post of Christianity, and where the kings of Castille are contending against the ever-menacing invasion of the Mussulmans, that Christian civilization gives welcome to the science and philosophy and art of the Arabs. There, in the Archbishop's palace, was founded a college of translators who, for three-quarters of a century, carried on this formidable task, and indeed to a happy conclusion. Englishmen, Italians, Frenchmen, and Germans worked side by side with Jews and christianized Arabs, under the encouragement and stimulus of the two learned Archbishops, whose names are

worthy of being engraved on tablets of bronze,—
Raymond of Toledo and Rodriguez Ximenes.

The actual acquisition of so much new knowledge
was made by the masters of Paris in comparatively
rapid stages. Its elaboration, however, took longer.
The first who came in touch with it were dazed.
In addition to the Greek thought, which took time
to master, there was that further world swimming
into ken, so new and enchanting, the Oriental philosophy of the Arabian people; born of Neo-Platonism, with its mystical, misleading conceptions, and its profound idealism, this philosophy
was very different from the cold, clear speculation
of the Neo-Latins and Anglo-Celts.

It was not until 1270, or thereabouts, that the
West completed its elaboration of these foreign
treasures, and the initial chaos gave place to order
and equilibrium; it was then that Thomas Aquinas,
the great systematizer among the intellectual giants
of that age, laid hold of his opportunity and won
his secure place in the history of thought.

V

We are now ready to enumerate the general results of the great network of causes which functioned in the philosophical development of the thirteenth century. Among these general *results* we
shall confine our attention to two outstanding facts
which dominate the entire thought of the thirteenth
century,—like two high peaks towering above the

rest in a mountain range. On the one hand, there is the predominance, in western Europe, of a great system of philosophy,—the scholastic philosophy; on the other hand, there is the impressive classification of human knowledge. It is important now to note carefully the significance of these facts; we shall seek to analyze them in the chapters that follow.

First, then, the scholastic philosophy. Numerous philosophical systems rose up on every side as if, as I said at the outset, a great variety of seed had been scattered on fertile soil by some generous hand. The thirteenth century is rich in personalities. But, among the numerous philosophical systems to which the century gave birth, there is *one* which overshadows and surpasses all others in its influence. It is the scholastic philosophy. This is the system of doctrines which attains the height of its perfection in the thirteenth century, and to which the majority of the ablest minds subscribe,—such as William of Auvergne, Alexander of Hales, Thomas Aquinas, Bonaventure, and Duns Scotus, to mention no others. There is a great fund of common doctrines, which each interprets in his own way, following his individual genius; just as there is also a common Gothic architecture, which appears in a great many cathedrals, each of which expresses its own individuality. This system of doctrines constitutes the binding tie in an important school of masters, who are thereby united like the members of a family. They themselves call it, in the manuscripts of the period, the *"sententia communis,"* the prevalent philosophy. This common fund of doctrine, to which I was the first to limit the name of "scholastic philosophy"[10] presents an imposing mass of ideas.

To be sure, there were rival and opposing philosophies. Never, at any time in the history of mankind, has contradiction lost its right. The thirteenth century is full of clashes of ideas and conflicts issuing therefrom. For instance, they experienced the shocks of materialism, of Averroism, and of Latin Neo-Platonism. Thus, Latin Averroism, which caused so much disturbance at the University of Paris, about 1270, denies the individuality of the act of thinking, by asserting that all men think through the instrumentality of a single soul, the soul of the race.[11] Again, the Neo-Platonic philosophies, which appear in the schools of Paris, deny all real transcendence of God by making creation an emanation from God, that is to say a part of God Himself.[12] Very naturally, therefore, against this common peril a coalition was formed, both defensive and offensive; and a legion of warriors,—such men as Roger Bacon, Bonaventure, Thomas Aquinas, Duns Scotus—forgot their quarrels and faced the common foe.

[10] *Cf.* my *Histoire de la Philosophie Medievale,* pp. 111 ff.
[11] See ch. XIII, iv.
[12] See ch. XIII, v and vi.

The scholastic philosophers of the thirteenth century also exhibits reasoning superior to all the systems which were trying to batter a breach in their systems of thought. A celebrated painting of the beginning of the fourteenth century, which is preserved at Pisa, furnishes a striking confirmation of this fact; for it reveals the recognition in society at large that the scholastic philosophy was the predominating philosophy of the time. The painter, Traini, represents Thomas Aquinas as crowned in glory and with Averroes at his feet crouching in the attitude of a defeated warrior. The triumph of Aquinas is the triumph of scholasticism, and the defeat of Averroes indicates the defeat of the entire Oriental and Arabian mentality. This painting of Traini, celebrating the triumph of Thomism, became a theme of the studio, that is to say a common opinion, a recognized fact.[13] It is reproduced in a host of well-known paintings. We find it splendidly developed, by an unknown painter of the Sienna school, in the Capitular Hall built by the Dominicans in 1350, at Florence (Chapel of the Spaniards). The subject attracted Gozzoli (in the Louvre); the Spaniard Zurbaran (Museum of Seville); then Filippino Lippi (Church of Minerva, Rome), who in turn directly inspired Raphael's "Dispute of the Blessed Sacrament.[14]

[13] See below ch. VII, ii, and ch. XIII, iv.
[14] Gillet, *Histoire artistique des ordres mendiants,* Paris, 1912, pp. 139 ff.

VI

The second great fact resulting from the intellectual life of the thirteenth century is the classification of human knowledge. All of the philosophical systems,—not only the dominating or scholastic philosophy, but also those anti-scholastic systems with which it was in perpetual struggle and contradiction—rested upon the conception of a vast classification, a gigantic work of systematization, the fruit of many centuries of speculation, and one of the characteristic achievements of the mediaeval mind. For more than a thousand years it has satisfied thinkers athirst for order and clarity. In what does it consist?

One may compare it to a monumental structure, to a great pyramid consisting of three steps,—with the sciences of observation as the base, with philosophy as the middle of the structure, and with theology as the apex.[14a] Let us consider each of these in order.

[14a] The general scheme is:
I. Particular sciences, such as botany, zoology, etc.
II. Philosophy. A. Theoretical a. Physics
                                    b. Mathematics
                                    c. Metaphysics
                B. Practical   a. Logic
                                    b. Ethics
                                    c. Social and political philosophy
                C. Poetical
III. Theology. A. Doctrinal a. Scriptural (*auctoritates*)
                                    b. Apologetical (*rationes*)
                B. Mystical

At the base are the natural sciences such as astronomy, botany, physiology, zoology, chemistry (elements), physics (in the the modern sense of the word); and instruction in these precedes instruction in philosophy. In this there is a very interesting pedagogical application of a ruling principle in the philosophical ideology of the Middle Ages; that is that since human knowledge is contained in the data of sensation, the cultivation of the mind must begin with what falls under the observation of the senses; *nihil est in intellectu quod non prius fuerit in sensu.*[15] But more especially there is implied, in this placing of the experimental sciences at the threshold of philosophy, a conception which inspires the scientific philosophies of all times; namely, that the *synthetic* or *total* conception of the world furnished by philosophy must be founded on an *analytic* or *detailed* conception yielded by a group of special sciences. These latter study the world minutely; and for this reason they are called *special* sciences. They investigate the world in one domain after another; the philosophers of the thirteenth century speak clearly concerning this method—the basis of the particularity of a science.

In every science, say the scholars of the thirteenth century,[16] it is necessary to distinguish the

[15] See ch. VIII, i.
[16] Thomas Aquinas, *Summa Theol.,* 1ª q. I, arts. 1-3, *passim; Contra Gentiles,* II, 4; Henricus Gandavensis, *Summa Theolog.,* art. 7, q. I-VI.

objects with which it is concerned (*materia*) from the point of view from which these objects are considered (*ratio formalis*). The objects with which a science is concerned are its material; for example, the human body constitutes the material of anatomy and of physiology. But every science takes its material in its own way; it treats this material from some one angle, and this angle is always *a point of view* upon which the mind deliberately centers, an aspect of things which the mind separates out,—"abstracts" (*abstrahit*) from its material. Thus the point of view of anatomy is not that of physiology; for anatomy describes the organs of the human body, while physiology, is concerned with their functions. The point of view of the one is static and of the other dynamic.

From this it obviously follows that two sciences can be engaged with the same material, or—to borrow the philosophical terminology of the Middle Ages—possess a common material object (*objectum materiale*); but they must possess in each case, under penalty of being confused, a distinct point of view, a unique formal object (*objectum formale*), which is the special "good" of each science. And, indeed, whatever group of sciences we may consider, we do, in fact discover everywhere the operation of this law, regulating the distinctions among the sciences; geology, inorganic chemistry, and physics are concerned with the same object— the inanimate world—but from different points of view. Biology, paleontology, anatomy, and physiology study the organism but in its different aspects. The material common to political economy, civil law, and criminal law is human action, but each of these sciences regards the complete reality of human action from a special angle. From this intellectualistic conception of the sciences, which bases the specific character of the science upon the point of view, it follows that a new science must be born whenever research and discovery reveal a new aspect, a point of view hitherto unsuspected in the unending pursuit of reality; the further the mind extends its view of things, the further does it penetrate into the secrets of reality.

This theory of science helps us to understand what makes a science "special," and how in the thirteenth century "special" sciences are opposed to "general" science. The particularity of the sciences rests upon two considerations which supplement each other, and an examination of a few of the sciences which we have named as examples will suffice to show in the concrete the value of these considerations. Anatomy and physiology, we said, are concerned with the human body, but they are not concerned about geological strata or stars. The material studied is a particular bit of reality; a restricted, specialized department or—to use again the mediaeval terminology—their material object (*objectum materiale*) is restricted. On the other hand, precisely because anatomy and physiology are concerned with only a particular group of existences, the point of view (*objectum formale*) under which they include this group of existences is also restricted; it is not applied to other categories of the real.

But,—and this is the second point—the detailed examination of the world for which the special sciences take up particular positions does not suffice to satisfy the mind; after the detail it demands total views. Philosophy is simply a survey of the world as a whole. The man of science is like a stranger who would explore a city bit by bit, and who travels through its avenues, promenades, museums, parks, and buildings one after the other. When at last he has wandered over the city in all directions, there will still remain another way for him to become acquainted with it; from the height of a platform, from the summit of a tower, from the basket of a balloon, from an aviator's seat, the city would disclose to him another aspect,—its framework, plan, and relative disposition of parts. But that way is the way of the philosopher, and not of the scientist. The philosopher is thus the man who views the world from the top of a lookout and sets himself to learn its structure; philosophy is a synthetic and general knowledge of things. It is not concerned with this or that compartment of existence, but with all beings existent or possible, the real without restriction. It is not a particular but a general science. General science or philosophy constitutes the second stage of knowledge. It is human wisdom (*sapientia*), science *par excellence*, ἐπιστήμη.

This generality has a twofold aspect; for in two ways the general character of philosophy is opposed to the special character of the particular sciences. In the first place, instead of dealing with one department of reality, philosophy plunges into the immensity of the real, of all that is. Its matter (material object) is not general of course in the sense of an encyclopedia (as was supposed in the early Middle Ages by Isidore of Seville and by Rhabanus Maurus, or by Vincent of Beauvais in the thirteenth century) into which is thrown pell-mell, and in a purely artificial order, a formidable array of information in regard to all that is known and knowable. An encyclopedia is not a science and does not pretend to be. If philosophy deals with all reality it does so by the way of viewing things in their totality. But, in the second place, these total views are possible only when the mind discovers, in the totality of reality, certain aspects or points of view which are met with *everywhere* and which reach to the very depths of reality. To return to the technical scholastic language, with which we are familiar, its formal and precise object is *the study of something that is found everywhere and which must be general because it is common to everything*. Philosophy is defined as the understanding of all things through their fundamental and universal reasons.[16a]

The thirteenth century directs us to the significance of synthesis or generality which belongs to philosophy, by taking up and completing Aristotle's famous division of philosophy, which was accepted as valid down to the time of Wolff in the seventeenth century. Philosophy is first, *theoretical,* second, *practical,* and third, *poetical.* This threefold division of philosophy into speculative, practical, and poetical is based upon man's different contacts with the totality of the real, or, as it was put then, with the universal order.

Speculative or theoretical ($\theta\epsilon\omega\rho\epsilon\tilde{\iota}\nu$, to consider) philosophy gives the results of acquaintance with the world in its *objective* aspect; it includes the philosophy of nature, mathematics, and metaphysics, which consider (*considerat sed non facit*) change, quantity, and the general conditions of being, respectively, in the material world. There are three stages through which the mind passes in order to secure a total view of the world of which it is spectator. The Middle Ages defines physics, or the philosophy of nature, as "the study of the material world in so far as it is carried in the stream of change, *motus.*" Change! Whether, indeed, it is a question of the inorganic kingdom or of the realm of the living, of plants or of human life, of the

---

[16a] Thomas Aquinas, *In Metaph.* I, lect. 2. "Sapientia est scientia quae considerat primas et universales causas."

atom or of the course of the stars: all that *is* in the sensible world, *becomes,* that is to say, *changes,* evolves; or, to use the expression of the Middle Ages, everything is in motion (*movere*). To study, in its inmost nature, change and its implications, in order to explain the movements of the material world,—this is the task of the philosophy of nature.[17] It is easy to see that this study is of a regressive and synthetic kind, that it is general, that is to say, philosophical, on account of the general character of the material investigated (material object), and the generality of the point of view from which the inquiry is undertaken (formal object). But through all their changes and transformations bodies preserve a common attribute, the primary attribute of body—*quantity*—so that the study of *quantity* forces us to penetrate reality still further. *Mathematics,* which studies quantity as regards its logical implications, was for the ancients a philosophical and therefore a general science, and in our day many scientists are tending to return to this Aristotelian notion. *Metaphysics* enters deepest of all into reality and deals with what is beyond motion and quantity,—for the sole purpose of considering the general determinations of being.

But practical philosophy is no less general in character, although it is not concerned with the universal order in its objective reality, but with the

[17] Be it observed that, since man is a part of the world of sense-perception, psychology also belongs to physics.

activities (πράττειν) of conscious life, *through which we enter into relation with that reality* (*considerat faciendo*). Hence, as Thomas Aquinas explains, practical philosophy is occupied with an order of things of which man is at once spectator (since he examines it by turning upon himself) and maker (since he forms it through his conscious function, that is, *knowing* and *willing*). Practical philosophy includes logic and ethics and politics. *Logic* sets up a scheme of all that we know, of the method of constructing the sciences; and there is nothing that the human mind cannot know in some imperfect way. *Ethics* studies the realm of our acts, and there is nothing in human life that cannot become the material of duty. *Politics* is concerned with the realm of social institutions, and there is nothing which has not its social side, since man is made to live in society (*animale sociale*). Going more deeply into the analysis of practical philosophy, one might show that logic draws in its train speculative grammar, for it invades the fields of grammar and rhetoric—its former associates in the trivium—to draw thence material for controversy. Furthermore, Paris saw the birth of some true philosophers of language, in the speculative grammars of **Siger of Courtrai** and of **Duns Scotus**;[18] and the lexicographical codes of **Donatus** and **Priscian**

---

[18] The authenticity of the *Grammatica speculativa*, attributed to Duns Scotus, has been doubted. However this may be, it is a remarkable work.

which had satisfied the twelfth century were finally rejected with scorn. Logic, ethics, and politics all claim to be in touch with the immensity of the reality with which man enters into relation.

The same quality of universality should pertain to the third group of the philosophical sciences, the poetical (ποιεῖν, to make) sciences, which study the order achieved by man *externally* through the guidance of reason. Man is at once the spectator and maker of an order which he creates. But this order is outside of him, in matter.[19] This third group is the least developed of all. It would seem as if the human product *par excellence, the work of art, endowed with beauty*, should here occupy a large place. But the thinkers of the thirteenth century regard the productive activity of the artisan,—maker of furniture or builder of houses—as on the same level with the human creative activity which inspires epics and which makes cathedrals to rise and stained windows to flame and granite statues to live. Dante has no special thought of beauty, when he speaks of the work of art, as "the grandson of God."[20] The professional philosophers bury their reflections on beauty in metaphysical studies; hence the fragmentary character of their thought in that realm. Possibly this omission as regards aesthetic theory has its explanation in the corporate character of their labors. The artisan was devoted

---
[19] *Cf.* Thomas Aquinas, *In Ethic. Nicom.*, I, 1.
[20] The *Inferno*, XI, 103, " . . . a Dio quasi nepote."

to his calling; and this devotion was such that every artisan was, or might become, an artist. The distinction between *artes liberales* and *artes mechanicae* did not rest upon any superiority of the artistic activity as such, but upon the difference in the processes employed; both were possessed of the *ratio artis* in like manner.[20a] Furthermore, we must bear in mind that the contemporaries of an artistic apogee do not realize the significance of the development witnessed by them; theories always come later than the facts which they are meant to explain. In any event, we should note how large and human is the philosophical conception of art in the Middle Ages; there is no work of man which it cannot clothe in the royal mantle of beauty.

It remains only to mention the last order of studies which is placed above philosophy, and which corresponds, in the comparison that we have been making, to the highest part of the structure, to the apex of the pyramid. This is *theology,* doctrinal and mystical.[21] The part relating to doctrines is an arrangement of dogmas founded upon the Christian revelation, and we shall see later[22] that it takes a double form,—being both scriptural and apologetical.

Theology aside, this classification of human

[20a] "Nec oportet, si liberales artes sunt nobiliores, quod magis eis conveniat ratio artis." *Summa Theol.,* 1a 2ae, q. LVII, art. 3, *in fine.*
[21] For its place in the general scheme see above, p. 85.
[22] See ch. VII.

knowledge is Aristotelian in origin. The Aristotelian spirit appears not only in the very notion of "science," which aims at unity; but also in the relation between the particular sciences and philosophy. Since the latter rests upon the former, it remains in permanent contact with the facts; indeed, it is anchored to the very rocks of reality. The abundant harvest of facts, supplied by Greeks and Arabians, was enriched by fresh observations in physics (in the modern sense of the word), chemistry (elementary), botany, zoology and human physiology. Moreover, Thomas Aquinas and Godfrey of Fontaines and others borrowed material from the special sciences which were taught in the other university faculties, notably from medicine and from law (civil and canon). Facts about nature and about the physical and social man,—indeed, observations from all sources—are called upon to supply materials for the synthetic view of philosophy. They all claim with Dominicus Gundissalinus, that there is no science which may not contribute to philosophy. *Nulla est scientia quae non sit aliqua philosophiae pars.*[23] Scholastic philosophy is thus a philosophy based upon science, and it is perhaps not superfluous to observe that we are now more than ever returning to these conceptions.

But in order to appreciate at their true worth the

[23] *De divisione Philosophiae, Prologus,* p. 5, edit. Baur (Baümker's-*Beiträge,* IV, 2-3).

applications made by the scholastics, we must make a twofold reservation. First, facts were studied much more for the purpose of furnishing material for philosophy than for their own sake; hence the Middle Ages never recognized the distinction between common experience and scientific experiment, which is so familiar to us. Second, this material secured out of observation and experience, represented a mixture,—a mixture of facts artificially obtained and of exact observation. The former necessarily lead to erroneous conclusions, examples of which we shall see later.[24] The latter, however, were adequate for establishing legitimate conclusions.

Finally, the Aristotelian spirit appears also in the inner articulation of philosophy itself. During the first centuries of the Middle Ages the Platonic division of philosophy into physics, logic, and ethics had been in vogue; and for a long time it persisted. The thirteenth century definitely rejects it, or rather absorbs it into new classifications. Compared with Aristotle—the most brilliant teacher whom humanity has known—Plato is only a poet, saying beautiful things without order or method. Dante was right when he called Aristotle *"the master of those who know."* But *to know* is above all *to order; sapientis est ordinare,*—it is the mission of the wise man to put order into his knowledge. Even those who do not accept the ideas of the Stagyrite acknowledge his kingship when it is

---
[24] See ch. V, ii.

a question of order or clearness. "Three-quarters of mankind," writes Taine,[25] "take general notions for idle speculations. So much the worse for them. What does a nation or an age live for, except to form them? Only through them does one become completely human. If some inhabitant of another planet should descend here to learn how far our race had advanced, we would have to show him our five or six important ideas regarding the mind and the world. That alone would give him the measure of our intelligence." To such a question the scholars of the Middle Ages would have replied by exhibiting their classification of knowledge, and they would have won glory thereby. Indeed, it constitutes a remarkable chapter in scientific methodology, a kind of "introduction to philosophy," to use a modern expression. Whatever may be one's judgment regarding the value of this famous classification, one must bow in respect before the great ideal which it seeks to promote. It meets a need which recurrently haunts humanity and which appears in all great ages: the need for the unification of knowledge. The thirteenth century dreamed of it, as Aristotle and Plato did in ancient times, and as Auguste Comte and Herbert Spencer have done in our day. It is a splendid product of greatness and power, and we shall see in the chapters that follow how closely bound up it is with the civilization to which it belongs.

[25] *Le positivisme anglais*, Paris, 1864, pp. 11, 12.

CHAPTER FIVE

UNIFYING AND COSMOPOLITAN TENDENCIES

i. Need of universality; the "law of parsimony." ii. Excess resulting from the felt need of simplifying without limit; the geocentric system and the anthropocentric conception. iii. The society of mankind (*"universitas humana"*) in its theoretical and practical forms. iv. Cosmopolitan tendencies.

I

We have seen that there are two outstanding results of the various causes that make for the great development of philosophy in the thirteenth century. On the one hand, there is the great classification of human knowledge, in which each science had its own particular place—a pyramid of three stages, or if one prefers the figure employed by Boethius,[1] a ladder for scaling the walls of learning. On the other hand, among all the clashing systems which rest upon that classification, there is one system of thought which prevails,—that is scholasticism; and it wins widest acceptance because it succeeds in reducing to one harmonious whole all of the problems and their solutions.

Bearing in mind these two great facts, we shall

[1] Boethius, *De Consolatione Philosophiae*, Lib. I, 1.

now proceed to show that they possess characteristics which are found in every sphere of the life of the times; and, indeed, as will appear, they are in organic connection with all the other factors of mediaeval civilization.

There is one fundamental characteristic, appearing in the scientific classification and the scholastic philosophy, which is found everywhere; I mean the *tendency toward unity*. The need of ordering everything in accordance with principles of unity and stability, the search for systems which extend themselves over vast domains, is one of the conspicuous marks of a century which saw in the large, and which acted on a broad plan. Wherever we turn, we find a prodigious ambition of initiators and everyone dreaming of universal harmony.

The policy of kings was filled with this ambition. For, at this time, the feeling for unity began to vivify great states such as France and England and Germany and Spain. Now, this unity could not be realized except by introducing principles of order, which would bring under a common régime social classes scattered over vast territories, and previously subjected to local and antagonistic powers. The thirteenth century was a century of kings who were all organizers, administrators, legislators; they were builders of stability, who all moulded their countries and their peoples: Philip Augustus and Louis IX in France; Edward I in England; Frederick II of Germany; Ferdinand III and Alphonso X in Spain; all had these traits in common.

In France, localistic and centrifugal feudalism became more and more feeble, and monarchical concentration grew steadily stronger. This concentration, which first appeared under Philip Augustus, became more and more evident under Louis IX, who perfected the work of unification begun by his grandfather. A lover of justice, respectful of the rights of others, and jealous of his own, he made no attempt to crush the feudal lords or the cities. There was nothing despotic in his rule, and he permitted all kinds of social forces to develop themselves.[2] His reign resembled the oak under which he held his court of justice; for the oak, the lord of the forest, likewise refrains from stifling growths of more fragile structure which seek protection under its shade.

Without attempting to establish a parallel between the policy and social condition of France and the neighboring countries, one must recognize that the stability realized by Louis IX recurs *mutatis mutandis* in England. When John Lackland rendered to England "the inestimable service of losing her French possessions,"[3] the country organized itself from within outward. The Magna Charta of 1215 established a rule of liberty in favor of the clergy and the nobility; it produced an equi-

[2] Luchaire, A., *Louis VII, Philippe Auguste, Louis VIII*, p. 203.
[3] See F. Harrison, *The Meaning of History*, etc., 1916, p. 161.

poise between the powers of the king and the representatives of the nation. Parliament came into being. Intelligent princes, like Edward I (1272-1307), completed the conquest of the Island and perfected the national institutions.

Much the same thing occured in the Norman kingdom of the Two Sicilies, and in the Catholic kingdoms of Spain, which grew powerful at the cost of the Arab states in the south of the peninsula, and in which later the Cortes checked the royal power. Like his relative Louis IX, Ferdinand III, king of Castile, had the centralizing idea. He organized a central administration of the state; and only his death prevented him from achieving legislative unity, which would have consolidated the mosaic of peoples living within the expanding confines of Castile.[4]

But while in France, in England, in the Catholic kingdoms of Spain, and in the Norman kingdom of the south of Italy, royalty was gaining in influence. the German Emperor was losing some of his power. The result was that the two types of government in the West, feudal particularism and German centralized authority, steadily approached each other, and the different European states became more like a single family. The German barons, bishops, and abbots were no longer the "valets" of the emperor;

[4] Altamira, *Historia de España y de la civilisacion espagnola,* 1913, I, p. 385.

the feudal nobility gained more independence; cities began to show their power.

Even in Italy, which the German Emperors had so long claimed as their own, Frederic II, son of Frederic Barbarossa, had to reckon with the Lombard cities which were powerful principalities, seeking to shake off his yoke. In his person the family of the Hohenstaufen underwent defeat at the hands of the Pope.

Above this process of beginning nationalization, states which were striving towards an autonomous national life, stood the Papacy, which assumed in the person of Innocent III its most perfect mediaeval expression. Its mission being above all regulatory, the Papacy followed a religious and international policy whose effect on the whole century will be defined later in this chapter.[5] It was Innocent III who affirmed the unitary rôle of the Papacy in the political life of his age: he was the first to set up as a *right* that which his predecessors had practiced in fact—that is, the nomination of the Emperor.[5a]

But politics, whether of kings or of popes, constitute only the body of civilization. Its inner life circulates in religious and moral feelings, in social, artistic, philosophical, and scientific doctrines.

[5] See below iii.
[5a] See the Bull *Venerabilem:* "jus et auctoritas examinandi personam electam in regem et promovendum ad imperium *ad nos* spectat."

Christian dogma and Christian ethics permeated the whole human fabric, no activity being exempted from their influence. They endued with a certain supernatural sanction the life of individuals, families and peoples, who were all on a pilgrimage (*in via*) towards the heavenly home (*in patriam*). Christianity gave a spirit of consecration to the workers in guilds, to the profession of arms (provided the war was just), to ateliers of painters and of sculptors, to the builders of cathedrals, to cloister-schools and universities. The new religious orders organized themselves in the new spirit of the age. While the Benedictine monks belonged to a particular abbey, as to a large family, the Dominicans and Franciscans belonged far more to their order as a whole,—they were delocalized, being sent out for preaching like soldiers to a battlefield.[6]

Similarly, in the whole field of art there was the same dream of universality, and the same attempt to realize rigorously the ideal of order.

The Gothic cathedrals, which are the most perfect flowering of mediaeval genius, amaze modern architects with the amplitude of their dimensions. "They were made for crowds, for thousands and tens of thousands of human beings; for the whole human race, on its knees, hungry for pardon and love."[7] At the same time, they astound the mod-

[7] Henry Adams, *op. cit.*, p. 367.
[6] *Cf.* E. Baker, *The Dominican Order and Convocation*, Oxford, Clarendon Press, 1913.

ern student of art by the logic of their plan. To make the edifice a mirror of nature, of the moral world, and of history, architecture calls to its aid sculpture, painting, and stained glass. Immense shrines populate themselves with statues, with figures of animals, plants, and foliage, with designs of every kind. The visible world was a veritable reflection of the thought of God for the mediaeval artists; hence they thought that all creatures might find a place in the cathedral. Likewise, the cathedral is the mirror of science, and, in fact, all kinds of knowledge, even the humblest, such as fitted men for manual labor and for the making of calendars, and also the highest, such as liberal arts, philosophy, and theology, were given plastic form. Thus the cathedral could readily serve as a visible catechism, where the man of the thirteenth century could find in simple outline all that he needed to believe and to know. The highest was made accessible to the lowest. Architecture has never been more social and popular at any other period of history.

As for literature, while the productions of the thirteenth century do not rank with their monuments of stone, nevertheless they represent great endeavor. A work like the *Roman de la Rose* is a sort of encyclopedia of everything that a cultured layman of the middle of the thirteenth century ought to know. The *Divine Comedy,* a work which has not been imitated and which is inimitable, is a symphony of the whole time. Dante's stage is the universe; he is a citizen of the world, and he informs us that he writes "the sacred poem to which heaven and earth put their hands."[8]

While the artists were thus giving birth to new life in art, the intellectual classes were hungering and thirsting to know all, to assemble everything within the domain of knowledge, and, after having completed the collection, to submit all to order.

There are different levels in that effort toward order. At the lower level the encyclopaedists express the desire of the time for an inventory of all that can be known. Thus Jacopo de Voragine, in the *Golden Legend,* gathers together the legends of the lives of the saints; William the bishop of Mende collects all that has been said about the Catholic liturgy. There are compilers like Bartholomeus Anglicus, author of a treatise *De Proprietatibus.* Above all there is Vincent of Beauvais, who wrote an enormous *Speculum Quadruplex,* a veritable Encyclopedia Britannica of the thirteenth century. Vincent calls attention to the *brevitas temporum* which is at the disposal of his contemporaries and to the *multitudo librorum* which they must read, in order to excuse himself for giving his ideas on all possible subjects.[9] Much the same may be said of the work of the jurists of Bologna and of the canonists—although doctrine

[8] *Divina Commedia,* Paradiso, XXV.
[9] *Speculum historiale,* cap. I (vol. I incunable, ed. Mentellini, 1473-6).

has begun to develop, and the unity of precision had made its appearance in their work. Thus, the jurists compiled the various theories of Roman law. The most famous of these jurists, Accursius who died in 1252, united in an enormous compilation (the *Glossa Ordinaria*) all the works of his predecessors. About the same time, the *legistes* of Philip Augustus translated the *corpus juris* into French; Edward I had a collection made of the decisions of his courts of justice; and James I of Aragon had a codification made of laws, called the *Canellas*. Furthermore, the canonists, at the wish of the Popes, continued the work of codification begun by Gratian in his *Decretum,* and brought together the decisions of the Popes (*Decretales*) and the decisions of the councils.

But in comparison with the philosophers, the encyclopedists, jurists, and canonists are as dwarfs by the side of giants. The philosophers, as we have seen,[10] created that vast classification of human knowledge, in which each kind of thinking found its place,—and in doing so they showed themselves to be, as lovers of order and clarity, in intimate sympathy with the demands of their time. Thus, all the particular sciences in existence at the time, and all those that might arise through a closer study of inorganic matter, or of the moral and social activities of man, occupy a place in the plan, marked out in advance.

[10] See above, ch. III, ii.

But the shining example of this urgent need for universality and unity appears in that massive system of thought which dominates and obscures all its rivals,—namely, the scholastic philosophy. Monumental *Summae,* collections of public lectures called *Quaestiones Disputatae,* and monographs of all kinds, display an integral conception of the physical and moral world wherein no philosophical problems are omitted. Questions in psychology, ideology, and epistemology; on the constitution of matter and corporeal bodies; on being, unity, efficiency, act, potency, essence, existence; on the logical construction of the sciences; on individual and social ethics; on general aesthetics; on speculative grammar and the philosophy of language—all of these vital philosophical questions receive their answer. The particular sciences are all pressed into service for philosophy, and they supply it with the facts and observations of concrete experience. Even the intellectual activities of the jurists and the canonists are also drawn within the scholastic synthesis. The scholastics of Paris especially, in their lectures and in their books, treat from their specific standpoint certain questions which the jurists treat by reference to their technical demands. For example, they commonly discuss and study questions of private property, of burial, of the right to make war, of the relations between Church and State; but such questions are approached not from the point of view of positive law, but rather from that of moral and natural law. Thus, just as the other departments of human knowledge furnish their several quotas of material, so civil and canon law bring their contributions.[11] In this way, philosophical thought is endlessly extended, and philosophy becomes an explanation of the whole.

But not alone are all vital questions answered; everywhere there is coherence, and in the full meaning of the word (σύστημα),—so that one may not withdraw a single doctrine without thereby compromising a group of others. Everything hangs together by implication and logical articulation; everywhere appears to the utmost that consuming desire for universality and order which lays hold of the savants and leads them to introduce the most comprehensive and rigorous schema possible. Thomas Aquinas, Duns Scotus, and, to a less degree, Alexander of Hales and Bonaventure are systematic minds; their philosophy is an intellectual monument, and the sense of proportion which it reveals is the same as that of the Gothic cathedral to which it has so often been compared. It is just because everything is so fittingly combined in the scholastic philosophy,[12] and because it does satisfy the mind's most exacting demands for coherence, in which its very life consists, that it has charmed through the ages so many successive generations of thinkers.

[11] *Cf.* above, ch. IV, vi.
[12] See below, ch. X, for an example of this doctrinal coherence.

We must also observe that scholastic philosophy accomplishes, by means of a limited number of ideas, that doctrinal order to which it is so devoted. It simplifies to the full limit of its power. Each doctrine which it introduces possesses a real value for explanation, and consequently it cannot be sacrificed. Thus, to take only one instance, the theories of act and potency, of matter and form, of essence and existence, of substance and accident are all indispensable to their metaphysics.[13] For them, philosophy as well as nature obeys the principle of parsimony. *Natura non abundat in superfluis,* writes Thomas Aquinas.[14] Indeed, the thirteenth century had already anticipated, in various forms, that counsel of wisdom which is usually attributed to William of Occam: not to multiply entities without necessity.[15] In its moderation, indeed, schol-

[13] See ch. IX.
[14] *Summa Theol.,* 1a 2ae, q. XCIV, art. 2. The Leonine edition of the *Summa contra Gentiles,* following the original text of Thomas (Rome, 1918), shows what pains the author took in this book to realize the internal order I refer to. The deliberate omissions, the additions, the studied improvements,—all of this reveals much labor. *Cf.* A. Pelzer, "L'édition léonine de la Somme contre les Gentils." *Revue Néo-Scolastique de philosophie,* May, 1920, pp. 224 ff.

[15] See below, p. 117, note 23, for an application of this principle made by Dante to universal monarchy. Duns Scotus is familiar with the principle. For a note on the formula: *pluritas non est ponenda sine necessitate,* see Mind, July 1918, by Thorburn, who observes that it does not originate in Occam. It is in fact a formula which moves through the whole thirteenth century, and which expresses just the felt need of unity that engages us in this chapter. All

astic philosophy is like the thirteenth century cathedral, which admits only those linear forms which are required by the *rationale* of the structure. It was not until the fourteenth century that those cumbersome theories appeared which weakened the doctrine.

The same systematic character marks also the theology of the time, which is simply a great grouping of Catholic dogmas, each of which is consonant with all the rest.

To sum it all up, then. Need of universality, need of unity, need of order: the whole civilization is athirst for them.

II

However, this passion for systematization, by its very fascination, sometimes led the ablest philosophers to excess,—and herein lies a reason for a certain peculiarity of the mediaeval mind. So great was this felt need of ordering things, that sometimes, in the lack of *reasons to prove,* recourse was had to *fiction to please.*

The astronomico-philosophical conceptions of the thirteenth century furnish a striking example of this fact. For the men of the time the earth is the centre of the universe, and man is the lord of the earth. The moon and the planets are conceived as fixed in their divers and distant spheres and as

philosophers invoke this principle, and each adapts it to his own doctrines.

describing their revolutions around the earth; with laborious care they seek to reconcile this conception with the apparent movements of the heavens. As regards the fixed stars, they form the last sphere of the world, beyond which "place or locus exists no more," following the assertion of Aristotle,— they think of them as held permanently in place by nails of gold in a sky of crystal, which the divine intelligences cause to revolve in their daily courses around this earth of ours, and around man who, in the last analysis, is the *raison d'être* of all. And here follows a series of postulates which are made simply to satisfy their demand for synthesis,— postulates which rest not on fact but on feeling. Thus, for example, it is thought to be fitting that the heavens, so impressive in their eternal mystery, should be made of an essence superior to anything here below. And being superior, it is equally fitting that they should have an influence upon terrestrial objects and direct human affairs. Does not the superior, writes Thomas Aquinas, command the inferior? The very order of things demands it. Or, once again, since unity is a more perfect thing than plurality, and creation is perfect, one must therefore believe in the unity of creation; consequently a plurality of worlds is rejected as discrediting the work of God. Undoubtedly men of clear vision saw through this fragile and naïve conception of the structure of the world; certainly in a few well known passages,[16] Thomas Aquinas and his disciple Giles of Lessines observe that the geo-centric system is only an hypothesis, and that the celestial movements are perhaps susceptible of explanation by theories yet to be discovered by man. To be sure, Thomas minimizes the influence of the action of the heavens; he restricts this action to the disposition of the human body, and rejects any such action upon the intellect and the will.[17] Nevertheless, the astronomico-philosophical doctrines are admitted as parts of the whole, because their incorporation satisfies the need of unity. Moreover, they are necessary for a proper understanding of their magic and alchemy,—or, again, of the interdiction by the University of Paris against the astrology of Roger Bacon, who exaggerated its directive influence in human affairs.

[16] Thomas Aquinas, *In lib. II de Coelo,* lectio 17. About 1322 an unknown teacher taught the following at Paris: quod si terra moveretur et coelum quiesceret, esset in mundo melior dispositio (*cf.* P. Duhem, "Francois de Mayronnes et la rotation de la terre," *Archivum Franscisanum Historicum,* 1913, pp. 23-25). Nicholas of Oresmes taught the same doctrine about 1362,—over a hundred years before the birth of Copernicus (1473).

It is important to observe, that in regard to astronomical questions the scholastics of the thirteenth century had more liberal ideas than had their successors of the seventeenth century. The latter refused to acknowledge the evidence of the discoveries made by the telescope,—and thus they helped to discredit the very philosophy of which they were such unworthy successors.

[17] *Summa Theol.,* 1a 2ae, p. IX, art. 5.

III

There is yet another mediaeval doctrine which sounds strangely to our modern ears, and which furnishes a further interesting example of their felt need of ordering things. I refer to their dream of a universal brotherhood, which they hoped to realize by organizing a kind of Christian republic, —a republic which should embrace all mankind.

If we wish to understand this "society of mankind," to grasp its essential point, we must more than ever think directly in the mental terms of the time. Let us look then at this *universitas humana* through the eyes of Dante the poet, Thomas Aquinas the philosopher, and Innocent IV the canonist. We shall find that in its *theoretical* form it is a brilliant manifestation of the centripetal tendencies of the time; and that also in its *practical* form it appears in a garb which well suits the thirteenth century.

God created all beings; all beings are subject to His providence. He is the Sovereign, the King of the universe. Everywhere in His kingdom there is a certain fixed hierarchy and order; yet in such wise that all depends upon Him and tends toward Him. The angels, who are pure spirit, are arranged in degrees of perfection, but are all in His service and contemplate His infinitude. Man, who is spirit united with matter, dwells in a corporeal space, the earth, awaiting a future day when he shall realize the supernatural destiny which the redemption of Christ has assured him.

Just as the earth is the centre of the universe, so man is the lord of the earth. He is the end of creation, and the most perfect image, here below, of God. Man is like a little world, a *microcosmos*. In the words of Dante as spokesman for his age, man resembles the horizon where two hemispheres seem to meet.[18] Made to be happy—for, all beings strive toward happiness—man has a twofold destiny: a temporal end, which he must realize here on earth, and a supernatural end, in which he obtains a perfect vision and love of God, but the right of approach to which he must gain in this life. Now, he cannot attain this temporal end and prepare himself for the supernatural end, unless he lives in society. Without society, he cannot meet the requirements of the material life, nor develop sufficiently his personality. He is a social animal, *"animal politicum."*[19]

The ideal, as Augustine says in the *City of God*, would be to have society on earth an exact copy of the divine city where all is peace and unity. In respect to political groups that are larger than the family, it would be best that there should be but one in the whole world. But such unity is impossible, because of discussions among men; masses of

[18] "Recte a philosophis assimilatur horizonti qui est medium duorum hemisphaeriorum," *De Monarchia*, L. III.
[19] See below ch. X, iii.

men, like masses of water, are the more dangerous the more abundant they are.[20] If there were no other reason, divergence in language alone would be sufficient cause of dissension—*hominem alienat ab homine*—for a man has a better understanding of his dog than of another man who does not understand his language. So, different kingdoms are required, and the rivalries between these involve wars and all their attendant evils.

The philosophers, theologians, canonists, jurists, and publicists of the thirteenth century reproduce all these doctrines of the *City of God,* which possessed such a fascination for the whole of the Middle Ages. But they wish to correct the defects arising from the plurality of the states, by a unifying theory, the universal community of men, *humana universitas,* as Dante says.[21] They wish, at any cost, to recover, in spite of the several kingdoms, a unity of direction, such as guides the revolution of the spheres, the general government of the universe.[22]

No one at that time doubted that man had a

---

[20] Post civitatem vel urbem sequitur orbis terrae, in quo tertium gradum ponunt societatis humanae, incipientes a domo atque inde ad urbem, deinde ad orbem progrediendo venientes: qui utique, sicut aquarum congeries, quanto major est, tanto periculis plenior. *De Civitate Dei,* XIX, ch. 7.

[21] *De Monarchia,* Lib. I.

[22] Humanum genus est filius coeli quod est perfectissimum . . . Et cum coelum totum unico motu, scilicet primi mobilis et unico motore qui Deus est, reguletur, etc. *Ibid.*

double end to fulfill; and consequently everybody admitted that there must be in human society two kinds of rule,—a temporal and a spiritual. The spiritual hierarchy is very clearly constituted: above the groups in parishes, directed by the rectors, are the bishops; above the abbeys directed by the abbots are the heads of the order; above all is the Pope, who represents Christ on earth. As for the temporal domain, above single states which were in process of formation, and which, for the most part, were governed by kings, the theorists proclaimed the rights of a Single Monarch. This was a political postulate. It was the Caesarian dream which, from the time of Charlemagne, had haunted the mediaeval mind, and which was never more brilliantly defended.

One may read, in the *De Monarchia* of Dante, the weighty considerations which the philosophical poet urges in defense of the universal monarchy, the political panacea which was to restore the golden age on earth. A single monarch, raised above the different kings of feudal Europe, was required to effect the unification of human society. There was no other method of establishing unity among the scattered groups of human kind, of subordinating the parts to the interest of all.[23]

[23] Constat quod totum humane genus ordinatur ad unum ... Partes humanae universitatis respondent ad ipsam per unum principium. ... Humanum genus potest regi per unum principem ... *quod potest fieri per unum melius est fieri per unum quam per plura.* Lib. I, *passim.*

After introducing these philosophical considerations, Dante enters upon the practical bearings of the problem. This is, he says, the only method of avoiding contentions in the world. Since he would be the most powerful ruler on earth, the Single Monarch must necessarily be just, and exempt from all covetousness,—just as Plato's ideal philosopher by very conception must practice justice. For, his jurisdiction would not be like those of the kings of Castile and Aragon, whose kingdom is limited; quite the contrary, he would rule from ocean to ocean.

Not that the universal monarch need occupy himself with each municipality. There needs must be a number of kingdoms; for the Scythians, who live in a country where the days and the night are unequal, cannot be ruled by the same laws as the Garamantes who live at the equinox. Still there are interests common to all peoples, and these can be entrusted only to a single ruler.[24] The universal monarch should therefore occupy himself above all with universal peace, and it is from him that the kings of the single states should receive rules for their conduct with this end in view. Once more recurring to a philosophical comparison, but in poetical form, he says that this rule of conduct, to insure harmony among mankind, should be prescribed by

[24] Ut humanum genus secundum sua communia quae omnibus competunt ab eo regatur et communi regula gubernetur ad pacem. *Ibid.*

the monarch to the individual kings, just as the speculative intellect furnishes to the practical intellect the principles which guide our actions.[25] And Dante's conclusion is that, just as a man's peace with himself is the condition of his personal happiness, so likewise universal peace, *pax universalis,* can alone realize the happiness of the human race. Apart from this, Dante says nothing as to the functions of this guide, arbiter, and judge. But he does say who this monarch shall be. He is to be the German Emperor, consecrated by the Pope, and regarded by Dante as the heir of the Caesars and of Charlemagne.[26]

But another question created a divergence of views between canonists and legists. We mention it only because it concerned this centripetal tendency of the time, this fascination of unity; and because, too, one of the best known quarrels of the thirteenth century seems to us clearly connected with the philosophical controversy about this ideal human society. The Empire and the Papacy being distinct, and involving two heads, there was again a new duality which must be reduced at any cost to an inclusive unity.

Canonists, such as Innocent IV, and Johannes

[23] Constat quod totum humane genus ordinatur ad unum ... Partes humanae universitatis respondent ad ipsam per unum principium. ... Humanum genus potest regi per unum principem ... *quod potest fieri per unum melius est fieri per unum quam per plura.* Lib. I, *passim.*

[26] Lib., III, *De Monarchia.*

Andreae, proclaimed the *subordination* of the Emperor to the Pope, that is, of the temporal power to the spiritual. Christ, they said, is the sole King of humanity, and the Pope is his viceroy on earth. Emperors and kings cannot exercise temporal power except by a delegated authority which is always revocable,—so that "the principle of separation was applicable merely to the mode in which those powers were to be exercised."[27]

Not so, replied Dante with all the legists. We are as desirous as you are of introducing unity of command over mankind, but this unity is the effect of a *co-ordination* between two distinct powers, each of which proceeds directly from God.[28] *"Imperium et Papae aeque principaliter sunt constituti a Deo,"* and *"imperium non dependet ab ecclesia"*[29] are the shibboleths of the legists. At best, adds Dante, since temporal felicity is subordinated to the eternal, the Emperor owes a certain kind of respect to the Pope, just as there is an obligation upon the eldest son to ensure a respectful understanding between himself and the head of the family.[30]

Thus, for the legists as well as for the canonists,

---

[27] Gierke, *Political Theories of the Middle Ages* (English translation by F. W. Maitland), Cambridge, 1900, p. 12.
[28] *De Monarchia.* Lib. III.
[29] Gierke, *op. cit.*, p. 17 and note 40.
[30] Illa igitur reverentia Caesar utatur ad Petrum qua primogenitus filius debet uti ad Patrem. Lib. III.

human society is conceived as a single association in which order prevails throughout.

Did the theory of the universal monarchy as maintained by the legists, and the theory of the omnipotence of the Pope as defended by the canonists, remain nothing more than a subtle academical thesis? Or did they descend from theory to living practice? History gives the reply to these questions, and it is sufficient briefly to recall the facts.

Under the name of the Holy Roman Empire, the Emperors of Germany sought to establish a hegemony over the peoples of the West. They maintained, as Dante teaches us,[31] that they were the heirs of Charlemagne, and that they were thus the heirs of the Roman Caesars. Hence their claims to the right of dominating Italy and of dictating to the princelings (*reguli*) of the West. Hence also the enforced claim, by the ambitious dynasty of the Saxons, and by the even more ambitious dynasty of the Hohenstaufen, of the right to nominate the bishops, the abbots, and even the Pope.

Everyone knows what the result was. At Canossa (1077) Gregory VII breaks the power of Henry IV, and delivers the bishops and the Papacy from the will of the Emperors; a century later Alexander III resists the claims of Frederic Barbarossa; a few years thereafter, Innocent III reverses the rôles, and disposes of the imperial crown to whomsoever he will. During the course of the

[31] *Ibid.,* Lib. II, III.

thirteenth century, the Emperor, in the person of Frederic II, is definitely defeated. The kings of Europe, however, continue vigorously their resistance to the interference of the Emperors. And even as late as the beginning of the fifteenth century, Antoninus of Florence points to the same fact, when he says: "Although all the secular lords and kings should be subjected to the Emperor, there are, however, many kings who do not recognize him as their superior, invoking either a privilege or another kind of right, or the simple fact, as for instance the King of France, the doge of Venice and certain other lords."[32] It might be added, that the German Emperor was not the only one who asserted a right to the title of heir of Charlemagne, and that certain kings—for instance Louis VII of France—laid claim, though in vain, to the same right. At all events, the Hohenstaufen did not succeed in playing the rôle of peacemakers, such as Dante assigned to the universal monarch. Far from being agents of peace, they passed their lives in making wars in all possible directions. Pangermanic supremacy in the thirteenth century suffered complete bankruptcy.

The fact was that the true agents of internationalism were the Popes, the representatives of the

[32] "Quum omnes domini et reges seculares deberent esse sub Imperatore, multi tamen reges non cognoscunt eum ut superiorem suum, tuentes se vel privilegio, sive alio jure vel potius de facto, ut rex Franciae et dux Venetiarum et alii domini." *Summa Theologica*, Titulus III. De dominis temporalibus, C. 1.

theocracy, which attained during the thirteenth century its greatest extent of authority. The kind of internationalism imposed by the Popes upon Christian nations, which were indistinguishable from the civilized world, was based upon the catholicity of the Christian faith and morality, and upon the discipline of the Roman Church. Catholicity means universality. One head recognized by all is the guardian of the great ideal by which the society of the time is guided. Gregory VII had already planned the deliverance of Jerusalem and the restoration of the Church of Africa.[33] His successors organized and encouraged the Crusades. Innocent III made use of the new mendicant orders for international and Catholic purposes. Doubtless there were plenty of heresies after the middle of the twelfth century; they underlay society like the ground-swell of the ocean, not breaking through to the surface. The thirteenth century had not yet heard the warnings of the great displacements which were to come, and the Catholic faith preserved its internationalism, thanks to the prestige of the Papacy.

As guardian of the faith and morality of the time, the Pope was also absolute master of discipline. The most autocratic form of the pontifical authority was attained by Innocent III. He in-

[33] Rocquain, *La cour de Rome et l'esprit de Réforme avant Luther*. vol. I. "La Théocratie, apogée du Pouvoir Pontifical," Paris, Thorin, 1893, p. 48.

tervened time and again in the government of the individual dioceses. All kinds of cases could be brought before him; his decisions were universal and supreme.[34] Innumerable appeals were made to his decisions. The moment came when Innocent III thought he could restore the schismatic Church of the Orient to his obedience. He could see upon the episcopal throne of Constantinople a partriarch who recognized his authority. The Serbs and the Bulgarians did him homage, and it seemed for a moment that the Russians would follow their example.

At this point, it is clear that the Pope not only affirmed his super-national rôle, as head of the Church, but also his rôle as arbiter of European politics, and as the guardian of international morality. He did not limit himself to the defense and extension of the temporal patrimony, but proclaimed himself the sovereign of all Christendom, by invoking the principle "that the church has the supreme right over the countries upon which she has conferred the benefit of Christian civilization." "Christ," as Gregory VII wrote in 1075, "substituted his reign on earth for that of the Caesars, and the pontiffs of Rome have ruled more states than the Emperors ever possessed."[35] By virtue of this doctrine, his successors recognize kings, or absolve their subjects from their duties of obedience; they

[34] *Ibid.*, 54, 412; Rocquain, *La papauté au moyen âge*, 1881, p. 162.
[35] *Ep.* II, 75. *Cf.* Roquain, *op. cit.*, p. 54.

confer feudal possessions; they make themselves the judges of the election of the German Emperors; they receive the homage of the great of the earth; those smitten with excommunication tremble with fear.

This political supremacy was far from being pleasing to all the secular princes. History is filled with the record of their resistance; and everyone knows the reply which Philip Augustus made to the legates of Innocent III: "The Pope has no right to interfere in the affairs which take place between kings."[36] But even when rising against the Popes, kings respected the Papacy. We see this clearly when Innocent protested against the divorce by Philip Augustus of his first queen, excommunicated the king, and obliged him to take back his lawful wife. Although in various other cases he abused his authority, this act of the Pope, in condemning the violation of the moral law by a great king, is one of the noblest instances of the exercise of his theocratic power. Likewise, he was respected when he intervened to prevent wars which he held to be unjust, and when he resorted to arbitration in order to put an end to dispute. Over the society of states as well as that of individuals he exercised supreme authority. "Each king has his kingdom," wrote Innocent III, "but Peter has the pre-emi-

[36] Paul Janet, *Histoire de la science politique dans ses rapports avec la morale,* Paris, 1887, vol. I, p. 350.

nence over all, inasmuch as he is the vicar of Him who governs the earth and all that is therein."[37]

After this statement of historical facts, it seems superfluous to point out that the *humana universitas* of the thirteenth century did not constitute a society of nations in the modern sense of the term. It could not be more than a society of the *European states as they then existed,* each more or less unformed and including heterogeneous races and diverse languages.[38]

Augustine has left to us this fine definition of peace: it is order which gives us tranquillity, *pax omnium rerum tranquilitas ordinis*.[39] Once everything is in place, and each thing is as it ought to be, a grateful repose hovers over all. The whole thirteenth century is under the influence of this formula. All the human sciences, present and to come, have their place marked out in the classification of knowledge; all the problems of philosophy had engaged them, and they had been worked out and co-ordinated in the dominating scholastic philosophy; all that art could endow with beauty was reassembled in the cathedrals; all the great social factors which enter into the life of a state were combined in equilibrium; and the theorists dreamed of a universal society of mankind. Everybody believed, and believed with conviction, that the world

[37] Rocquain, *op. cit.,* p. 358.
[38] Compare below ch. XI.
[39] *De Civitate Dei,* Lib. XIX, cap. 13.

had arrived at a state of repose as the end of its destined course. To them as to the contemporaries of Augustus, or of Louis XIV, a stability approaching close to perfection seemed to have been attained. A general feeling of content prevailed, and this state of complacency continued for a full hundred years after the middle of the thirteenth century.

IV

In the light of this tendency toward unity, we can better understand another aspect of the mediaeval civilization; an aspect which permeates all departments of their social life, and which appears also in the two outstanding facts of their philosophical activity already noticed. This other aspect is: cosmopolitanism,—their tendency to evaluate by a universal standard.

The classification of knowledge which we have referred to[40] is not a matter of some individual conception, as was the effort made by Auguste Comte or Ampère or Herbert Spencer; on the contrary, the results are accepted by the general consensus of learned opinion.

The twelfth century groping has disappeared,— the attempts of Radulfus Ardens, and even of the *Didascalion* of Hugo of St. Victor, and of the numerous anonymous classifications of that century. The treatises of the thirteenth century deal

[40] See above ch. IV, v.

definitely with methodology. Thus, for example, the *de divisione philosophiae*,[41] which Dominicus Gundissalinus wrote at Toledo about 1150 under the influence of Aristotle and the Arabs, pursues in detail the relation of the sciences to philosophy and the superposition of the various branches of philosophy. And the work of Michael Scot, one of his successors at the Institute of Toledo is inspired by the ideas of Gundissalinus. Again, there was the important work of Robert Kilwardby, the *de ortu et divisione philosophiae*[42] (written about 1250, and perhaps the most noteworthy introduction to philosophy produced in the Middle Ages); this work perfects the outline of his master of Toledo, and while it introduces certain distinctions, it adds nothing new, and does not pretend to do so. Further, the same classification is found in the *compilatio de libris naturalibus*,[43] written by an anonymous author of the thirteenth century, which makes a place therein for the works of Aristotle and of the Arabians; and the plan therein followed is in accord with the program of the University of Paris which was published in 1255.[44]

[41] L. Baur, "Gundissalinus, De divisione philosophiae," Baümker's-*Beiträge*, 1903, IV.

[42] L. Baur, "Die philosophische Werke des Robert Grosseteste, Bischofs von Lincoln," Baümker's-*Beiträge*, 1912, IV.

[43] M. Grabmann, "Forschungen über die lateinischen Aristotelesübersetzungen des XIII Jahrhunderts," Baümker's-*Beiträge*, 1916, XVII, h. 5, 6.

[44] See further my study: "The Teaching of Philosophy and the Classification of the Sciences in the Thirteenth Century," *Philosophical Review*, July, 1918.

In short, one finds the same classification in all the writers of the period,—in Robert Grosseteste, Thomas Aquinas, Bonaventure, Siger of Brabant, Duns Scotus, Roger Bacon and others; their knowledge is all run into the same mould. Dante refers to this classification at the beginning of his treatise *De Monarchia*. It exists not only in the program of studies at the University of Paris, but it is found also at Oxford and at Cambridge;— moreover, it is the basis of private instruction. I have found it also in a treatise as yet unedited, the *speculum divinorum et quorumdam naturalium* which was written toward the end of the thirteenth century, by Henry Bate of Malines, for the use of Count Gui of Hainaut, whose instruction he had undertaken; it is one of the few pedagogical treatises of that century written for the use of a lay prince.[45] This classification constitutes the framework for the various doctrines; and, indeed, such divergent philosophical systems as those of Thomism and Averroism, for example, are readily included within it,—much as plants essentially different may grow in the same soil. It is, so to speak, the atmosphere in which all the systems are immersed, the common mental life which hovers over systems and parts of systems. It was not the habit in those days for one set of thinkers designedly to destroy the presuppositions built up by another

[45] See my study: "Henri Bate de Malines" (*Bulletin de L'Académie royale de Belgique*, 1907).

set; they lacked that spirit of negation which later became so characteristic of modern philosophers.

This cosmopolitan tendency in evaluating was also the result of the remarkably widespread agreement with the one dominant philosophy,—that is, the scholastic philosophy. This great system had its rise at Paris, the "cosmopolis of philosophy," and there, after a crisis in its development, it attained its full growth and displayed the plentitude of its power. The existence of this common centre of learning, especially of speculative thought, contributed in a large measure to safeguard for a century and a half the unity of doctrine. From Paris this philosophy spread in great waves to Oxford and Cambridge, to Italy, to Germany, to Spain and everywhere. Borne on the wings of French influence, it became international. It reunited the numerous host of those who were loyal to philosophy, and so it can lay claim to the greatest names,—in England, Alexander of Hales and Duns Scotus, in Italy, Bonaventure and Thomas Aquinas, the Flemish Henri of Ghent, and the Spanish Lully, each of whom gave it his own interpretation and marked it with his own personality. Thus, the entire West accepted the same explanation of the world, the same idea of life. Of course the same was true for theology, both speculative and mystical. Such unity of thought has seldom existed in the history of mankind. It occurred in the third century of our era,—at the time of the glory of the

Neo-Platonic philosophy. And since the thirteenth century, this phenomenon has never repeated itself.

Far from being an anachronism, this remarkable fact of universal agreement in the West satisfies the profound aspirations of the time. For, there was one system of education for princes, lords and clerks; one sacred and learned language, the Latin; one code of morals; one ritual; one hierarchy, the Church; one faith and one common western interest against heathendom and against Islam; one community on earth and in heaven, the community of the saints; and also one system of feudal habits for the whole West. Customs, characteristic of the courtesy and chivalry which were born in France in the preceding century, had spread to all countries, and had created among the nobility of the various nations a sort of kindred spirit. The network of feudalism embraced all social classes, and everywhere the system had common features. The Crusades had taught the barons to know each other. Commerce, also, established points of contact between the French and the English and the Flemish and the Italians, and predisposed men to a mode of thinking, which was no longer local. Everywhere work was organized on the principles of guild and corporation.

The rapid expansion of Gothic art is another example of the felt need of a conception of beauty not limited to any one people. A marvelous architecture and sculpture saw the light of day in the Isle of France. The cathedrals of Sens, Noyon, Senlis, Laon, Notre Dame de Paris, Chartres, Auxerre, Rouen, Rheims, Amiens, Bourges were then either in process of building or completed. The garland of masterpieces, begun under Louis VII in northern and central Europe, and by Henry II Plantagenet in the West, was completed and enriched under Philip Augustus; and the forms of the pointed arch attained then a purity and a beauty which have never been surpassed. The new style of art passed almost immediately to the English cathedrals of Canterbury, Lincoln, Westminster, and York. In Spain, the cathedral of Burgos (1230) was inspired by that of Bourges; the cathedral of Toledo was due to a French architect; the cathedral of Léon, the most perfect of all, was built on the basis of French ideas;—and the same is true also of the German Gothic style generally,—thus, for example, the cathedrals of Münster, Madgeburg, Cologne, and Bamberg were patterned after French standards, and the pointed arch is definitely called "French style" by the builders of the Wimpfen cathedral, *opus francigenum*.[46] As Mâle has so well shown, the new art became "oecumenical."[47]

[46] Compare the interesting work of E. Mâle, *L'art allemand et l'art français du moyen âge*, Paris, 1917. At Wimpfen, the priest Richard summons an architect "qui tunc noviter de villa parisiensi e partibus venerat franciae, *opere francigeno* basilicam e sectis lapidibus construi jubet," p. 148.

[47] Mâle, *L'art religieux du* 13ᵉ *siècle en France*, p. 5.

We also observe a kind of uniformity, the cosmopolitanism of which we have been speaking, in the political institutions of the European states which were then in process of formation. Everywhere this process proceeds on the same general principle,—the feudal monarchy, a representative system of government.

Finally, as we have already seen,[48] the Popes were genuine cosmopolitan forces of a practical kind; for in their view the society of mankind was to be extended universally.

In conclusion, it should be stated, the foregoing does not imply that the mentality of the thirteenth century was on a dead level of uniformity. By no means. Human nature is always complex; and no matter how general a phenomenon may be in any condition of society, there always arise by the side of it certain secondary phenomena of a contradictory character. Of these account should of course be taken,—but without exaggerating their significance or bearing. It will always be true that mothers in general love their children, notwithstanding the fact that some heartless mothers exist. Just so, respect for authority was prevalent in the thirteenth century, in spite of the evidence of some germs of rebellion against the discipline of the Church and the power of the State. The unity of the catholic faith was not prejudiced by the various heresies and superstitious practices; nor did the ex-

[48] See above, pp. 122-126.

cesses of some barons weaken the virtues of the feudal customs. The protests of a small group of zealous mystics against the rich decoration of the churches did not annul the delight of the whole age with the beauty of their original art; nor did the low morality of some of the clergy serve as a general detriment to the purity of life in that class.

The spirit of the Middle Ages cannot be gathered accurately out of a mere catalogue of anecdotes, nor from the exclusive perusal of satirists, preachers and fable-writers, nor again from the history of certain chroniclers and writers, whose temperament or office might prompt them to exaggerate. On the contrary, the real task and point is to ascertain whether these facts and anecdotes and caricatures (whose name is legion) describe the usual or the exceptional instances; whether they are mainly characteristic of the period; and whether they reach and express the real depths of the mediaeval soul.

So also in philosophy, a few isolated instances of scepticism do not derogate from the general doctrinal assurance which is characteristic of the mediaeval philosophers. And similarly the great number of systems of thought, and the atmosphere of emulation in which they were conceived, can be readily reconciled with the predominance of a philosophy which was truly cosmopolitan,—as was the scholastic philosophy.

CHAPTER SIX

Optimism and Impersonality

i. Optimism in philosophy, in art, in religion. ii. Impersonality. iii. History of philosophy and literary attribution. iv. Perenniality.

I

The optimism of the mediaeval mind is another feature which stands out as distinctive of the whole civilization. The thirteenth century is a constructive period in every domain. But such exercise of constructive powers and such realization in practice involved confidence in human resources and capacities. That confidence the age possessed abundantly. Not only had it a passion for ideals, but it knew how to realize them in concrete form and in practical life.

When dealing with scientific classifications and philosophical systems, optimism means confidence in the powers of reason, serenity in intellectual work. Without such confidence, could they have found the courage to set in order all the human sciences, and especially could they have spent their energies in meticulously ordering the manifold parts of a system so extensive as is the scholastic philosophy?

They were in no doubt concerning the power of the reason to grasp external realities, to know everything to some extent.¹ Subjectivism, which confines the mind within the closed circle of its impressions, was foreign to the spirit of the times. Thus, when Nicholas of Autrecourt, called sometimes the Hume of the thirteenth century, taught in Paris that the existence of the external world cannot be demonstrated, that the principle of causality is without objective validity, he was plainly an exception; and so he was regarded as an amateur in paradoxes. The cultivated minds of the age relied upon human reason unanimously. Frankly dogmatic, the scholastic philosophy considers human intelligence to have been created to know the truth, just as fire was made to burn. To be sure, the philosophers of the thirteenth century believe that human intelligence has its limits,—it knows all things in a very imperfect manner—but within these limits they give it full credence; it is for them a spark lighted at the torch of eternal truth. This conception of certitude neither includes nor excludes our modern epistemology; like all that belongs to the mediaeval genius it is *sui generis*.

Scholasticism is not less optimistic in its moral teachings. It makes happiness to consist in the fullest possible development of personality. It teaches that nothing can efface from conscience the fundamental principles of moral law. It maintains,

¹ See ch. VIII, i and ii.

accordingly, that even the most wicked man still retains a fundamental tendency toward goodness,— a tendency which renders his improvement always possible.[2]

In the realm of art, optimism and serenity are still more evident; for art springs from the heart, which realizes joy even better than the spirit. There appear in the *Chansons de geste* a joy of living and a freshness of imagery which enrich the love between knights and ladies, an exhalation of nature which reveals the profound happiness felt in living in the midst of its bounties and wonders. We all know what clear and vibrating poems the "Little Flowers" of St. Francis are, and how they express as does the *Divine Comedy* of Dante, not only a glorification of the Divine Creation and of the Redemption, but also songs of delight in the presence of the spectacle of nature.

Is it necessary to mention the Gothic cathedrals, as they too sing a hymn of joy, the triumph of nature and of God? Their lofty arches flooded with light, their windows sparkling in the sun like oriental tapestry, their noble and expressive vaults, their profusion of paintings and of figures and of symbols,—this is not the work of men who are skeptical of life. The sculptors of the Middle Ages "looked on the world with the wondering eyes of children." They depict nature in its perfection of beauty.

[2] See below, p. 270.

Finally, a still more elevated motive stimulates the optimistic view of life in society at large. It is Christian idealism,—the hope of future happiness, the belief in the religious value of work accomplished. Can we explain in any other way, the wonderful exploits of optimism shown in the Crusades? How closely they press upon each other in that long succession! In spite of the hugeness of the enterprise, or the lack of success in each of those attempts, still the Crusades continued to arouse an ever-recurring enthusiasm. They have been well called "epopées of optimism."

II

Another feature which is closely connected with the optimism of the scholastics and which requires equal emphasis, is the *impersonal* character of their work, a certain spirit of personal detachment which pervades also their scholarly labors,—whether in the classification of human knowledge, or the great system of scholastic philosophy. Both their optimism and their impersonalism are simply the product of a consciously progressive and collective effort.

Indeed the thirteenth century was possessed of a significant conception regarding truth. Truth is a great edifice to be gradually built up. This work is necessarily co-operative and over a long period of time; and therefore it must be entered into impersonally by each worker. The truth, and the knowledge which expresses it, is not considered as the *personal property of him who finds it*. On the contrary, it is a great common patrimony which passes from one generation to the next, ever increased by continuous and successive contributions. "So shall it be to the end of the world," says Roger Bacon, "because nothing is perfect in human achievements." And he goes on to say: "Always those who come later have added to the work of their predecessors; and they have corrected and changed a great deal, as we see especially in the case of Aristotle, who took up and discussed all the ideas of his predecessors. Moreover, many of the statements of Aristotle were corrected in turn by Avicenna and by Averroes."[3] Nor does Thomas Aquinas speak otherwise of the *impersonal constitution* of philosophy and of its improvement. Referring to Aristotle's Metaphysics, he writes: "That which a single man can bring, through his work and his genius, to the promotion of truth is little in comparison with the total of knowledge. However, from all these elements, selected and co-ordinated and brought together, there arises a marvelous thing, as is shown by the various departments of learning, which by the work and sagacity of many have come to a wonderful augmentation."[4]

[3] Nam semper posteriores addiderunt ad opera priorum, et multa correxerunt, et plura mutaverunt, sicut patet per Aristotelem, maxime, qui omnes sententias praecedentium discussit. Et etiam Aviccenna et Averroes plura de dictis ejus correxerunt, *Opus Majus*, Pars I, c. 6 (ed. Bridges, vol. III, p. 14).

[4] *In lib. II Metaphys.*, Lectio 1.

Do not these declarations call to mind the beautiful thought of Pascal, who also reflected deeply and shrewdly on the rôle of tradition in the continuity of philosophy. "It is owing to tradition," he says, "that the whole procession of men in the course of so many centuries may be considered as a single man, who always subsists, who learns continually."[5] There is, then, no break in the continuity of philosophy, any more than there is in the other departments of civilization; and a chain of gold joins the Greeks to the Syrians, the Syrians to the Arabs, and the Arabs to the Scholastics.

The impersonality of scholastic philosophy is further revealed in the fact that those who build it disclose nothing of their inner and emotional life. Works like the autobiography of Abaelard are as exceptional as the *Confessions* of Augustine. Only the mystics speak of that which passes in the soul's inmost life. In the voluminous works of Thomas Aquinas, for instance, there is only a single passage where the philosopher exhibits any emotions;[6] everywhere else his thought runs without haste or emotion, as tranquil and as majestic as a river.

III

The thirteenth century drew from these principles, in the form of corollaries, its characteristic

[5] Pascal, *Opuscules,* édit. Brunschvigg, p. 80.

[6] *De unitate intellectus contra Averroistas,* (in fine), where his indignation is deeply stirred.

views concerning the history of philosophy and literary attribution. The determination of historical fact and authorship is subordinated to the truth which the scholastics are concerned to advance; the determination of fact has no absolute value as such. Consequently, they confine themselves to seeking, from the authorities they refer to, a support for the thesis they wish to defend.

From this attitude arises the tendency of the mediaeval thinker to attenuate, and even to suppress, all doctrinal divergencies,—such as those of Plato, of Aristotle, of Augustine, of Isidore of Seville, of the venerable Bede, of Anselm of Canterbury. Are not all these co-workers in a common task? To understand this, one must study not the common and stock phrases quoted by all, but rather the difficult and more subtle texts, to which they succeed in giving so many different meanings. The thirteenth century has characteristic expressions to describe this procedure,—for example, *"in melius interpretari,"* to interpret in a better way; *"reverenter exponere,"* to explain with respect; *"pium dare intellectum,"* to give a dutiful meaning. These are euphemisms of which the greatest make use, when it is necessary to adapt some embarrassing passage to their own theories on a given subject. We recall here the astute words of John of Salisbury concerning the philosophers of his day, eager to bring Plato and Aristotle into agreement,—how they worked in vain to reconcile dead people who contradicted each other all their lives!

Such being the fact, it seems difficult to admit that the philosophers of the thirteenth century were the slaves of tradition and the scrupulous servants of authority. In judging of their critical attitude, and of their attitude towards the ancients, one should not tie fast to the mere letter of their statements; on the contrary, one should judge by their interpretation of the texts which they are citing, for or against their doctrines. If they sin against the spirit of criticism, it is due to excess of liberty and not to the lack of it. The most eminent philosophers took great liberties with their authorities. "What else is authority but a muzzle?" wrote Adelard of Bath to his nephew.[7] "Authority has a nose of wax, which may be turned in any direction," said Alan of Lille.[8] And Thomas declared, as is so well known, that the argument from authority is the weakest of all,—where the *human* reason is involved.[9]

On the other hand, their attitude has a significant practical implication. If philosophical work is directed to the collective and progressive construction of a fund of truth, as its aim, then of course only

[7] "Quid enim aliud auctoritas dicenda quam capistrum?" Adelardi Batensis de quibusdam naturalibus quaestionibus, *op. cit.*, fol. 76 V^b.

[8] *Contra Haereticos*, I, 30. "Auctoritas cereum habet nasum . . . i.e., in diversum potest flecti *sensum.*"

[9] *Summa Theol*, 1^a, q. VIII, ad secundum. Locus ab auctoritate *quae fundatur super ratione humana est infirmissimus.*

the work matters, and the name of the worker necessarily disappears in face of the grandeur of truth. Hence their philosophy attaches little importance to the name of its collaborators. *"Unus dicit," "aliquis dicit,"* they say in speaking of contemporaries. It is, as it were, the law of humility and silence. It was necessary for a writer to be known by everyone to have his name mentioned at all (*allegari*). One can count on one's fingers those who received such an honour in the thirteenth century.

On such principles the textual interpolations made by the copyists were not regarded as any violation of the original; rather they were intended and taken to improve the expression of truth which the author sought to convey.[10] Similarly, literary theft was not stealing; it was the utilization of a common treasure. In the twelfth century a monk by the name of Alcher of Clairvaux had written a small book on psychology, and in order to ensure it a wide circulation the copyists of the time ascribed it to Augustine. William of Auvergne, Bishop of Paris in 1229, reproduced almost word for word in his *De Immortalitate Animae* the similar work of Dominicus Gundissalinus, the archdeacon of Toledo. There are numerous examples of the same kind. If we recall, further, that the

[10] For a striking example of such interpolation, in the *Summa contra Gentiles* of Thomas, see A. Pelzer, *Rev. Néo-Scol.,* May, 1920, p. 231.

negligence of copyists or the modesty of authors set in circulation a mass of manuscripts without any well-determined status, we can readily understand some of the insurmountable difficulties which the recorder of mediaeval ideas faces; for instance, in identifying opponents or in attributing texts or in detecting literary theft.

With this understanding of the matter, we are little surprised to learn that the predominant scientific classification represented such an amalgamation that the names of all those who were connected with its origin or perfection or promulgation were either neglected or forgotten. As with popular music, so here; each composer appropriates and fashions in his own way.

This same understanding also enables us to see just why and in what measure the scholastic philosophy itself is the soul of a collective body, made up of men belonging to different peoples. To be sure, there were some among them who opposed their mighty personalities to this fund of ideas which was the common heritage of all,—for example, Thomas Aquinas, Duns Scotus, Henry of Ghent, and others. But apart from these, as the documents show, the great host of men of average ability taught and developed the same doctrine, without either opposing it or adding anything of their own. They were ennobled by it; their littleness was redeemed by its grandeur. Like dwarfs on the shoulders of giants, they enjoyed a prominence which they did not deserve.

IV

One last corollary—and not the least important—is born of this impersonal character of learning and its progressive constitution. Philosophy is not something essentially mobile, some dazzling chimera, which disappears or changes with the succeeding epochs, but it possesses a sort of perenniality. It forms a monument, to which are always added new stones. The truth of the time of the Greeks is still the truth of the time of Thomas Aquinas and of Duns Scotus. Truth is something enduring. Of course, there is left a place for progress and extension in human knowledge, there are adaptations of certain doctrines to social conditions; this appears, for example, in the scholastic doctrine of the mutability of ethical laws. But the principles which rule the logical, ethical and social activities remain unchanged; they are like human nature of which they are expressions, and which does not change,[11] or like the order of essences which is ultimately based on divine immutability. Nothing is more contrary to the spirit of scholastic philosophy than the modern temper of displacing preceding contributions with one's own, doing away with tradition, and beginning *de novo* the upbuilding of thought. From this standpoint we may say that the philoso-

[11] See below ch. XII, i.

phers of the thirteenth century are conscious of the responsibility of *building for eternity*.

Nor is it different in the other branches of knowledge,—in civil and canon law, and in the social and political realm. Thus Dante, who on so many questions reveals the spirit of his time, begins his *De Monarchia* with a significant statement in this connection. I give the opening sentences of that unique treatise. "All men," he says, "whose superior nature inculcates the love of truth, have, as their chief care, it seems, to work for posterity. Just as they themselves were enriched by the work of the ancients, so must they leave to posterity a profitable good. Now, of what use would that man be who demonstrated some theorem of Euclid anew; or he who tried to show again, after Aristotle had done so, wherein happiness lies; or again, he who attempted after Cicero the defense of the aged? . . . This wearying superfluity of work would be of no avail." And then he continues: "Now as the knowledge of the temporal monarchy is to be considered as the most useful of the truths which still remain hidden, and as it is extremely obscure, my object is to bring it out into the open with the twofold end of giving humanity a useful witness of my solicitude and of gaining for myself (keeping in view my own glory) the reward which such a work deserves." Like all the rest, though with a modest store of ambition besides, Dante dreams of *writing for eternity*.

This impersonal and eternal note is also found in the hymns of the Catholic liturgy, that collection of spiritual outpourings, wherein so often the author remains unknown.

And must not the same be said of the works of art? One does not know the names of the artists who illuminated the manuscripts of the thirteenth century, nor of the glass-makers. Since many of these works were made in the cloisters, doubtless the monks who did the work were moved by their rule of humility to hide their names.[12]

Similarly, the epic poems contain numerous themes which are like a treasure of folk-lore upon which all may draw alike.

Above all, this impersonal character is found in the Gothic system, which in every respect resembles the scholastic philosophy and helps us to understand it. For, the Gothic system is the property of everyone; while each architect may interpret it in his own way, it belongs in reality to no one. Even now, we do not know the names of all those who conceived the plans and directed the work on the great cathedrals; or, if they were once known, they have since fallen into oblivion. Who now speaks of Petrus Petri, the director at the building of the cathedral of Toledo? Armies of sculptors chiselled the virgins and saints which occupy the portals and niches, yet how few of these have sealed

[12] Rule of St. Benedict, cap. 57. Artifices si sint in monasterio, cum omni humilitate facient istas artes.

their works with their names! The builders of cathedrals also were builders for eternity; and in their minds, the materials of their structures were to survive for centuries; they were to last not for one generation but for all generations to come.

CHAPTER SEVEN

SCHOLASTIC PHILOSOPHY AND THE RELIGIOUS SPIRIT

i. Common definition of scholastic philosophy as a religious philosophy. ii. Reflective analysis of the distinction between philosophy and theology. iii. The religious spirit of the epoch. iv. Connections of philosophy with religion not affecting the integrity of the former. v. Subordination of philosophy to Catholic theology in the light of this analysis. vi. Solution and adjustment of the problem. vii. Influences of philosophy in other fields. Conclusion.

I

Regarding western scholastic philosophy in the Middle Ages, every one repeats the laconic judgment, that it is "philosophy in the service, and under the sway and direction, of Catholic theology." It could be nothing else, they say, and it seems that one has said everything after pronouncing this clear-cut formula. This current definition, susceptible of the most varied meanings, is found in nearly all the books which deal with scholastic philosophy. Whether their authors give an extreme or a moderate interpretation of it, it is offered to the reader as an abridged thesis, containing in condensed form all that is worth knowing of the subject. "Scholasticism is philosophy placed in the service of doctrine already established by the Church, or at least philosophy placed in such a subordination to this doctrine that it becomes the absolute norm for what they have in common."[1]

Now this current definition of scholastic philosophy in the Middle Ages defines it very badly, because it contains a mixture of truth and of falsehood, of accuracy and of inaccuracy. It must be distrusted, like those equivocal maxims which John Stuart Mill calls "sophisms of simple inspection," which by force of repetition enjoy a kind of *transeat,* or vogue, in science without being questioned.

To eliminate the ambiguity we must attend to the historical setting, and view both philosophy and theology in the midst of the civilization whence they evolved. For this we must consider what results they attained; and the study of this will disclose a new relational aspect, wherein the scholastic philosophy and its classification of knowledge appear in vital and organic harmony with the general mentality of the epoch.

[1] "Die Scholastik ist die Philosophie im Dienste der bereits bestehende Kirchenlehre oder wenigstens in einer solchen Unterordnung unter dieselbe dass diese auf gemeinsamen Gebeite als die absolute Norm gilt," p. 196. Dr. Mathias Baumgartner, in the last (10th) edition of the Ueberweg-Heinze *Grundriss der Geschichte der Philosophie,* Zweiter Teil, "Die mittlere oder die patristische und scholastische Zeit," Berlin, 1915.

II

That philosophy was a science distinct from theology, had been universally recognized since the middle of the twelfth century;[2] and the masters of the thirteenth century laid emphasis upon this distinction. The sharp separation of the personnel in philosophy (*artistae*) and in theology is one of the first indications that the distinction of the two disciplines was clearly maintained. The University of Paris simply took over the methodological classifications of the twelfth century, as one finds them in the treatises of Dominicus Gundissalinus, Hugo of St. Victor, Robert Grosseteste, and many others. The tree of knowledge has the form of a pyramid, with the particular sciences at the base, philosophy midway up, and theology at the top, as we have already explained.[3] What is new at this stage of the development is the reflective and reasoned study of the mutual independence of philosophy and theology.

This independence rests on the difference in the points of view (*ratio formalis objecti*) from which philosophy and theology regard the materials with which they are occupied (*materia*).[4] Bearing in mind this principle of methodology, we can understand the declaration with which Thomas Aquinas opens his two *Summae* on the *raison d'être* of the-

[2] See above, ch. III, p. 50.
[3] See above, ch. IV, pp. 85 ff.
[4] *Cf.*, ch. IV, p. 87.

ology outside the philosophical sciences (*praeter philosophicas disciplinas*) and its distinction from philosophy. "It is," he says, "diversity in the point of view of knowledge (*ratio cognoscibilis*) which determines the diversity of the sciences. The astronomer and the physicist establish the same conclusion, that the earth is round; but the astronomer uses mathematical arguments abstracted from matter, while the physicist uses arguments drawn from the material condition of bodies. Nothing, then, prevents the questions of the philosophical sciences, so far as they are known by the light of natural reason, from being studied at the same time by another science, in the measure that they are known by revelation. Thus theology, which is occupied with sacred doctrine, differs in kind from theodicy, which is part of philosophy."[5]

A contemporary of St. Thomas, Henry of Ghent, also maintains this doctrine, accepted by all the intellectuals of the time: "Theology is a distinct science," he says. "Though theology is occupied with certain questions touched on by philosophy, theology and philosophy are none the less distinct sciences, for they differ in the aim pursued (*sunt ad aliud*), the processes (*per aliud*), and the methods (*secundum aliud*). The philosopher consults only reason; the theologian begins by an act

[5] *Summa Theol.*, 1ᵃ, q. I, art. 1.

of faith, and his science is directed by a supernatural light."[6]

It is easy to show that such principles were widely applied in the thirteenth century. Philosophers reasoned on the origin of ideas, on human liberty, on causality and finality in nature, on the relations between will and knowledge, and on many other problems of a purely rational kind. One would seek in vain a religious veneer or a theological *arriére pensée* in the solutions given; their constant reliance upon Aristotle is the simple fact that makes this impossible. On the other hand, theologians discuss the Trinity, the Redemption, the supernatural end of man, and like problems, and they invoke Scriptural authority. When certain matters are common to the two orders of study, such as the existence and the nature of God, there is a difference in the point of view, from which the philosopher and the theologian respectively discuss them. Their arguments meet, like the rays of light which set out from distinct foci and are received on the same screen; but they are no more confused than—in our comparison—the luminous sources are confused. Hence numerous philosophic systems could arise, remarkable explanations of the world

[6] *Summa Theol.*, art. VII, q. 1, Nos. 10-13. "Adhuc philosophus considerat quaecumque considerat, ut percepta et intellecta solo lumine naturalis rationis; theologus vero considerat singula ut primo credita lumine fidei, et secundo intellecta lumine altiori super lumen naturalis rationis infuso.

and of life, capable of being judged and set forth as one sets forth and judges the philosophy of Aristotle, or of Plato, or of Descartes, or of Kant.

It is important to observe that this distinction was universally recognized by the scholastics of the thirteenth and fourteenth centuries. That the public itself was of like mind in the matter is evidenced by the painting by Traini, preserved in the Church of St. Catherine of Pisa, to which we have already referred.[7] In this picture, entitled the Triumph of St. Thomas, the great artist of the fourteenth century has symbolized in drawing and in color all the intellectual movements of the time. What interests us especially here is the diversity of the sources by which Thomas is inspired, as he sits upon a golden throne in the centre of the composition, the *Summa Theologica* open on his knees. From the top of the picture Christ sheds upon him rays of light, which are reflected by six sacred personages —Moses, the four Evangelists, and St. Paul—who are placed in a semicircle; then, further, by Plato and Aristotle arranged on the two sides after the same plan. Luminous waves spread the doctrines over the world, whilst Averroës, in the attitude of one conquered, lies at Thomas's feet. We have here a synthetic picture, as it were, which presents a striking résumé of intellectual speculation in the thirteenth century; and it reveals the impression received by men like Traini, who was placed in a

[7] *Cf.* above, p. 84.

position that enabled him to see in broad outline.
It teaches us that theology and philosophy are in
different planes, with a subordination like that of
the personages who symbolize the one and the
other; it shows us that both are joined, as complementary, in the work of Thomas, that famous
thinker whom the contemporaries of Traini called
"doctor sanctus." Moreover, the writers of the
Renaissance and the Reformation,—for the most
part so curt in their treatment of the Middle Ages
—have clearly distinguished the scholastic theologians and the scholastic philosophers, reserving
rather for the latter the name of scholastics: *"Cum
vero duplicem eorum differentiam animadvertamus
theologos alios, alios philosophos, quamquam illis
hoc nomen potius tributum sit."* This judgment,
which I take from the treatise *De doctoribus scholasticis* of Busse, 1676, is confirmed by Binder,
Tribbechovius,[8] and by all those who belong to that
curious category of detractors of scholasticism, on
whom Rabelais and so many others have rested their
sarcasm. These "distributers of injuries" are better
advised than some of our contemporary historians,
for whom the speculation of the Middle Ages is a
chaos, a hodge-podge of philosophy and theology,
and who make the history of mediaeval philosophy
a department of the history of religion.

Not to understand the fundamental distinction

[8] Tribbechovius, *De doctoribus scholasticis et corrupta per eos divinarum humanarumque rerum scientia.* Giessen. 1665.

between the order of nature and that of grace, between the rational conception of the world and the systematization of revealed dogmas, would be to misunderstand the speculative work of the Middle Ages, and to substitute arbitrary conceptions for the indisputable declarations of its greatest doctors.

III

The freedom of philosophy from dependence on theology rests then on solid methodological grounds. But while philosophy and theology are objects of speculation, we must not forget that both are vital parts of the civilization in which they appear and whose effects they feel. Hence they are both touched,—the one more than the other of course—by the religious spirit.

Could it be otherwise in an epoch in which Catholicism leaves its mark on all civilization? To judge of this impression it is not enough to turn to the *Golden Legend,* or the Apocryphal Gospels, which furnished food for the piety of the people. It is not enough to collect popular superstitions,— such as the charges and stories of Caesar of Heisterbach. It is not enough to note the excesses caused by the veneration of relics, the conflicts between abbots and bishops or the bourgeois of the towns and the feudalists, whom material interests divided. These many oddities pale before the great fact that the Catholic religion inspires society throughout and regulates its morals, its art, and its thought. The most individualistic statesman—Philip Augustus or St. Louis in France, Simon of Montfort or Edward I in England, Frederick II or Rudolph of Hapsburg in Germany, Ferdinand of Castile—all recognized the Catholic Church as the necessary foundation of the social structure, even when their politics led them into conflict with the Papacy in order to shake off its patronage. The same ardent faith which had aroused the Crusades also gave birth to the new monastic orders of Dominicans and Franciscans, who came from the most diverse social strata, and so raised the level of belief and morality in the masses. Even the heretical movement that appeared in Languedoc and Champagne and Flanders shows the vitality of the religious sentiment. In spite of the spirit of opposition to the Church, the century of Philip Augustus remains an epoch of Catholic faith.[9] By its dogmas and its morality, Christianity penetrates the lives of individuals and families and peoples. Under the influence of Christian ideals and canonical law, usury and the taking of interest are forbidden; just prices and just wages rule trade and commerce. In the corporation, work is a holy thing, masters are equal, art is allied to handicraft, the institution of the masterpiece guarantees the quality of the product. It was because one worked for God that the thirteenth century could cover,

[9] Luchaire, *op. cit.*, p. 318.

first the soil of France and then that of Germany, with gigantic cathedrals, chiselled like jewels.

Likewise, the intimate union between religion and beauty shines forth in the work of the period. The *"Rationale divinorum officiorum"* of William (Durand) Bishop of Mende, shows in detail how the cathedrals are at once marvels of art and symbols of prayer. The church of Amiens, which was the most perfect of the great French monuments, is a striking demonstration of the aesthetic resources of the original scheme. That of Chartres no less brilliantly exhibits its iconographic resources. Each stone had its language. Covered with sculpture, it presents a complete religious programme. It is for the people the great book of sacred history, the catechism in images. Think of Amiens or Chartres, Paris or Laon. In every line appears the function of a temple destined for the masses; from every angle the gaze is drawn towards the altar, which sums up the idea of sacrifice. The frescoes and the glass windows of Giotto breathe forth the perfume of religious life; the poems of St. Francis, singing nature, raise the soul towards God; and Dante wrote to Can Grande della Scala, tyrant of Verona, that he wished by means of his poems to snatch away the living from their state of wretchedness and put them in the way of eternal happiness.[10]

[10] Dicendum est breviter quod finis totius et partis est removere viventes in hac vita de statu miseriae et perducere ad statum felicitatis. See Dantis Alighieri Epistola X, in *opere Latine di Dante,* ed. G. Giuliani, Firenze, 1882, Vol. II, p. 46.

Art, in all of its forms, shows the unfailing bonds between religion and beauty.

The religious spirit that penetrated everything was bound to be felt also in the domain of science, and notably philosophy. We shall see this question—so complicated and so badly understood—under new aspects, in seeking to understand the precise relations of scholastic philosophy and the Catholic religion. In what does the bond between philosophy and the religious medium consist? How can one reconcile it with that doctrinal independence which philosophers so fiercely claim?

IV

It is easy to make the reconciliation for a certain group of ties, which I shall call external, and which therefore cannot really affect philosophical doctrine. They are not less suggestive of the mentality of the time, and they show the perfect harmony existing between scholastic philosophy and mediaeval civilization. One can, it seems to me, reduce these extra-doctrinal relations to three classes, which we must examine briefly.

The first class results from the social superiority of the theologians; and this indicates that philosophy is for the most part a preparation for theological studies. That theology holds the place of honor in the complete cycle of studies, and that it is the topmost in the pyramid of knowledge ought not to surprise us; for all study whatever was subservient to the clerical estate. The thirteenth century in this only continued the traditions of the earlier Middle Ages. The University of Paris, issuing from the schools at Nôtre Dame, counted only clerics among its professors, and these professors had the closest relations with the Chancellor of Nôtre Dame and with the Papacy. Many were themselves canons, either of Paris or of the provinces or from abroad. Not to mention the Franciscans or Dominicans, who were the most brilliant masters in the University, the translation of Greek and Arabic works—so momentous for the West— was due to clerks of Toledo or monks of Greece and Sicily. In short, all the co-workers in the great awakening of the thirteenth century are ecclesiastics.

It is natural that the masters in the Faculty of Theology (*sacrae paginae*) took precedence of all other masters, and notably of philosophers. In this, University discipline was only the reflection of social life. The intensity of Catholic life makes intelligible why so many of these "artists," or philosophers, desired to undertake the study of theology, after taking their degrees in the lower faculty. So much was this the case that the mastership of arts was a direct preparation for the grades of the Theological Faculty. The documents make this clear: "*Non est consenescendum in artibus sed a liminibus sunt salutandae,*"[10bis]—One does not grow old in philosophy; one must take leave of it finally and engage himself with theology. It is the intensity of this Catholic life which makes us understand how Robert of Sorbonne, founder of the famous college of that name, could compare the Last Judgment,—in his short treatise *De Conscientia*[11]—to the examination for the degree at Paris, and pursue the comparison into a thousand details. In that "supreme trial" for the Doctorate, for example, the judge will not be accessible to recommendations or presents, and all will pass or fail strictly in accordance with the requirements of justice. It is, moreover, the intensity of religious life at that epoch which alone can explain certain controversies among theologians which contravene our modern ideas,—such as that on the subject of Christian perfection. While ordinary people are enthusiastic for a religion that is simple and sturdy, the learned at Paris sought to determine whether the life of the regulars is nearer to perfection than that of the seculars. Between 1255 and 1275 all doctors in theology were obliged to declare themselves on this question. Certain secular masters treated it with an asperity and a passion which served as an outlet for their ill-humor against the Dominicans and Franciscans, whom they never forgave for having taken the three chairs in the Faculty of Theology.[12]

[10bis] *Cf.* Denifle, *Die Universitäten des Mittelalters bis 1400*, Bd. I, pp. 99-100.
[11] Edited by F. Chambon, *Robert de Sorbon*, Paris, 1903.
[12] *Cf.* above, p. 76.

If, for all these reasons both social and religious, more credit or honor or importance was attached to theology and to religious discussion than to philosophy, this fact could in no wise change the position of philosophy, which remained what it is and must be—a synthetic study of the world by means of the reason alone.

The second class of ties results from the penetration of philosophy into speculative theology, and from its being constituted an apology for Christianity,—the penetration affecting theology alone, and philosophy not at all. This method which was so dear to the masters of Paris, has been commonly called by modern authors the dialectic method in theology. We already know that speculative theology, which achieved its greatest renown in the thirteenth century, aimed at the co-ordination of Catholic dogma; therefore its chief method was necessarily based upon the authority of the sacred books. But by the side of this principal method, the theologians employed another one, as accessory and secondary. In order to make dogmas intelligible, they sought to show their well-founded reasonableness,—just as Jewish theologians had done in the days of Philo, or Arabian theologians had done with the Koran. In the twelfth century, Abaelard, and Hugo of St. Victor, and Gilbert de la Porrée, had founded this apologetic method; and in the thirteenth century it had attained the widest extension. The same Thomas Aquinas who taught the clear distinction between philosophy and theology, wrote on the subject: "If theology borrows from philosophy, it is not because it needs its help, but in order to make more obvious the truths which it teaches."[13]

The application of philosophy to theology I call *apologetics.* Just as the application of mathematics to astronomy affects astronomy alone, so also the application of philosophy to theology affects only theology. On this historical point, which I have long sought to establish, the writers of the thirteenth century give ample support; for they distinguish the two theological methods of authority and of reason, *"auctoritates et rationes."*[14]

It clearly follows that the use of philosophy for theological ends arises by the side of pure philosophy, while the latter remains unchanged. If you will recall the religious mentality of the thirteenth century, you will readily understand how the application of philosophy to dogma led many minds into theology. The result was that most philosophers became theologians; and mediaeval apologetics arose in the most varied forms. In a society where heresy itself sprang from an excess of re-

---

[13] "Ad secundum dicendum quod haec scientia accipere potest aliquid a philosophicis disciplinis, non quod ex necessitate eis indigeat, sed ad majorem manifestationem eorum quae in hac scientia tiaduntur." *Summa Theol.,* 1ª, q. I, art. 5.

[14] This distinction between "auctoritates et rationes," appears as early as Peter of Poitiers. *Cf.* Grabmann, *Gesch. d. schol. Methode,* I, 33.

ligious zeal and under color of purifying belief, no one dreamed of opposing dogma; on the contrary, it was explained—and in all sorts of ways. The wisest, following the traditions of Anselm and of the Victorines, posited a domain of mystery reserved to the advantage of theology. Thomas Aquinas does not admit the philosophical demonstration of mystery itself; he allows philosophy to prove only that mystery contains nothing irrational. Duns Scotus goes further; from fear of actual conflict, he withdraws every theological question from the empire of reason. But others did not follow these wise examples. Raymond Lully wished to support all the contents of revelation by the syllogism—as formerly Abaelard had done; and Roger Bacon even confused philosophy with apologetics. Mediaeval rationalism, in its scholastic form, vindicates for reason the power of demonstrating dogma in every way; and in this it is in striking contrast with the modern rationalism which would deny dogma in the name of reason.

Where could the profoundly religious spirit of mediaeval speculation appear more luminously than in these rash attempts? It was religious to the point of folly. There is no better word to characterize the attitude of the latin Averroists, who stirred so deeply the University of Paris in the thirteenth and fourteenth centuries. Not wishing to deny either the Catholic faith or the compact mass of philosophical doctrines which were in flagrant contradiction with this faith, they hit upon an ingenious device; this was the astonishing doctrine of the twofold truth: "What is true in philosophy," they said, "may be false in theology, and vice versa."[15]

Whatever these different attitudes may have been,—and the religious concern which inspired them—they had a very important effect on the relation of philosophy and theology. For, the theologian was wont to enter into a great number of philosophical questions for the purpose of his apologetics. Since no science bears more than does philosophy the impress of him who treats it, each theologian thus retained and developed his own philosophic attitude. Moreover he might feel again the attraction of certain philosophic problems, or he might refresh the memory of his hearers—*"propter imperitos,"* says Henry of Ghent; in both cases he made deep and prolonged incursions into the ground reserved for philosophy. The result was that philosophy became employed in both the Faculty of Arts and the Faculty of Theology,—definitely disinterested in the former and frankly apologetic in the latter.

This is the simple explanation of that pedagogical phenomenon, peculiar to the Middle Ages, which has perplexed historians so much—the mixture of matters philosophical and theological in the *Summae,* the **Quodlibeta,** the **Quaestiones Dispu-**

[15] *Cf.* ch. XIII, iv.

tatae, and in almost all mediaeval works. To consider only the title of *Summa Theologica* given to their chief works by Alexander of Hales, Thomas Aquinas, Henry of Ghent and others, one would think they are great works in which philosophy has no place. But let there be no deception. Genuine philosophical treatises are contained in these vast productions. It will suffice to refer to a part of the great *Summa* of Thomas Aquinas, wherein are to be found integral treatises on psychology and ethics and law.[16]

The religious mentality of the time created also a third class of ties, existing not between philosophy and theology but between the subjective intentions of philosophers and the objective end to which they subordinated all their studies,—which was no other than that of obtaining happiness. The eye of all was fixed on the future life. On the margin of the *Summa Contra Gentiles,* in the rough draft by Thomas himself, we find various pious invocations (*ave, ave Maria*).[17] As Dante wrote the *Divine Comedy* "to snatch the living from the state of wretchedness and to lead them to the state of happiness," so also the intellectuals of the thirteenth century refer their researches, whatever they are—astronomy, mathematics, the science of obser-

---

[16] See *Summa Theol.*, 1ª, qq. LXXV-XC; 1a2ae, qq. I-XXV; *ibid.*, qq. XC-XCVII.

[17] *Summa contra Gentiles,* ad codices manuscriptos praesertim sancti Doctoris exacta, Romae, 1918, Praefatio, p. VIII.

vation, and philosophy also—to their personal striving for Christian happiness. There was here no difference between them and the painters or sculptors or architects, who also worked for the glory of God and their own salvation, or even princes and kings, who were all moved by the desire to avoid hell and to merit heaven, and who did not conceal this in their official acts. But the intention was a matter of moral consciousness; it changed in no respect either the politics of kings or the beauty of works of art or the value of philosophical systems. Scholastics would have applied to their case the famous distinction of *"finis operis"* (the work itself) and *"finis operantis"* (the intention with which it was done).

To sum up: Neither the social superiority of theologians nor the constitution of theological apologetics nor the religious tendency of thinkers was an obstacle to the independence of philosophy. However, these three facts make perfectly plain just how philosophy also in the thirteenth century was bathed in a general atmosphere of religion which pervaded everything else.

V

But, since we have raised in general terms the question of the relations between philosophy and religion in the thirteenth century, there is a last class of ties of which it remains to speak, and which touch very closely philosophic doctrine itself—

the prohibitive or negative subordination of philosophy to theology. Profoundly convinced that Catholic dogma is the expression of the infallible word of God; convinced, on the other hand, that the truth cannot overthrow the truth, without overthrowing the principle of contradiction and involving all certainty in this ruin, the scholastics drew this conclusion: that philosophical doctrine cannot in reality contradict theological doctrine,—therefore it is prohibited from doing so.

To understand the precise meaning of this prohibition we must note three points: First, that it is based on the principle of the solidarity of truth; second, that it involves the denial of contradiction, and not the assertion of positive proof; and, third, that it affects philosophy in part only, namely, so far as its domain belongs at the same time (but from another point of view) to theology. Let us consider each of these in turn.

Truth cannot contradict truth. Music, writes Thomas Aquinas, depends on the application of mathematical principles, which it cannot, therefore, contravene; but it is not concerned with their foundation,—that is not its affair. Assuming the fact of a revelation—and in the heart of the Middle Ages no one doubted it—the attitude of the scholastics is logical. Henry of Ghent puts the matter concisely, when he says: "If we admit (*supposito*) that theological doctrines are true, we cannot admit that other doctrines can contradict them."[18]

That the prohibition is solely negative in character, appears from a statute of the Faculty of Arts of 1272. This statute simply enjoins the "artists" (*artistae*) from "*determinare contra fidem*"; but it does not instruct them "*determinare pro fide.*"[19] No one followed this simple precept with greater breadth of mind than did Thomas Aquinas; and his famous position regarding the eternity of the world is ample evidence of this fact. Thus, the Bible teaches that God created the world in time. To avoid contradicting this dogma, Thomas eliminates the thesis that the world is eternal. But he does maintain that the idea of eternal creation is not contradictory,—because the eternity of the world would not be in opposition to its contingency.[20]

Finally, as regards its limited effect on philos-

[18] "Supposito quod huic scientiae non subjacet nisi verum . . . supposito quod quaecumque vera sunt judicio et auctoritate hujus scientiae . . . his inquam suppositis, cum ex eis manifestum sit quod tam auctoritas hujus scientiae quam ratio . . . veritati innititur et verum vero contrarium esse non potest, absolute dicendum quod auctoritati hujus scripturae ratio nullo modo potest esse contraria." *Summa. Theol.*, X, 3, No. 4.

[19] *Chartularium Univers. Parisiensis,* ed. Denifle et Chatelain, I, 499.

[20] Mundum non semper fuisse sola fide tenetur et demonstrative probari non potest. . . . Demonstrari non potest quod homo aut caelum aut lapis non semper fuit . . . unde non est impossibile quod homo generetur ab homine in infinitum. *Summa Theol.*, 1ª, q. XLVI, art. 2.

ophy, this prohibition applies only to matters expounded by both philosophy and theology. The interdiction has no force unless both domains are involved; therefore philosophy was affected only to a very limited extent.

With this understanding of the scholastic conception before us, we might seek to estimate the truth of their view concerning the relation of philosophy to theology. The result would of course vary, according to the acceptance or rejection of Christianity and the particular meaning given to the idea of revelation. But we are here concerned with an historical problem. Certainly, from that point of view, there can be no doubt concerning the position in fact taken by the scholastics of the thirteenth century.

VI

We are now in position to evaluate the commonly accepted view of scholastic philosophy, which was given at the outset of this lecture. The definition which was then quoted,—accepted by most historians of mediaeval philosophy—conceives of scholastic philosophy as essentially religious.

Of course, one can say of scholastic philosophy that it is largely inspired by religion. However, this is true in so general a sense that the fact turns out to be *irrelevant* for purposes of definition. Their philosophy evolved in a social atmosphere in which religion was dominant. Under the spell of this mentality theological studies enjoyed a prestige superior to that which was granted to philosophical studies. The proximity of the faculties of theology and philosophy introduced a kind of passion for combining (but not confusing) philosophical and theological questions in the same work. Finally, as regards the realm of morals, philosophy was regarded by the intellectuals of the Middle Ages as a preliminary step in aspiring to happiness. But this religious inspiration affects all the other activities that make up the civilization of the thirteenth century—politics, art, morals, family, work. The religious inspiration is a relational characteristic along with many others; but precisely because this characteristic belongs to the civilization, it belongs to all its factors and is not peculiar to philosophy, which is only one factor. Hence it is as inadequate to the definition of their philosophy as would be, for example, the description of the oak by reference merely to the nature of the soil, which its roots share with those of the elm and the beech and the other trees of the forest. One can understand why historians who study expressly the civilization of the Middle Ages,[21] should single out for criticism the dominant preoccupation with salvation, in the thirteenth century scholasticism, and should regard this as sufficiently characteristic. But it seems incredible that works which treat

[21] As does, for example, H. O. Taylor in his remarkable work, *The Mediaeval Mind*, vol. II, ch. XXXV.

solely of the historical exposition of philosophical doctrines should be content with such a superficial judgment; and the procedure seems to me inadmissible.

In addition to the general criticism which we have just made of this definition, on the ground of insufficiency, some special criticisms may be considered on the basis of our preceding study.

Scholasticism, others say, is philosophy placed in the service of doctrine already established by the Church. Not at all. To place philosophy in the service of theology is to use apologetic; and apologetic, which proposes to show the rational character of dogmas fixed beforehand, comes from scholastic theology and not from scholastic philosophy. To define, according to the explicit procedure of Aristotle, is to say what a thing is, and not only what it is not.

Is scholasticism, then, placed in such dependence on theology as to follow it without any contradiction whatever? The reply to this question is in the affirmative, provided the ground is a common one. But the question is whether this dependence is enough to constitute a complete definition, and one must reply in the negative. In the first place, because this dependence simply places boundaries or limits beyond which one cannot pass. It does not treat of what is beyond, or of numerous philosophical doctrines in which theology is not interested, but in which our definition should be interested.

Scholastic philosophy includes vast domains which are not in conflict with the realm of theology.[22] Now definition involves not merely the outlining of limits, but also the penetrating of the field itself. We object further, because this dependence does not establish any doctrinal content, but simply forbids contradiction. It can therefore only establish a negative—that is to say, an imperfect—definition of philosophical doctrine, which is the thing itself to be defined.

VII

We conclude then that need of universal order, cosmopolitan value, optimism, impersonality, and religious spirit are so many *harmonious* relations which exist between scholastic philosophy and all the other spheres of the civilization in which it appears.

But in addition to these harmonious relations, which reveals this civilization rather in its static aspect, there are also relations which are distinctly dynamic. For, scholasticism had a very profound

[22] Even Mr. Taylor (*op. cit.*) recognizes that scholastic philosophers are devoted to the pursuit of knowledge for itself. Beside the joy of working for their salvation, they have the joy of study. Men like Roger Bacon, Albertus Magnus, and Thomas Aquinas, could not have done what they did, says he, without the love of knowledge in their souls. Similarly, it has been shown by Mâle, that in addition to the *symbolic sculpture*, which is based on religious doctrine, there are many sculptural designs and motives in the Gothic cathedrals which are introduced solely for the sake of artistic beauty. See E. Mâle: *L'art religieux du 13'e s. en France*, pp. 70 ff.

influence within the various departments of psychical life; and from this angle of its efficacy it acquires a new value for our consideration.

What has been said concerning mediaeval apologetics constitutes an example of the penetration of philosophic doctrine within the domain of theology. In the same way one can show that this doctrine reacted in the spheres of canon law and of civil law and of political economy and of mysticism. Moreover, like a musical sound in its harmonic scale, the same doctrine reverberates throughout the forms of artistic and common life. And it could be pointed out readily how the literature of the period is permeated with it,—how the *Roman de la Rose* read in the feudal castles; how great didactic poems such as the *Bataille des Septs Arts* of Henri d'Andeli, the *Renart Contrefait*, the *Mariage des Septs Arts et des Septs Vertus*; how Chaucer's *Parlement of Foules* or his *Canterbury Tales* are filled with philosophical theories borrowed from Alan of Lille, Avicenna, Thomas Aquinas, Thomas Bradwardine and others.[23] The same may be said of the Canzone of Guido Cavalcante[24] and of the poems of Dante.

Thus, for example, Dante's *De Monarchia* draws its inspiration from the theory of the four causes; it invokes the scholastic theory of the *proprium*, in

---

[23] For instance, Chaucer's "Nun's Priest Tale" reproduces the theological determinism of Thomas Bradwardine.

[24] For instance, *Canzone*, p. 123, ed. Ercole Rivalta: *La Rime di Guido Cavalcante*, Florence, 1902.

order to justify its claim that man's good consists in the development of his intelligence;[25] it takes as its authority Gilbert de la Porrée, *"magister sex principiorum"*; it constructs "polysyllogisms in the second figure";[26] it sets forth at length the theory of liberty for which it employs a definition which expresses the feudal mentality (*suimet et non alterius est*) ; it observes that it is easier to teach philosophy to one who is utterly innocent of knowledge about it than to those who are replete with erroneous opinions; it rests at one point, on the precept which expresses so admirably the unifying tendency of the time: *"quod potest fieri per unum melius est fieri per unum quam per plura"*;[27] it likens the relation of petty prince and monarch to that of the practical and the speculative intellect, inasmuch as directions for conduct pass to the former from the latter. As for the *Divine Comedy*, it is full of philosophy, notwithstanding the poetical transformation which suffuses the thought with its magical charm. While Dante is no systematic philosopher, nevertheless he is eclectic and the influence of philosophical systems is everywhere evident in his thought; in hands so expert the work of art receives every doctrinal impression like soft and pliable wax.

One could show how the statues of the cathedral churches of Chartres or of Laon or of Paris, for ex-

[25] Pars Prima.
[26] "Iste polysyllogismus currit per secundam figuram."
[27] See above, p. 110.

ample, and the frescoes and miniatures of the thirteenth century generally, reflect in design and in color the philosophical thought of the period; how the great painters from the fourteenth century to the seventeenth century owe much of their artistic inspiration to scholastic themes; how the terminology of that same philosophy makes no small contribution to the ever increasing modern vocabulary, especially in philosophy;[28] how scholastic definitions have entered into English literature and French literature; how some of the thirteenth century hagiographers make use of the methods of division and the technical terms of scholasticism; and how entire doctrines drawn from scholasticism are con-

[28] The scholastic terms become "current coin," as Saintsbury observes; and he adds: "Even the logical fribble, even the logical jargonist was bound to be exact. Now exactness was the very thing which languages, mostly young in actual age . . . wanted most of all." *Periods of European Literature,* vol. II (The Flourishing of Romance and the Rise of Allegory), p. 16, *cf.* pp. 20, 21. *Cf.* Brunetière: "Les définitions de la scholastique n'ont rien de *scientifique* au sens véritable du mot; mais elles n'en ont pas moins discipliné l'esprit français en lui imposant ce besoin de clarté, de précision et de justesse qui ne laissera pas de contribuer pour sa part à la fortune de notre prose . . . A coup sûr, nous ne pourrons pas ne pas lui être reconnaissants de nous avoir appris à *composer;* et là, comme on sait, dans cet équilibre de la composition, dans cette subordination du détail à l'idée de l'ensemble, dans celte juste proportion de parties, là sera l'un des traits éminents et caractéristiques de la littérature française." *Manuel de l'histoire de la littérature française,* Paris, 1898, pp. 24-25.

Shakespeare is acquainted with scholastic doctrines. For example, the "quiddities" of Hamlet (Act V, sc. i, "Where be his quiddities

densed in the terse sayings of popular speech. Indeed, these influences are so far reaching and so diverse that no student of history or of political and social science or of art or of literature in the Middle Ages can safely ignore the philosophy of that period.

But however important and interesting these influences (the dynamic relations) may be, they are not more significant for our proper understanding of the scholastic philosophy than is the harmonious equilibrium (the static relations) considered in the preceding chapters. And hence, to comprehend fully and to estimate that philosophy aright we must proceed to consider what belongs to it in its own constitution. To that end we shall enter into its doctrinal content.

It will be impossible of course to consider all of the manifold and extensive doctrinal realms which scholastic philosophy covers. We shall therefore limit ourselves to those doctrinal realms which are

now?") is a scholastic term; it means 'realities' and not 'subtilities' (common glossary). Again Hamlet (Act I, sc. v) speaks of "table of my memory" and
"All forms, all pressures past
That youth and observation copied there."
This is an allusion to the *"formae et species impressae."* And again, he is using scholastic thought when he says:
"Sense sure you have,
Else could you not have motion." (Act III, sc. iv)
recalling the doctrine that movement presupposes sense-perception. That "godlike" reason differentiates man from beast (Act. IV, sc. iv) is also scholastic doctrine.

most intimately connected with the civilization. Namely, intellectualism because it permeates the entire life of the century, although it belongs properly to psychology (Chapter VIII); metaphysics, because it is the foundation of the whole scholastic philosophy (Chapter IX); social philosophy because it is intimately bound up with the political and religious life (Chapters X and XI); and, finally, the conception of human progress, because for them as for all energetic humanity it is the mainspring of life (Chapter XII).

CHAPTER EIGHT

INTELLECTUALISM

i. Intellectualism in ideology. ii. In epistemology. iii. In psychology (free volition). iv. More generally (psychology, logic, metaphysics, ethics, aesthetics). v. In other forms of culture.

I

Intellectualism is a doctrine which places all the nobility, all the intensity, the whole value of psychical life in the act of knowing. No philosophy is more "intellectualistic" than mediaeval scholasticism. It is a doctrine of light. Long before Descartes,—but from another point of view—Thomas Aquinas and Duns Scotus emphasized the importance of clear intellectual insight. The scholastic conception of clear knowledge is not only prominent in their psychology; it also penetrates all the other departments of their philosophy, so that intellectualism is at the same time a doctrine and a method.

Considered in its ideological aspect, scholastic intellectualism is a brilliant form of idealism,[1] and

[1] With the term, *idealism*, I refer to the ideological conception which establishes a difference in kind between sense perception and intellectual knowledge.

places the philosophers of the Middle Ages in the family of Plato, Plotinus, Descartes, Leibnitz, and Kant. This will appear from a simple example. I look at two black horses drawing a carriage. All that my senses perceive in these external data receives a particular dress, which is temporal and spatial.[2] But I possess another power of representing to myself the real. The intellect draws out of this sensible content the ideas of motion, of muscular force, of horse, of life, of being. It does away with the concrete conditions which, in the sensible perception, bind the real to a particular state; it "abstracts" the *"quod quid est,"* the *what* of a thing.

One might multiply examples at will; but they would only bring out the more clearly that we have abstract ideas without number,—ideas, for example, of qualities and forms and quantities and action and passions and so on. Indeed one possesses a very treasure of these abstract ideas; they are as manifold as the kinds of reality implied in the complex data of sense perception,—out of which the abstract idea is always drawn. *Nihil est in intellectu quod non prius fuerit in sensu.* For, in the scholastic view, to abstract is the law of the intellect; its function of abstraction is as normal as is the bodily process of digestion. The moment the intellect enters into contact with reality, it reacts upon that reality,—its food, as it were—by as-

---

[2] Sensus non est cognoscitivus nisi particularium. Thomas Aquinas, *Summa Contra Gentiles*, lib. II, cap. LXVI.

similating it to itself and therefore by divesting it of every particularized condition.

The question naturally arises, just how does the intellect form these *abstract* ideas through contact with *concrete* objects of sense? The scholastic would reply by reference to his theory of the *intellectus agens*. But this would take us too far afield for our purposes here.[3] Their conclusion alone is significant for our present study; namely, abstract knowledge differs from sense perception not in degree but in kind. For, the *content* of our abstract ideas,—the motion and force and life of our horses and carriages, in the above illustration—is quite independent of the particular ties of time and space, and of all material conditions in which reality as perceived by the senses is involved. Consequently, abstract knowledge is superior to sense perception; abstraction is the royal privilege of man. This superiority of intellect is as much a matter of grateful pride to the scholastics as it was to Plato and to Aristotle.

II

Intellectualism furnishes also a solution in the field of epistemology,—the problem of the value of knowledge; for it establishes truth on a firm foundation, while at the same time it fixes the limits of reason. Truth is something which pertains to the

[3] For detailed account of this conception see D. Mercier, *Psychologie*, Louvain, 1912, vol. II, pp. 39 ff.

intellect. "For truth consists in saying that a being is when it is, or that it is not when it is not."[4] Consequently certitude, which is nothing but a firm assent to truth, is a possession of understanding and reason; it does not depend on will or on sentiment or on pragmatical efficiency. Here is one of the basic differences between scholastic philosophy and an important contemporary tendency in epistemology, which insists on some "non-intellectualistic" criterion of certitude.[5]

The intellect grasps "being"; it can somehow assimilate all that is: *intellectus potest quodammodo omnia fieri*. Moreover, when it grasps being, it is infallible. "In the figure of Ezekiel, "writes Meister Eckhart, who with his wonderful power for imagery expresses splendidly this particular idea, "the intellect is that mighty eagle, with wide reach of wing, which descended upon Lebanon and seized the cedar's marrow as its prey,—that is to say, the constitution of the thing—and plucked the topmost bloom of foliage."[6] There is no error in the understanding itself; it is always true as regards being,

[4] Thomas Aquinas, *Perihermeneias*, I, 3.

[5] For fuller details, see my *Histoire de la Philosophie Medievale*, p. 246.

[6] Intellectus enim est in figura aquila illa grandis Eze. 17 longo membrorum ductu, que venit ad Lybanum et tulit medullam cedri, id est, principia rei, et summitatem frondium ejus avulsit. Edit. Denifle (*Archiv für Litteratur und Kirchengeschichte des Mittelalters*, 1886, p. 566).

its object proper.[7] Error lies only in the judgment, when we combine two concepts and declare that their contents coincide, although in reality they are in disagreement. It follows from this that reason in our life has genuine worth; it is not a wayward will-o'-the-wisp which leads him astray who trusts to it,—it is a torch which illumines.

But that which the intellect understands is only a small measure of reality; therefore, one must understand the limits of reason. Intellectual knowledge is imperfect and inadequate. First, because our ideas are derived from the content of sense-perception, from which follows that we cannot know properly more than the realities of sense; accordingly, the supersensible can be known only by analogy. From this point of view, the human intelligence is no longer the powerful eagle, but the winged creature of night, the bat (*noctua*), which faces with difficulty the full light of the sun,—the supersensible realm. Moreover, even the corporeal reality is apprehended by imperfect processes. We know only the general determinations of being, notions of what is common, for instance, to live or to move in various living or moving beings. The nature of the individual as such escapes us,—even though, with Duns Scotus, we derive a kind of con-

---

[7] Intellectus circa proprium objectum semper verus est; unde et seipso numquam decipitur; sed omnis deceptio accidit in intellectu et aliquo inferiori, puta phantasia vel aliquo hujusmodi. Thomas Aquinas, *Summa Theol.*, 1ᵃ, q. XCIV, art. 4.

fused intuition of the concrete and singular. Furthermore, these general notions do not even manifest what is specific in the essences which are known; indeed, we employ the same common notion of life for plants and animals and men, and we are condemned to ignorance of the innermost reality peculiar to the life in each class of these living beings. On all sides, therefore, reality surpasses knowledge; the unknowable encompasses us round about.

III

Yet this very same reason, at once so glorified and humbled, is the queen of conscious life. It rules the appetitive life, by restraining the passions and lower appetites. Reason shines as a torch which lights and directs the will, necessary or free. We will only what we know as good—*nihil volitum nisi cognitum*—and already this precedence of intellect over will establishes a dependence of the will on the intellect.

It is because we are reasonable beings that free volitions are psychologically possible. Thomas Aquinas, and Duns Scotus too[8]—so long regarded as holding here a different view—gives a remarkable intellectual explanation of liberty which is not found in any preceding system.

[8] See P. Minges, Ist Duns Scotus Indeterminist? Baümker's-*Beiträge*, 1905, V, 4. *Cf.* my *Histoire de la Philosophie Médiévale*, p. 460.

We are drawn to the good. This means that we are inclined to will whatever reality is presented as capable of satisfying a certain indwelling tendency, —our tendency, namely, toward what is *considered* to be suitable to us. Just as the intellect conceives being in the abstract, as integral being, so it conceives the good as such, the general good. For when the intellect acts, it obeys the law of its activity; and in doing so it abstracts the good as such, and sees in this (or any) being the good which it contains. Only the complete good can draw us irresistibly, because it alone satisfies this intellectual tendency of our nature.[9] It is then impossible for the will *not* to will it. If the Infinite Good should manifest Himself, the soul would be drawn towards it, as iron is attracted by the magnet. The attractions which the martyrs felt for the benefits of this life, at the very moment when they preferred to die, remarks Duns Scotus, is the sign and effect of this necessary tendency toward the good, the good as a totality.

But during our earthly life the good never appears to us unadulterated; for every good is limited. The moment we reflect, the limitation is perceived; every good is good only under *certain* aspects; it contains deficiencies. Then the intellect places me before two intellectual judgments. For example,

---

[9] Objectum autem voluntatis quae est appetitus humanus, est universale bonum, sicut objectum intellectus est universale verum. Thomas Aquinas. *Summa Theol.*, 1ª2ᵃᵉ, q. II, art. 8.

it is good for me to undertake a journey; not to undertake it contains also some good. Behold, I am called upon to judge my own judgments. Which judgment shall I choose? The will must decide,— and it decides freely, for neither judgment enjoins a necessary adhesion. We will freely the good which we choose, not because it is the *greater* good, but because it is *some good*. In a sense we may say that our choice stops with the good which we consider the best. But, in the last analysis, this is true only if we add, that the will *freely intervenes* in the decision. In other words, it is under the influence of the will that the practical intellect makes its judgment, that the one or the other course of action is the better. The will can in reality give its preference to either of the alternatives. At the moment of definite choice, *deliberation* ceases and gives place to *decision*. So Thomas and Duns Scotus avoided the psychological determinism which puzzled other scholastics,—such as Godfrey of Fontaines and John Buridan.

Thus, liberty resides in the will, but it has its roots in the judgment. Consequently, a free act is a deliberate act, and entirely reflective. An act of this kind is not a common thing. Indeed, whole days pass during which we do not make intellectual decisions,—that is, in the scholastic meaning of the word.

IV

Scholastic intellectualism is quite evident, not only in the remaining branches of psychology, but also in logic, in metaphysics, in aesthetics, and in morals.

Abstraction, which is the fundamental operation of the intellect, establishes the spirituality of the soul; for a being capable of producing thoughts, the content of which is free from the chains of matter, is itself above matter.[10] It justifies the natural union of soul and body, because the normal function of the organism cannot be dissociated from the act of thinking. It furnishes an argument in favour of a new union of the soul with the body in the resurrection, because the body is the indispensable instrument of intellectual activity.

Is it necessary to observe that every theory of science, or scientific logic, is incomprehensible without intellectualism? Scientific judgments are necessary judgments, laws; and they are not of necessity without abstraction and generalization. On abstraction is based the theory of the syllogism, the value of first principles, of definitions, of divisions, and of everything which enters into constructive procedure. Before Henry Poincaré, the scholastics had said, "Science will be intellectual or it will cease to be."

The perception of a work of art, and of its beauty,

[10] Thomas Aquinas, *De Anima,* lib. III, lect. vii.

is also an act of the intellect. Beauty ought to be resplendent, *claritas pulchri,* it ought to reveal, and in a striking way, the internal order that governs beauty. It speaks to the faculty of knowing, and above all to the intellect.

What is true of the perception of a work of art is true also of its production. Man's artistic faculty,—by virtue of which the carpenter and the sculptor achieve their results—consists in a right use of reason; for the reason alone can subordinate the means to the end. *Ars nihil aliud est quam ratio recta aliquorum operum faciendorum.* The "virtue of art," *virtus artis,*—for the humble artisan as for the gifted artist—consists far more in a perfection of the spirit than in any virtuosity or muscular dexterity.[10a]

A like sovereignty obtains in the moral realm. Reason teaches us our duties and guides our conscience. Reason gives a characteristic significance to destiny and happiness. To be happy is above all to know, because happiness consists in the highest activities of our highest psychical power, which is understanding.[11] Even in this life, knowledge is a great consolation. Beatitude, or the perfect

[10a] *Summa Theol.*, 1a2ae, q. LVII, art. 3: Utrum habitus intellectualis qui est ars, sit virtus. Read all of arts. 3, 4, and 5, for interesting suggestions on the intellectualistic theory of art. *Cf.* my study, *L'Oeuvre d'art et la Beauté,* Louvain, 1920, ch. VI.

[11] Oportet quod (beatitudo) sit optima operatio hominis. Optima autem operatio hominis est quae est optimae potentiae respectu optimi objecti. Optima autem potentia est intellectus, etc. *Summa Theol.*, 1a2ae, q. III, art. 5.

goodness destined for man,—that alone which philosophy considers—would be a "happiness of abstractions," a goodness founded on abstract knowledge of the laws and the being of the sensible world, a knowledge and love of the Creator in His works.[12]

The supremacy of reason appears also in metaphysics, where it explains the fundamental order of things, which rests entirely on Divine Reason. It manifests itself in the immutability of natural as well as moral law, which God could not change, without contradicting Eternal Reason, that is to say, without destroying Himself. No will, not even the will of God, can change the nature of truth; and truth can no more contradict truth than a circle can be quadrate.

Finally, this same supremacy of reason is apparent in their whole theory of the state, where government is conceived as being properly a government of insight; from whose laws everything arbitrary ought to be excluded; where the elective system is justified because it favours the exercise of reason.[12bis]

[12] Compare the following excerpt from an unedited text of the thirteenth century (as in Grabmann, "Forschungen über die lateinischen Aristoteles-Uebersetzenigen d. XIII Jhr.," p. 76 in Baümker's-*Beiträge,* 1916, XVII, 5-6): "Cum omne desiderii compos et maxime creatura rationalis appetat suam perfectionem, summa vero et finalis perfectio hominis sit in cognitione unius intellectualis veri et in amore unius incommutabilis boni, quod est nosse et amare suum creatorem, et medium praecipue inducens ad cognoscendum et amandum creatorem sit cognitio consideratione operum creatoris, etc."

[12bis] See Ch. XI.

V

But this clear-cut intellectualism and love of precision, appears also in other forms of culture of the thirteenth century. It inspires even the smallest detail of that doctrinal structure elaborated by the doctors of theology, giving to each element of belief an apologetic and rational interpretation. It is found in the works of canonists, who reason out the ecclesiastical law, just as jurists reason out the Roman law. Intellectualism is found also in the explanation of rites and symbols, the manifold meanings of which such a man as William of Mende endeavoured to unfold in his *Rationale Divinorum*. It is further found in the *Roman de la Rose* of the poet Jean de Meung, where *Reason* is personified and fills the poem with long discourses, as she filled with her dictates the lives of mediaeval men.[13]

The same intellectualism and the same clearness appears also in the Gothic architecture and sculp-

[13] It is, then, not surprising that Dante, educated in scholastic circles, wrote these words in his *De Monarchia* (lib. 1): "Reason is to the individual what the father is to the family, or what the mayor is to the city. It is master. In all matters reason makes its voice heard." The *Banquet,* or *Convito,* addresses itself to those who hunger for knowledge, and contemplates making all humanity participate in knowledge,—that "good desired of all," that supreme form of happiness. In the *Divine Comedy* Dante exalts the man who sacrifices his life in the promotion of knowledge. Virgil represents human knowledge, which the soul must acquire in its plentitude before being admitted to the divine mysteries. And in the *Paradiso,* each of the elect enjoys to the full that beatitude "which he can conceive."

ture, where everything is reasoned and rational. Has it not been said with justice that Gothic architecture is an application of logic in poems in stone, that it speaks as forcibly and clearly to the mind as to the eye? It is nothing more than the most logical application of the laws of gravitation. The pointed arch windows and the double arched vaults express their function admirably, as do also the supports and the buttresses. Everywhere we find beauty rationalized; no superfluous ornaments, nothing of that fantastic decoration which spoiled the Gothic idea in the fifteenth century. In those lines of clearness and purity which we see in the naves of the cathedral of Rheims, Paris, Amiens, and Chartres all is sober and reasonable. The walls have let themselves be cleft in order to admit the light,—the light filled first, however, with those dreams imparted by the glass; and the felt need of light issued finally in creating churches that are transparent, as it were, where all is subordinated to the idea of illumination.

Nor is it otherwise with the sculpture of the thirteenth century, the form of which is vivified by clear and severe concepts. "The iconography of the thirteenth century," writes M. Mâle, "aims to speak to the intelligence and not to the feelings. It is doctrinal and theological, that is to say, logical and rational; but there is nothing pathetic or tender about it. The great religious compositions speak to the *mind*, and not to the heart. Consider, for instance, how the artists of the thirteenth century conceive the Nativity: Mary reclines on a couch with head averted; the Child is not in a crib, but upon an altar; a lamp is suspended over His head between parted curtains."[14] Every point directs the mind to dogma and to doctrine. Human emotion is silent before such a conception, and the same is true when the tranquil Virgin bears in her arms, or upon her knees, the Infant Saviour; or when she assists, in her grief, but without weakness, at the crucifixion of her Son. It is only after the fourteenth century that art becomes *tender,* that the Virgin smiles and weeps, and "the symbolic apple which the serious Virgin of the thirteenth holds in her hand to remind us that she is the second Eve, becomes a plaything to prevent the child Jesus from crying."[15]

Society is also intellectualized, in its entirety, in the sense that the whole age craves for order. Of course the thirteenth century is filled with quarrels and revolts, and hostilities break out everywhere; this signifies only that it was no more possible to realize fully a social ideal in that age than in any other. But the ideal existed none the less and it was efficacious. The relations of vassals and suzerains and of the subjects and kings, the participation of the feudal classes in the prerogatives of government, the establishment of national parliaments,

[14] Mâle, *L'art religieux du 13'e siécle en France,* 1910, p. 221.
[15] *Ibid.,* p. 239.

the codification of civil and canon law, the organization of crafts and guilds, the absolute and international hierarchy of the Church, the subordination of states to the moral authority of the Pope,—all of these were regarded by the intellectual classes as the best means of establishing things in their proper places. Order, said Thomas Aquinas, reveals in every case the intervention of mind. *"Intellectus solius est ordinare."*[16] Only the mind is able to set things in order. Naturally, therefore, intellectualism makes its appearance in everything.

[16] *In Ethic. ad Nicomach.*, Lect. I, 7.

CHAPTER NINE

A Pluralistic Conception of the World

i. What metaphysics is. ii. Static aspects of reality. iii. Dynamic aspects; the central doctrine of act and potency. iv. Application to substance and accident; to matter and form. v. The problem of individuation. vi. Human personality. vii. God: as pure existence.

I

To inquire into the conception of the world offered by the scholastics is to enter into the realm of their metaphysics. Real beings exist outside of us. We know them first by means of sense-perception. Then the intellect divests the realities offered by sense-perception of their individualizing and particular features, so that the object is laid hold of as abstract and permits generalization. Metaphysical inquiry is thus based upon abstract knowledge both of what lies at the heart of corporeal beings and of determinations which belong to all being.

What is reality? To make clear the scholastic answer to this question, I propose to consider reality successively under two aspects: first, the static aspect, or reality in the state of repose; second, the dynamic aspect, or reality in the state of change. I use these technical expressions provisionally; they will become clearer as we proceed.

II.

Let us suppose for the moment an impossibility; namely, that the whirling universe in the midst of which we live should stop suddenly, and that in this state of universal repose we could take a snap-shot of this static universe. In this state, of what would the real world consist? Scholasticism would reply: of *an indefinite number of beings, independent, in their existence, each from the other.* Each man, each animal, each plant, each mono-cellular organism, each particle of matter exists by itself, in its impenetrable individuality. *The individual alone exists.* Such is the fundamental doctrine of scholastic metaphysics and it was inherited from the twelfth century. It belongs to natural science, and not to philosophy, to tell us what that individual is. Is it the atom, the ion, the electron? Scholastic metaphysics would follow modern science to the innermost division of reality. Whatever it may be, it is only the individual that exists.

Thus, scholasticism is a pluralistic philosophy, and the sworn enemy of monism, which teaches the fusion of all realities in one. Accordingly, Thomas Aquinas speaks of the *Fons Vitae* of Avicebron, an apologetic of Neo-Platonic and Arabian pantheism, as being a poisoned well rather than a fountain of life.

Let us consider more closely one of these myriad individual realities, which surround us on all sides, —for example, that oak-tree planted yonder. The individuality here presented includes many elements: it has a determinable thickness and height, a cylindrical form of trunk, a roughness of bark, a somber color of foliage, a place which it occupies in the forest, a certain action of its foliage upon the ambient air, a specific subjection to influence as it absorbs the nourishing sap from the ground. These are all so many determinations of being or, to use the scholastic language, so many classes, *categories,*—categories of quantity, quality, action, passion, time, space and relation.

Now, all of these classes, or categories, presuppose a yet more fundamental one. Can you conceive, asks Aristotle, the reality of walking without some one who walks? Can you conceive quantity, thickness, and the rest, without something,— our oak-tree above—which possesses it? Neither the action of walking nor the extension of quantity can be conceived apart from a subject in which they exist. And it is such a subject which Aristotle and the scholastics call *substance,*—the fundamental category, as distinguished from the other classes, which they call accidents (*accidentia*).

Not only do we *conceive* corporeal realities in terms of substance and accidents,—and no philosophy denies the existence in our minds of these two concepts—but also the substance and the accidents exist independently and outside of our minds. In the order of existence, as in the order of our thought, substance and accident are *relative* to each other. One who succeeds in proving the external existence of the accident[1] (for instance, the thickness of the tree), also proves the existence of the substance (that is, the tree). If the act of walking is not an illusion but something real, the same must be equally true of the substantial being who walks, without whom there would be no act of walking. The substance, or subject, exists in and by itself; it is self-sufficient. But it is also the support of all the rest, which therefore are called *accidentia* (*id quod accidit alicui rei*).

As for my own substance, the substance of myself as a human being,—that is personality—there is the witness of consciousness, by its several activities, to the existence of just such a substantial Ego. In thinking and speaking, and so on, I attain to my own existing substance. The scholastics were essentially familiar with the *cogito ergo sum*. Without permanence of personality, memory would be inexplicable. If I were only a collection of

---

[1] Scholasticism proves the objectivity of our external sense-perception by the mark of *passivity* (of which we are conscious) and by the principle of causality: *quidquid movetur ab alio movetur*. We are conscious of being *passive* in external sensation; consequently we do not create it,—therefore it must come from a non-ego.

ephemeral activities, what Taine calls a collection of *sky-rockets of consciousness* (*"gerbes lumineuses"*), how could one sky-rocket remember another? How could I then remember in maturity the acts of my boyhood? But, not only do I remember such acts, I am also conscious of being the same *personality;* my acts disappear, my body changes, but I remain a subject independent of these acts and changes.

The frequent misunderstanding of the scholastic theory of substance rests upon two misconceptions of what that theory involved: first, that one knows wherein one substance differs from another; second, that substance is something underlying accidental realities. Now, as regards the former, scholastic philosophy never pretended to know wherein one substance differed from another in the external world. It thought of substance as an idea resulting from reasoning, which does not instruct regarding what is *specific* in each of the substances;[2] one knows that they are and must be, but never *what* they are. Indeed, the idea of substance is essentially thin. And the same may be said of the Ego, as the substance best known to each individual person; consciousness witnesses to its existence, but never to its *nature,*—as Descartes erroneously supposed. A proof that consciousness alone does not instruct us regarding our own *nature,* says scholasticism, is the discussion among philosophers on

[2] See above, p. 184.

the nature of the soul. The second misconception above mentioned, may be readily disposed of. To imagine that something lies behind or underneath the accidents, as the door underlies the painted color, is simply a misinterpretation of the scholastic theory. Locke especially was here in error; of course he had no difficulty in criticizing this conception as ridiculous. But this interpretation is totally wrong. In the scholastic view, substance and accidents are really one and the same concrete existing thing. Indeed, substance is that which confers individuality upon the particular determinations, or accidents. It is therefore the substance of the oak-tree which constitutes the foundation of its individuality, and which thus confers individuality upon its qualities, the dimensions of the oak and all the train of accidental determinations which belong to its concrete individuality.

This *"tout ensemble"* of substance and accidental determinations, both taken together, exists by virtue of *one* existence alone, the existence of the concrete oak-tree which we have considered as fixed and motionless in the static instant above described.

III

But such a picture of the world is not a possible picture; for *nothing is motionless*. Reality is involved in change and in evolution. Chemical bodies are in constant change, in all stages of their existence, be it liquid or gaseous or solid; living organisms are changing; our globe as a whole is ceaselessly borne along in a twofold movement; the sun with its train of planets is subject to the law of change, and the same is true of the stars scattered throughout the immensity of space. Substance and accident: all is becoming. The oak springs from the acorn, it becomes tall and massive, its vital activities are forever changing, and the tree itself will disappear. In order to understand the full meaning of metaphysics, it is necessary to throw *being* into the melting pot of change.

Thus the static point of view, or the world considered in the state of repose, must be supplemented by the dynamic point of view, or that of the world drawn into becoming. Here appears a further scholastic conception; namely, the well-known theory of *act* and *potency,* which forms, in my opinion, the key-stone in the vault of the metaphysical structure. This theory is a general analysis of what change implies. The scholastics get it from Aristotle, but give to it a breadth and extension unknown to the Greek philosopher. What is change, any change? It is the real passage from one state to another. Now, they observe, when one being passes from state A to state B, it must already possess in A the *germs* of its future determination in B. It has the power, the potency, to become B before it actually does so. This is demanded by the principle of sufficient reason—an absolute principle to which all that is must be obedient, under penalty of not being at all. To deny this sort of preëxistence is equivalent to denying change from one state to another, the evolution of reality. What we call change would then be a series of instantaneous appearances and disappearances of substances, having no internal connections whatever, each with duration infinitesimally small. The oak is potentially in the acorn; if it were not there potentially, how could it ever issue from it? On the other hand, the oak is not potentially in a pebble, rolled about by the sea, and which outwardly might present a close resemblance to the acorn. *Act* or *actuality* (the ἐντελέχεια of Aristotle, the *actus* of the scholastics) is any present sum-total of perfection. *Potency* (δύναμις *potentia* of the scholastics) is the aptitude to become that perfection. It is imperfection and non-being, if you will; but it is not mere nothing, because non-being considered in an already existing subject is endowed with the germ of future actualization.

The coupling of act and potency therefore penetrates reality in its inmost depths. It explains all the great conceptions of scholastic metaphysics. Especially does it explain those two great doctrines, in which we shall follow the play of act and potency,—namely, the doctrine of substance and accident, and the doctrine of matter and form.

IV

The doctrine of substance and accident is thus rounded out and clarified by the coupling of act and potency; indeed, an adequate understanding of the former requires the latter. Thus, to say that a being already constituted in its substantial determination is changing, means that it is *actually realizing its potentialities*. A child is already potentially the powerful athlete he will some day become. If he is destined to become a mathematician, then already in the cradle he possesses this power, or predisposition, whereas another infant is deprived of it. Quantitative and qualitative change, change in the activities brought about by actual being and in the activity undergone,—all of this was able *to be* before being in fact.

Considered in the light of this theory, the doctrine of substance and accident loses its naïve and false significance. A growing oak, a living man, a chemical individuality of any kind, each of the myriad individual beings, is indeed an individual substance becoming, because its quantity, qualities, activities, relations are the becoming of its potentialities. Leibnitz was really following this thomistic doctrine when he said: "The present is pregnant with the future." But more than this. While Leibnitz also taught the eternity and the immutability of substances, which he called monads, Thomas and the scholastics go further into the heart of change. It is not only the accidents which change when, for example, the oak grows, or its wood becomes tougher, or its place changes when it is transplanted, or its activities are renewed as it develops; but the very *substances themselves* are carried into the maelstrom of change, and nature makes us witness to the unceasing spectacle of their transformations. The oak dies; and from the slow work of its decomposition are born chemical bodies of most diverse kinds. An electric current traverses the molecule of water; and behold hydrogen and oxygen arise.

All of this is essentially scholastic doctrine. When one substance changes into another, each has a *quite different specificity.* Substances differ not in degree but in kind. An oak never changes into another oak, nor a particle of water into another particle of water. But out of a dying oak, or a decomposed particle of water, are born chemical bodies, which appear with quite different activities, quantities, relations, and so on.[3] The differences of all these activities, quantities, and the rest, are for us the *only means* of knowing the substances of things, because the activity of a thing gives its measure of perfection and springs out of it: *"agere sequitur esse."* And hence corresponding to irre-

---

[3] "There is not the slightest parity between the passive and the active powers of the water and those of the oxygen and the hydrogen which have given rise to it," says Huxley in *Lay Sermons,* ("The Physical Basis of Life"), New York, 1874, p. 136.

ducible activities and qualities there must be irreducible substances. Of course, the scholastics were unable to observe, as we can, the chemical activities of corporeal bodies. But this is simply a matter of application and the principle remains. The substance of hydrogen is quite different from that of water; this is what I have called the specificity of objects. A corporeal substance cannot be more nor less than what it is. Water is plainly water or it is something quite different; it cannot have degrees of being water. Just as a person cannot be more or less man than another man. *"Essentia non suscipit plus vel minus."* Accordingly, the world offers the greatest diversity of irreducible substantial perfections.

But let us consider more closely this phenomenon of basic change, from one substance into another or into several other substances,—for instance, water becoming hydrogen and oxygen. If Thomas had been invited to interpret this phenomenon, he would have said: *that the substance of the water transformed itself into new substances,* hydrogen and oxygen, and that the hydrogen was in the water potentially, or in promise. But then, he would add, every substance that comes into being consists at bottom of two constituent elements; on the one hand, there must be something common to the old state and to the new, and on the other hand there must be a specific principle. That which is common to the two stages of the process is an indetermination found equally in the water and in the hydrogen-oxygen. Otherwise the one could not change into the other; no transformation of water into its component parts would occur, but instead there would be annihilation (of the water) followed by creation (of the hydrogen-oxygen). As for the specific principle, this must exist at each stage of the process as a peculiar and proper factor whereby the water as such differs from the hydrogen-oxygen as such.

With this we come to the theory of *primary matter* and *substantial form,*—so often misunderstood. This is really nothing but an application of the theory of act and potency to the problem of the transformation of bodies. Primary matter is the common indeterminate element or substratum, capable of receiving successively contrary determinations. The substantial form determines this unformed and potential fundament, and fixes the being altogether in its individuality and in its specific mode of existence. Each man, each lion, each oak, each chemical individual, possesses its form; that is, its principle of proper perfection. And the principle of perfection, or of the form which is immanent in the oak, is not reducible to that which belongs to the man, or to the molecule of hydrogen.

All that belongs to the perfection of a being (its existence, its unity, its activities) is more closely related to the form, while all that belongs to its imperfect state (its indetermination) is more closely related to the matter,—and especially is this true of the quantitative extension of corporeal being. To be extended in space, in divisible quantity, is an imperfection; and no really distinct beings could exist, were it not for the unifying function of form assembling the scattered elements of extended matter. No doctrine really better explains the mixture of perfection and imperfection, of good and evil, which are rooted in the depths of all corporeal being.

Thus the corporeal world mounts stage by stage from one species to another, nature passes from one step to another, from one species to another, following a certain definite order. Nature changes water into hydrogen and oxygen, but it does not change a pebble into a lion; nor can one make a saw out of wool. It evolves bodies according to affinities and successive progressions, the deciphering of which is the mission of the particular sciences, which we can know only by patient observation. If there are any saltations in nature, they are never capricious. In every corporeal substance, at every stage and at every instant, the germs of the substantial states are found which are to be born out of it. This is the meaning of the formula repeated by the scholastics, "that primary matter contains potentially, or in promise, the series of forms in which it must dress and redress itself, in the course of its becoming." To ask, as some do, where the forms are before their appearance and after their disappearance, is to reveal a complete misunderstanding of the scholastic system. One has no right to require of a doctrine a solution which it does not pretend to give. We simply know, by reasoning, that there *must* be matter and form,—just as we know that there *must* be substances and accidents. In their explanation of facts, the scholastics taught that a given thing *must* be; but they did not always teach *what* that thing is.

This doctrine represents a definitely teleological interpretation of the universe. For, the successive stages of change in each of the becoming substances, and the recurrence of the same transformations in the corporeal world, require the inclination on the part of each being to follow a definite order in its activity.[3a] Such inclination in each substance is immanent finality.

To sum up. Two kinds of change suffice to explain the corporeal world. First the becoming of constituted substance; thus, an oak is in process of becoming, in its activities, its quantity, its qualities, its relations, but it retains the same substance. Second, a change of one substance into another (or into many other substances); such as the change of an oak into a collection of chemical bodies, when, under external influences, the disposition of the

---

[3a] The term *natura* is used to signify the individual substance as far as it possesses such definite inclination.

primary matter requires a new substantial becoming of the whole.

V

It is impossible here to give a detailed survey of such an interpretation of the corporeal world. Let us merely apply this conception of the world to the famous scholastic problem of "individuation," and show how all of these doctrines are employed for an explanation of humanity.

The problem of individuation (*individuatio*) in the scholastic philosophy has a peculiar but restricted significance. The problem is: How can so many distinct *individualities* of the same substantial perfection, and therefore of the same kind, exist? Why are there millions and millions of oaks, and not only one oak, one *forma querci?* Why should there be millions and millions of human beings, and not only one man? Why myriads of molecules of water, and not only *one* molecule of water? Why not one molecule or ion or electron of each kind? If this were in fact the case, the world would still represent a scale of perfection, differing degree by degree; but there would be no two corporeal beings of the same kind. One thing would differ from another, as the number three differs from the number four.

The monads of Leibnitz realize in some aspects such a conception of the world. But the thomistic solution is more profound and lies in this thesis:

That extended matter, *materia signata,* is the principle of individuation. In other words, without *extension,* and extended matter, there would be no reason why several individuals of the same kind should exist.

Indeed, a substantial form as such, is foreign to and indifferent to reduplication; and, as long as one considers *form,* one cannot find any reason why there should be *two identical* forms, why one form should limit itself, instead of retaining within itself all the capacity of realization. *Forma irrecepta est illimitata.* But the question takes on a new aspect when this form must unite with matter, in order to exist, and so take on extended existence. My body has the limitation of extension, and therefore there is place for your body and for millions of bodies besides yours and mine. An oak has a limited extension in space, and at the point where it ceases to fill space there is also place for many more. And the same may be said of all corporeal beings in the endless species within the cosmos.

There is an important consequence, which follows directly from this philosophy. *If there exist* some limited beings which are not *corporeal* beings, and therefore are pure perfections, pure forms, (pure Intelligences for instance), then no reduplication is possible in that realm of being. They differ from one another as the oak-form differs from the beech-form or the hydrogen-form.

This last consideration explains why the problem

of individuation is different from the problem of individuality. Each existing being is an individuality; and therefore a pure Intelligence, if existent, is an individuality.[4] But individuation means a special restriction of individuality, that is to say a reduplication of several identical forms in *one* group,—hence called specific groups, species.

VI

All the doctrines which we have sought to explain are to be applied to human beings or human personalities. We are impenetrable and incommunicable substances, or personalities. No philosophy ever insisted more than did the scholastic philosophy upon this independence, and upon the dignity and value of human life,—by virtue of this doctrine of personality. All kinds of relations exist between men; for instance,—the family and political relations. But, as we shall see,[5] they do not touch directly our innermost substance, which with Leibnitz we may call "ferociously independent."

A human personality is composed of body and

[4] This theory is all too frequently misunderstood. Thus Henry Adams erroneously writes as follows: "Thomas admitted that the angels were universals" (*Mont St. Michel and Chartres*, p. 364). This is of course a misunderstanding; incorporeal beings are not deprived of individuality because they are without matter. Thomas Aquinas seems to have written the following in direct contradiction: "Non est verum quod substantia separata non sit singularis et individuum aliquod; alioquin non haberet aliquam operationem." See his *De unitate intellectus contra Averroistas*, edit. Parme, 1865, vol. XVI, p. 221.

[5] Ch. X, v.

soul, and the most inward unity of man results from this combination; the body is primary matter, the soul is substantial form, and each completes and permeates the other. Therefore, our soul is not at all in an unnatural state, when united to our body. The soul is not to be compared, as does Plato in the *Republic,* to the sea-god Glaucus, as impossible to recognize under the grimy accretions of the seashells and creeping things. On the contrary the union of soul and body is such that the former requires aid from the latter in all her activities.

The becoming of human beings, and their individuation in mankind, must also be explained by the doctrines already exposited. The generation of a child is the becoming of a new substance; but it includes several stages of a specific kind, each more perfect than the preceding. The soul is united to the embryo only when the dispositions of the new organism are sufficiently perfect to require union with a *human* soul. Thus, in the scholastic philosophy, it is really the human body, as a product of human generation, which is the principle of individuation; it is indeed the precise reason why such and such a soul, with its greater or lesser treasure of potentialities, is united to such and such a body. And although the spiritual and immortal soul is not a product of generation, nevertheless the parents as givers of the body to the child assume the responsibility of fixing the potentialities of the whole being. The soul may be compared to the wine which varies in quantity according to the size of the cup.

There is, however, one very important difference between the human soul and the form of other beings in the corporeal world. For reasons which we cannot develop here, founded especially upon the superiority of human knowledge, the human soul is of a *spiritual* nature, that is, it is superior to corporeal things and therefore *immortal*. Accordingly, a human soul, although it constitutes a whole with the body, is not the result of the chemical, physical, and biological activities which explain organic generation. Aristotle had said that the intellect came from without ($\theta\acute{v}\rho\alpha\theta\epsilon\nu$). Thomas adds: the soul is created by God.

VII

We shall now consider, in conclusion, the place given to the idea of God in the scholastic metaphysics. Their natural theology, or theodicy, is closely connected with their conception of the world. It is drawn from the theory of change, which has been explained above. It is intimately connected with their whole idea of change,—but especially with the doctrine of *efficient causality*.

Change, as we have seen, is the passage from one state to another, a sort of oscillation by which the real in potency becomes the real actually, and so obtains a new perfection. Now the principle of efficient causality says: *No being which changes can give to itself, without some foreign influence coming from without, this complement of reality,* by virtue of which it passes from one state into another. *Quidquid movetur ab alio movetur.* The principle of contradiction requires this; and the principle of contradiction, according to which a thing cannot in the same aspect both be and not be, is a law of mental life, as well as a law of reality. For, if a thing could change its own state (whether substantial or accidental) unaided from without, it would possess before acquiring,—it would already be what is not yet. This is of course absurd. The water is in potency of changing into oxygen; but without the electric current,—without the intervention of something else—the water could not, by itself, give to itself new determinations. This other thing by which water changes into oxygen and hydrogen is called the efficient cause.

However, this active cause is itself carried into the nexus of becoming. The electrical energy could not appear without undergoing, in its turn, the action of other efficient causes. The whole process expands, very much as when a stone is thrown into still water the waves spread out from the centre, each acting upon the next in succession. Moreover, the process becomes complicated, for every action of a being A on a being B is doubled by a reaction of B on A. Nature is an inextricable tissue of efficient causes, of becomings, of passages from potency to act. Newton's law of gravitation, the law of the equilibrium of forces, the law of the conservation of energy,—these are all so many formulas which state in precise form the influence of one being upon another.

But,—and there is of course a but—we cannot continue the process to infinity. For, in that case, change would be an illusion, and this would involve denying the very evidence itself. The initial motion demands a starting point, an original impetus. This absolute beginning is possible only on the condition that a Being exists who is beyond all change,—in whom nothing can become, and who is therefore immutable. That being is God. Now, God cannot set in motion the series of changes, constituted of act and potency, except by an impulse which leaves free and undisturbed His own impassibility. For, however slight the modification which one supposes this act (of changing others) to cause in Him, it would still be a change, and hence something *new* and requiring explanation afresh,—by recourse to the intervention of a still higher being. Thus the process would be endless, unless God is the "prime mover unmoved."

Let us suppose that one decides to build a house, and that one wants it to be supported solidly. To this end he lays deep the foundations which must support the building. Deep he digs, and still deeper, and ever deeper, in order to obtain a base of absolute fixity. But he must finally call a halt in this work of excavation, under penalty of not ever beginning the work of building. Thus we must conclude, from the very existence of the house, that the builder did in fact halt at some point in the earth, there to set his first stone.

Just so with the scholastic argument which we are considering. Change exists as a fact even as the house exists as a fact. The fact is there; it stares us in the face; it fills the universe. If there were not a halting place in the chain of efficient causation, the change itself could not exist. One is in no position to choose whether the world shall evolve or not; for evolution is the law of the universe itself. To conceive that one may make an endless regressus in the causal nexus, would be like conceiving that he might suspend a weight to the one end of a chain whose other end requires the ceaseless adding of link upon link, to lengthen out the chain to infinity!

It all comes then to this: if any fact is real, the totality of things, without which the reality of that fact would be compromised, is no less real. It follows, therefore, that scholastic philosophy demonstrates God's existence by making His existence a necessary condition of the explanation of reality. Accordingly, from the standpoint of metaphysics, He exists only for the world. Hence God is not, as one might suppose, a further mystery requiring explanation, in addition to the general mystery of the world. The scholastic argument for the existence of God has just the value of the principles of contradiction and of efficient causation. The first is a point of support; the second is a lever which thought employs to lift the things which change to the plane of the Being who changes not. Remove the point of support or destroy the lever, and thought falls impotent before the world's enigma.

God, adds Thomas Aquinas, having in Himself no potentiality, is *infinitude,* absolute perfection; and at this point his mind is suddenly lifted and borne upwards, and it attains to the most penetrating insight concerning divinity. In order to bring this home to our full realization, I shall avail myself of a simile,—although in such matters comparison is inadequate.

Imagine a series of vessels, with different capacities, which are to be filled with water; let there be tiny vessels, and vessels that will contain gallons, and great receptacles which are to serve as reservoirs. Clearly the volume of water, which may be stored in each vessel, must be limited by the capacity of the vessel itself. Once a vessel is filled, not a drop can be added to its content; were the very ocean itself to flow over it, the contents of the vessel would not increase.

Now *existence* in a finite being may be likened to

the water, in our simile; for *existence* too is limited by the capacity of every recipient being. This capacity is the sum total of the *potentialities* which from moment to moment become actual realities, by being invested with existence. That oak of the forest which is invested with the most beautiful qualities of its species, and with the most perfect vital forces; that man of genius who is endowed with the most precious gifts of mind and body,—these possess the maximum of *existence* that can possibly be found in the species of oak and of man. But, be it remembered, the capacity for *existence* in each of these is limited and circumscribed by the very fact of the apportioned potentiality, or "essence." In this beautiful conception of Thomas, a vigorous oak has a larger measure of existence than a stunted one; a man of genius possesses *existence* in a larger sense than a man of inferior mind,— because the great man and the vigorous oak possess a larger measure of powers and activities, and because these powers and activities exist. But, once more, there is a *limit* even to their existence.

On the other hand, to return to our simile, let us picture to ourselves an existence indefinitely uncircumscribed, say the ocean, without shore to confine or to limit it. Such existence, pure and unqualified, is that of God. God *is* existence; He is nothing but the plentitude of existence; He *is* the one who *is*,— *Ego sum qui sum*—whose very essence is His existence. All other beings *receive* some degree of existence,—the degree increasing in measure with their increasing capacity. But they receive, in each instance, this degree of existence from God. The created agents, or secondary causes, determine the capacity of the vessel, and the size varies unceasingly; God alone fills it to the full capacity of existence.

It is God who is the direct dispenser of existence, from that of pure spirits to that of atoms. It is He who sustains everything, that is anything, short of pure nothing. It is He who directs the world toward the goal, which is known to *Him alone;* and presumptuous, nay rash, would it be for men to seek to penetrate the mystery. In short, God *is* existence; other beings *receive* existence—an existence distinct from His own—just in proportion as they have the power to receive it. No one can say what Infinity implies. "The highest knowledge which we can have of God in this life," writes Thomas Aquinas, "is to know that He is above all that we can think concerning Him."[6]

Scholastic metaphysics thus finds its culminations in theodicy. Starting out from the study of the changing corporeal world, it rises to the Being without whom change would be inexplicable. But its main object is none the less a study of the corporeal beings which surround us. Hence one may

[6] *De Veritate,* q. II, art. 2.

IN THE MIDDLE AGES 219

say that it is based on observation and anchored to the very rock of reality.⁷

[7] The following schema may aid in clarifying the metaphysical doctrines and the relations explained in this chapter:

Essence
(*essentia*)
- Substance (*substantia*)
  - Prime matter (*materia prima*)
  - Substantial form (*forma substantialis*)
- Accidents (*accidentia*)
  - Qualities, for instance: shape, power, habit (*habitus*)
  - Quantity
  - Action
  - Passion
  - Relation
  - Time
  - Space
  - Posture (*se habere*)
  - State

Existence (*esse*)

CHAPTER TEN

INDIVIDUALISM AND SOCIAL INDUSTRY

i. Social theory the last addition to scholastic philosophy. ii. Fundamental principle: the group exists for its members, and not conversely. iii. Ethical foundation of this principle. iv. The idea of the group in the teaching of canonists and jurists. v. Metaphysical basis: the group not an entity outside of its members. vi. Comparison of the group with the human body. vii. Conclusion.

I

Social philosophy is the last addition to the edifice which the scholastic thinkers reared. In point of fact, it is unhistorical to speak of a social philosophy before 1260, the year in which William of Moerbeke's translation of the *Politics* of Aristotle came into circulation among scholars. Prior to that time we find, to be sure, discussions on isolated questions, such as natural law or the divine origin and the moral function of political authority. But these questions were not combined in any philosophical *system,*—although they received remarkable elaboration in the works of Manegold of Lautenbach and of John of Salisbury especially (in his *Polycraticus,* 1159).

However, in saying that social philosophy is

one of the last additions to the scholastic edifice, some explanation is necessary, in order to make valid this temporal comparison. A philosophy does not grow as a house, to which a wing is added from time to time, nor as a landed estate to which one adds gradually adjoining fields. For, new doctrines that are introduced in philosophy must not destroy those which have been already adopted; on the contrary, they must be suited to form with the doctrines adopted a coherent whole, and to this end each and every addition must be carefully rethought.

The *systematic* character of scholastic social philosophy is striking in the works of Thomas Aquinas. He is the first to succeed in constructing, out of the new material, a doctrine in which everything holds together, and which is entirely impregnated with the social mentality of the thirteenth century. This doctrine appears in his *Summa Theologica* and in his commentary on the *Politics* of Aristotle; we know that he also intended to write a treatise *De Regimine Principum,* for the education of a ruling prince, Hugh II of Lusignan, king of Cyprus.[1] Other philosophers followed his ex-

[1] See *Summa Theol.,* 1a 2ae, qq. XCIII-CV. Thomas himself commentated only Books I and II and III (part only chs. 1-6) of Aristotle's *Politics.* This is now clear from an ancient MS cited by Grabmann (See "Welchen Teil der Aristotelischen Politik hat der hl. Thomas selbst Kommentirt?" in *Philos. Jahrbuch,* 1915, pp. 373-5). As for the *De Regimine Principum,* only Book I and part of Book II (chs. 1-4) were written by Thomas. The authenticity of

ample and his teachings; they addressed their works to princes and kings, in order to enlighten them regarding both their rights and their duties. Thus, for instance, the Franciscan Gilbert of Tournai wrote, at the request of Louis IX of France, a treatise *Eruditio Regum et Principum*, which has been recently published;[2] and Gilles of Rome composed a similar work for the king's son.

II

As preliminary to a discussion of the more important questions with which scholastic social philosophy concerned itself—a subject which we reserve for the next chapter—I wish here to examine its basic principle. This principle constitutes the broad foundation of political and social theory, and upon it the superstructure of the state was laid, very much as the stories of a house are made to rest upon the main floor. The principle may be briefly stated as follows: The State *exists for the good of the citizen,* or obversely, *it is not the*

---

even so much has been doubted by J. A. Endres ("De regimine principum des hl. Thomas von Aquin," in Baeumker's *Beiträge,* Festschrift, 1913, pp. 261-267). However, his reasoning is not at all conclusive; and the oldest and best catalogues attribute this portion to Thomas himself. It is my own opinion that Thomas was the author of the beginning of the work (Bks. I and II, chs. 1-4), and that the remainder was inspired by his doctrine.

[2] A. De Poorter,—in the series: *Les Philosophes Belges, collection de textes et d'études,* vol. IX, Louvain, 1914.

citizen who is for the good of the state. This statement is susceptible of enlargement. Any group whatever,—be it family, village, city, province, kingdom, empire, abbey, parish church, bishopric, or even the Catholic Church—justifies itself in the good which it accomplishes for its members. In other words, the members do not exist for the good of the group. The question is the more interesting because the professors of Roman law at Bologne and the other jurists, who argued on behalf of the sovereigns (the Hohenstaufen, and the kings of England and France), and the canonists, following the *Decretum* of Gratian, had touched upon these delicate questions; but the philosophers attained to a clearness and precision which had been denied to experts in law on the same questions.

In very fact, this principle—that the state exists only for the good of the citizen, or obversely, that it is not the citizen who exists for the good of the state—is closely connected with the whole scholastic system. While it is a foundation for the doctrine of the state, this principle itself rests upon an *ethical* ground. In its turn, this ethical ground rests upon the deeper lying basis of *metaphysical* doctrine. Thus, social philosophy in reality rests upon a twofold basis, the ethical and the metaphysical. Let us consider briefly the part played by each of these bases.

III

First, the ethical foundations of the principle. Why should the group, in particular the state, be subordinated to the good of the citizens? Is not the citizen an instrument for the good of the state? Scholastic ethics replies: because every human being has a certain sacred value, an inviolable individuality, and as such he has a personal destiny, a happiness, which the state must aid him to realize. Let us see more fully what this means.

Each man seeks in his life to attain some end. Our activities would lack even ordinary meaning, if they did not reach forward to a goal, if they did not aim—consciously or unconsciously—to realize the *good*, that is to say the perfection of the individual who is the source of the activities involved. This is true not only for man, but for all created things. Human finality is simply an application of universal finality; and therefore the scholastics repeat with Aristotle: "That is good which each thing seeks" (*Bonum est quod omnia appetunt*). Man's possession of his good means human happiness.

As a matter of fact, men seek the good in the most diverse objects, and they frequently deceive themselves; but that is only a question of application, which does not affect the main thesis. Even the man who hangs himself is yielding to inclinations which he believes will issue in his benefit. But this illustration only shows that one should pursue one's good according to rational judgments, and follow where they lead him, without letting himself be deceived by appearances. Man, indeed, is distinguished from the stone which falls, or from the wild beast which follows its instincts, by the fact that he has the privilege of reflecting on his ways and choosing them freely; he has the power of mistaken choice. Man's counsels lie in his own hands. The philosophers of the thirteenth century have no difficulty in proving, that neither riches nor honour, nor glory, nor power, nor sensual indulgence can satisfy the demands of the *good,* the *summum bonum* for men; there he is free to seek or not to seek them as the chief end of life.[3]

Moreover, every destiny is necessarily personal; the good is *my* good. If, for example, I make it to consist in pleasure, it is quite evident that the pleasure is *my* pleasure. A fortiori must destiny be personal for the scholastic ethics which maintains that happiness results from the employment of that which is the noblest and the highest in human life,— namely, *knowledge* and *love.* Nothing is more personal than knowing and loving. Happiness is so personal a matter, that the good of another only enters into it incidentally, and not essentially. It takes a noble soul to include the destinies of others within the domain of his own preoccupations.

Now, the individual left quite to himself, as a

[3] See above, p. 186.

solitary being, is not sufficient to attain to his proper end. He will find himself deprived of material means, of intellectual directions, of moral support. This impotence of the solitary individual, says Thomas Aquinas, is the sole reason for the existence of society. "Man is called by nature" he writes[4] "to live in society; for he needs many things which are necessary to his life, and which by himself he cannot procure for himself. Whence it follows that man naturally becomes part of a group (*pars multitudinis*), to procure him the means of living well. He needs this assistance for two reasons. First, in order that he may obtain the elementary necessities of life; this he does in the domestic circle of which he is a part. Every man receives from his parents life and nourishment and education; and the reciprocal aid of the family members facilitates the mutual provision of the necessities of life. But there is a second reason why the individual is helped by the group, of which he is a part, and in which alone he finds his adequate well being. And this is, that he may not only *live* but live the *good life,*—which is enabled by the opportunities of social intercourse. Thus civil society aids the individual in obtaining the material necessities, by uniting in the same city a great number of crafts, which could not be so united in the same family. And civil society also assists him in the moral life."

[4] *Comment in Ethic. Nicom.,* lib. I.

The scholastic philosophers of the thirteenth century unanimously agree with Aristotle and Augustine that it is a natural necessity for man to live in society, *naturalis necessitas*. This social life involves degrees. There are groups, more or less extensive, which are logically and chronologically anterior to the state. Man is of necessity born into a family (*domus*). Several families grouped under a chief constitute a village—community, *vicus*, whose raison d'être, says Dante,[5] is to facilitate an exchange of services between men and things. The city (*civitas*), continues Dante, is a wider organization, which allows one to live with moral and material sufficiency, *bene sufficienterque vivere*. But, whereas Aristotle had stopped with the city, Thomas considers (in the *De Regimine Principum*) a wider group, the province,—which corresponds to Dante's kingdom (*regnum*). Perhays we may see in the province those large feudal fiefs, which were important units, such as the Duchy of Normandy or the Duchy of Brabant, with which Thomas was actually acquainted. As regards states, some were growing up under his very eyes, notably in Italy, where the princes of the house of Anjou were governing the Two Sicilies, while the main European states, France, England, Spain, and Germany were taking on their various characteristic features. A kingdom (*regnum particulare*), writes Dante, provides the same advantages as the city, but gives a

---

[5] *De Monarchia*, lib. I.

greater feeling of security, *cum majori fiducia suae tranquilitatis*. In this Dante repeats the thomistic thought that the kingdom, better than the city, responds to the needs of war, when it is attacked by enemies.[6]

Now, since the group exists only for the benefit of its individuals, the good of the group *will not be of any other kind than that of the individuals*. Thus Thomas says: "The end of the group is necessarily the end of each individual who composes the group,"—*oportet eundem finem esse multitudinis humanae qui est hominis unius*.[7] And Dante, in a similar vein, writes: "Citizens are not for consuls or kings, but kings and consuls are for citizens,"—*non enim cives propter consules nec gens propter regem, sed e converso*.[8] The group would be an absurdity, if the rôles were reversed, and the state or any other group should pursue a course, which no longer coincided with the happiness of each of its subjects; and if the individual be treated as a worn-out machine, which one scraps when it has become useless.

This conception is at once *new* and *mediaeval*. For, while the city or the state appears in Aristotle as an end in itself, to which the individuals are subordinated, the scholastic philosophy, on the contrary, conceived of the states as subordinated to the

[6] *De Regimine Principum*, lib. I, cap. 1. *De Monarchia*, lib. I.
[7] *De Regimine Principum*, lib. I, cap. 14.
[8] *De Monarchia*, lib. I.

good of the individuals. For Aristotle the prime duty is to be a *good citizen,* and to increase one's civic virtue. But for the scholastic philosopher the prime duty is to give to life a human value, to be a *good man,* and the state should help each of its members to become such.

It follows from this teaching that as against the state the individual should hold himself erect, conscious of his crown of rights, which the state cannot infringe upon, because their validity is derived from the worth of personality itself. These are "the rights of man." Their foundation is the law of nature, that is to say, the essence of man and the eternal law,—the eternal relations which regulate the order of beings in conformity with the decrees of uncreated wisdom. These are the right to preserve his life, the right to marry and to rear children, the right to develop his intellect, the right to be instructed, the right to truth, the right to live in society. These are some of the prerogatives of the individual which appear in the thirteenth century declaration of the rights of man.[9]

Thus, scholastic philosophy justifies from an ethical point of view the conception of the worth of the individual, as against the central power. But we see at once how it also conforms to the feudal temperament. For, knight and baron and vassal and citizen had all been consumed for two centuries past with the idea of living each his own life.

[9] Thomas Aquinas, *Summa Theol.*, 1a2ae, q. XCIV, art. 2.

IV

But, in its turn, the ethical doctrine rests upon a metaphysical foundation. Why, indeed, does the human person possess the right to realize his happiness, of which no state can deprive him? Metaphysics replies: because human personality alone is a genuine *substantial reality*. On the other hand, any group whatever, the state included, is not a *real* being; it is simply a group of human persons (*multitudo hominum*).

This doctrine interested the jurists and the canonists as much as it did the philosophers. Since its nature is such as to throw light upon the political mentality of the period, let us consider briefly the conceptions of the jurists and theorists in civil and canon law. This will be a helpful preliminary to dispose of, before passing to the conclusions of the philosophers.

The legalistic theorists simply took over from Roman law the concept of the *corporation* (*universitas*) and applied it,—as civil theorists to the state, and as canonists to the Church. Now, the Roman corporation (*universitas*) is *nothing but an association of individuals*. To be sure, it is the seat of private rights, and it can possess and acquire property; but, as Savigny has emphasized, it is not a real person, and in consequence it has no soul, no intelligence, no will. The Roman jurists were too realistic, too amenable to common sense logic, to conceive of a collective soul,—a reality distinct from the individuals—in these associations, whose purposes were plainly commercial and industrial.

Similarly, the parish churches and the monasteries and the universal Church had not been regarded by the canonists as *real entities,* as beings distinct from the members who compose them. Innocent IV, who had the name of being an eminent jurist, is the first who would have spoken of the corporation as a *"persona ficta"* a *fictitious* person—an excellent formula, which is not found in the *Digest* of Justinian, but which expresses admirably the thought of the thirteenth century. Gierke calls him the "father of the fictitious person theory."[10] Thereafter the corporation is definitely no thing-in-itself, no living organism, in the real sense of the word, since it has neither intelligence nor will. The canonists, indeed, declare that it cannot commit crime or misdemeanour of any kind; hence a political group as such need not fear hell or wrath to come.

Nor do the mediaeval lawyers conceive otherwise of the state-corporation. In the same manner they explain the artificial personality of the kingdom or of the empire. The state (*universitas*) is the collective mass of individual men, who constitute the *populus;* and its functions,—says the author of a

[10] Otto von Gierke, *Die Staats- und Korporations- lehre des Altertums und des Mittelalters und ihre Aufnahme in Deutschland,* Berlin, 1881, p. 279, n. 102: "cum collegium in causa universitatis *fingatur una persona*" (Innocent IV).

treatise *De Aequitate* which is ascribed to Irnerius, —is to care for the individual men who are its members.[11] Likewise, the society of states is considered by Dante as a grouping of individuals, a *respublica humana* rather than as a group of governments. The universal monarch is the servant of all, *minister omnium*, precisely as the Pope is the servant of the servants of God. He wills the welfare of each man; he is nearer to each citizen than is any particular sovereign.[12] And in the fourteenth century Baldus writes: *"Imperium non habet animum, ergo non habet velle nec nolle quia animi sunt."*[13]

Does this conception of the state (as being no entity outside of the members who constitute it) really represent a failure[14] of the mediaeval jurists and canonists? Is it not rather the triumph of good sense and healthy thinking of men who were seeking loyally for truth and not for originality? Personally I do not believe that the state is a real being, a real substance outside of its citizens, and I agree with Paul Bourget in one of his latest novels (*Le Sens de la Mort*), when he places in the mouth

[11] Irnerius, *De Aequitate*, 2: universitas, id est populus, hoc habet officium, singulis scilicet hominibus quasi membris providere. *Cf.* Carlyle, *op. cit.*, vol. II, p. 57.

[12] *De Monarchia*, I. *Cf.* above, ch. V, 111.

[13] Cited by Gierke, *Political Theories of the Middle Ages*, (English translation by Maitland), Cambridge, 1900, p. 70. This translation is only a small part of Gierke's work cited above.

[14] Gierke, *Ibid*.

of Doctor Marsal these suggestive words: To die for France is not to die for a collective entity, but for all Frenchmen present and to come. To climb the ladder and go over the top, is to mount the scaffold. They did it. For whom? For France. But France is the sum total of all those who are destined to be Frenchmen. It is our very selves, you and I,—we Frenchmen, I repeat.[15]

V

The underlying reason for this doctrine,—that the state large or small is not a "thing-in-itself," an entity distinct from the citizens who compose it—is furnished by the scholastic philosophy itself, and we have already seen what it is. For scholastic philosophy the world is pluralistic, the only real beings existing are individual beings,—for instance, such and such oak, such and such bee, such and such man.[16] And since unity follows being (*ens et unum convertuntur*), individuals alone have a physical and internal unity. A forest of oaks, a hive of bees, a team of horses, a steamboat, a house, an army, a parish, a city, a state,—none of these designate real, physical beings; in consequence they have not the *unity* that belongs to a real substance.

[15] Sortir de la tranchée, sur l'échelle, c'est monter à l'echafaud. Ils y montent. Pour qui? Pour la France. Mais la France, c'est la somme des destinées françaises. C'est nous, je vous répète," p. 173, edit. 1915, Paris, Plon.
[16] See ch. IX, ii.

In what then does this unity of the group consist? The metaphysics of Thomas Aquinas give us light on this subtle question. After having shown why the individual must become a member of a family and of a civic community, he writes: "Now we ought to know that this totality, of the civil or the domestic group, *possesses only the unity of (external) order,* and consequently it is not endowed with the unity that belongs to a natural substance. This is the reason why a portion of this totality can carry on activities which are not the act of the group. A soldier, for example, carries out actions which do not belong to the army; but such actions of the soldier do not prevent the group from carrying on its activities,—activities which do not belong to each part but to the whole. Thus, a battle is the activity of the whole army; the towing of a barge is the activity of the totality of the men who pull on the rope."[17]

There is then a profound difference between the

[17] "Sciendum est autem quod hoc totum, quod est civilis multitudo vel domesticia familia, habet solam *unitatem ordinis,* secundum quam non est aliquid *simpliciter unum.* Et ideo pars ejus totius potest habere operationem quae non est operatio totius, sicut miles in exercitu habet operationem quae non est totius exercitus. Habet nihilominus et ipsum totum aliquam operationem, quae non est propria alicujus partium, puta conflictus totius exercitus. Et tractus navis est operatio multitudo trahentium navem." *In Ethic. Nicom.,* L. I. I understand *"unitas ordinis"* to mean the unity resulting from a combination of independent beings, realizing an external order, as distinguished from the physical unity which results from internal order, in a being where there is a plurality of elements.

unity of the individual,—the organic and internal *"indivision"* (*unum simpliciter*) which belongs to the human person—and the external unity which is the outcome of social grouping among a certain number of individuals. Internal unity introduces coherence within the individual substance, so that all of its constituent parts or elements have neither independent value nor existence of their own. Hence there is a contradiction in the very idea of a *collective-person.* Either the members who are supposed to compose such a collective person, remain substantially independent,—in which case there is no *one* person but a collection of persons— or they are dependent of the whole, and then each member loses his individuality. It is quite different in the case of the external unity that appears in a group of persons, since this unity does not affect the individuality that belongs to each member.

You will ask then: Is the family or the state a mere nothing? To make such an assertion would be to overstate the doctrine. For, the *unity* of the group, of which Thomas speaks, is functional in character and *rests on performing in common certain human activities,* of which each member contributes his share. Such activities are endowed with reality, but a reality different from the incommunicable and inalienable substantial being which each member preserves. In towing a barge, the muscular activities of the men who tow are directed in common; in a game or a club or any friendly association, each member places a portion of his activities at the disposal of the common life,—and in all of these cases withdrawal is always possible.

But in the family or the community, on the contrary, this mutual pooling of activities is imposed by nature; there can be no such withdrawal, for certain basic activities of the individual are absorbed by the community. Indeed, in certain crises, for the common good and the common safety, the family or the state can demand the entire activity of its members. But even so, the man who gives all his *activities* nevertheless preserves his *individuality*. The individual man never surrenders the sovereignty of his own personality.

This doctrine could not have been stated more clearly than it was by Thomas Aquinas in these fine words: "The law should take account of many things as to persons, as to affairs, and as to times. For, the community of the state is composed of many persons, and its good is procured by *varied activities*."[18]

Accordingly, from the point of view of scholastic metaphysics, there is no difference between the unity of a group of men towing a barge and the unity of the family or of the state or even of a whole

[18] Bonum autem commune constat ex multis, et ideo oportet quod lex ad multa respiciat et secundum personas et secundum negotia et secundum tempora. Constituitur enim communitas civitatis ex multis personis et ejus bonum per *multiples actiones* procuratur. *Summa Theol.*, 1a2ae, q. XCVI, art. 1.

civilization. The only question of difference is that which attaches to the excellence of the activities displayed. The proper functioning of the state depends upon the diversity of activities, and a state becomes more perfect, as does a whole civilization, in proportion as these activities are more complete, more varied, and more intense. The *bonum commune,* the commonwealth which the state has to provide, results from the sum total of activities performed to unite and to harmonize.

These considerations make clear how one can speak at the same time of the *unity* of the civilization of the thirteenth century and of the *pluralism* which is so basic in their thought. The unity of a civilization is the result of common aspirations, common beliefs, common sentiments both moral and artistic, common language, common organization of life; and such a unity is no more than a community of activities. At the same time, unity of substance, or physical unity, belongs to each of the *numerous personalities* which are the agents of this civilization, and to them only.[19]

[19] Through failure to perceive this distinction between the unity of order and the physical unity, many historians deny individualism in the Middle Ages, and misconceive that fundamental teaching of thirteenth century metaphysics,—*"nihil est praeter individuum."* Thus, struck by the unitary character of the civilization, Mr. E. Barker writes: "We can hardly say that the Middle Ages have any conception of the state. The notion of the state involves plurality, but plurality is *ex hypothesi* not to be found." See, "Unity in the Middle Ages," in *The Unity of Western Civilization,* p. 112, ed.

In this thomistic and scholastic view, the group life acquires dynamic meaning. It rests upon a sharing of *activities* for the good of all. Possessing all a similar human nature, with its train of inalienable rights, the individuals present the greatest diversity in their talents, their faculties, and the activities which result from them. *Equal in human nature,* men are *unequal in capacity for action;*[20] such is the metaphysical law which governs the play of the social group, in all of its degrees.

VI

After this precise and substantial argument, to which the whole body of scholastic philosophers of the thirteenth century subscribe, it is easy to give just value to a certain favourite comparison of that age,—a comparison to which publicists. canonists, legalists, theologians, and even poets, frequently recur, for the purpose of explaining the problem of the individual in relation to the group. It is the comparison of the state with the human body. John of Salisbury works out the comparison in detail, and he likens each member of the human body

Marvin, Oxford, 1915. This statement is preceded by this other erroneous assertion: "The prevalence of Realism, which marks mediaeval metaphysics down to the end of the thirteenth century, is another Platonic inheritance, and another impulse to unity. The universal *is* and is a veritable thing in which the particular shares and acquires its substance by its degree of sharing." Nothing is more contrary to scholastic philosophy of the thirteenth century.

[20] *Cf.* ch. **IX, iv and vii.**

to some part of the state. The prince is the head; the senate is the heart; officers and judges are the eyes, ears, and tongue; officials are the hands; the peasants and the workers are the feet of the state,— so that, remarks this English writer, the state has more feet than a centipede or a scolopendra. The function of protecting the people becomes the "footwear" of the state. Indeed, there is no reason why one might not continue this little game of anthropomorphic comparison without end.[21]

The idea is no discovery of John of Salisbury's. He himself refers it to a letter written by Plutarch to Trajan (falsely so far as we yet know). The comparison is repeated in the thirteenth century, but it has lost its literal value. Each state, each church, each city, even each guild, is compared to a natural body. But the philosophers of that century are not misled by its purely figurative value, and Engelbert of Volkersdorf, abbot of Admont, who writes about 1290 a treatise concerning the rule of Princes, speaks of a moral and political body, in contrast with the body of nature.[22] Further, when Thomas Aquinas calls the collectivity of the citizens a public person, *persona publica*,[23] there is no doubt possible about his true meaning.

Reduced to the rôle of an imaginative instrument, the comparison is not wanting in elegance;

---

[21] *Polycraticus,* lib. V, cap. 1 and 2.
[22] Gierke, *op. cit.,* p. 24.
[23] *Summa Theol.* 1a2ae, q. XC, art. 3.

it shows in a striking way that, in a political or ecclesiastical organism, the members do not occupy the same place; that there are diversities of functions; that there are intermediate articulations; that a healthy organ can help or supply a weak or defective organ. The comparison is well suited to the mediaeval mind with its delight in symbols, and to an age which speaks of the mystical marriage of Christ with the Church and of the bishop with his diocesan church, and which likens to daughters the various abbeys which have grown out of the mother abbey. Such symbols, and many more, deceived no one. Nor do we today take literally Tennyson's comparison of "the million-footed mob,"[24] or the expression "adopted towns," which was given to certain cities crushed during the war, or "mother-towns" as the name proudly assumed by certain other cities which undertook the adoption. The philosophers of the thirteenth century did not mistake the straw of words for the grain of ideas. The organic theory, made fashionable today by certain German philosophers is contrary to the genius of scholastic philosophy, as it is opposed to the juridical doctrine of the thirteenth century; both would have regarded it as a seductive mirage.

VII

A short time before the war, I made a brief stay at Strasbourg. In visiting its magnificent cathe-

[24] The Fleet.

dral, I observed that a crack had appeared in one of the walls of the finished tower, and that it had been necessary to erect a support, in order to prevent the tower from collapsing. A friend explained to me that the architects of the thirteenth century had erected the cathedral on a foundation of strong oak piles, which had lasted for centuries because they were driven into marshy ground, but that the recent drainage works in the city had brought about the unforeseen consequence of drying out these ancient water-soaked timbers, and so undermining the cathedral. *Invisible* and *underground,* up to that time they had sustained the façade of this marvelous Gothic gem, without anyone realizing how fundamental was their presence and their function.

So it is with the metaphysical doctrine, which may be called the *invisible and underlying support* of the social philosophy of the thirteenth century. Upon this foundation reposed morals, as upon morals is based the guiding principle that the state is made for the citizens, the group for its members. If the metaphysics of the scholastics should settle or fall, then in turn their ethics would be compromised, and an ominous cleft would appear in their social philosophy. This close interdependence of doctrines furnishes a striking example of the coherence and unity of the scholastic system, which we have above pointed out.[25]

[25] See ch. V, i.

CHAPTER ELEVEN

THE THEORY OF THE STATE

i. Sovereignty from God. ii. It is a function; morality of governors not different from that of the governed; what the function implies. iii. Sovereignty resides in the people who delegate it. iv. The best form of government according to the philosophy of Thomas Aquinas. v. Making of laws the essential attribute of sovereignty; natural law and human law. vi. This form of government compared with the European states of the thirteenth century; with the modern nationalities; with the theories of preceding centuries.

I

The state exists for the good of the individuals, and not conversely. It is in the light of this principle that all the problems, which the study of state organization raises, are solved; and, as thinkers are agreed on the principle, so they will be agreed also upon the majority of solutions which issue from it, by way of application or of corollary. These problems can all be arranged under some aspect of the notion of sovereignty or power. No social life is possible,—whether in the family, the village community, the state, the monastery, the parish, the diocese, the universal Church—unless there exists an authority to which the members owe obedience.

What then is the source of sovereignty, in what does it consist, to whom does it belong, what are its attributes? These are some of the specific problems in the philosophical discussion of political life.

Whence comes sovereignty, this superiority of one man, who rules over his fellow men? Like their predecessors of the preceding centuries, the thirteenth century philosophers answer: All power comes from God. And their reasoning is as follows. The entire universe is under a providential plan; it is governed by an eternal law (*lex aeterna*), which is nothing but the order of things, the sum of relations which result from the nature of beings.[1] To realize his end as a rational being, and to attain to his happiness, is man's unique part in cooperating with the universal cosmic finality, ordained by God. Now, the rationale of governing others, *ratio gubernationis,* is instituted to make easy for each person the realization of his end. It must therefore be, in the final analysis, a divine delegation, a command according to which the rulers carry out those necessary functions which will enable the individual members to occupy their assigned places in the divine economy.[2]

Accordingly, rulers hold divine power by dele-

---

[1] See below v of this chapter.

[2] "Cum ergo lex aeterna sit ratio gubernationis in supremo gubernante, necesse est quod omnes rationes gubernationis quae sunt in inferioribus gubernantibus a lege aeterna deriventur." Thomas Aquinas, *Summa Theol.,* 1a2ae, q. XCIII, a. 3.

gation. This theory is independent of the further question: In what way does this power, divine in its essence, come to those who hold it, and to whom is it given? Let the rulers hold this power from God directly, as the legalists and the *De Monarchia* teach, or let the delegation of temporal power pass through the Papal channel, as the partisans of *mediate* divine power maintain; let sovereignty be in the hands of a monarch or a representative republic,—in any case, it always derives back to God as its source. The demands of metaphysics link it up with God.

II

The raison d'être of sovereignty therefore fixes its nature. And this brings us to our second question: In what does sovereignty consist? Legalists and canonists and philosophers all agree in the reply. Sovereignty is a *utility,* a *function,* an *officium;* it is dedicated to the well-being of all. The applications of the leading principle, already explained, are easy to understand. Since the state is made for the individual, sovereignty in the state can be only an advantage for its members. Princes of the earth, according to Thomas Aquinas, are instituted by God, not for their own advantage, but in order that they may serve the common good.[3] The kingdom, says Ptolemy of Lucques, is not made

---
[3] *De Regimine Principum,* I, c. 1-3.

for the king, but the king for the kingdom.[4] Even under the theocratic papal rule, the idea persisted of an *officium,* duty, fused with that of power. The Pope is the servant of the servants of God, *servus servorum Dei.* It is just because the state is an association of individuals, and instituted for their welfare, that there is no difference between the morality of the governors and that of the governed. For instance, fidelity to treaties and observance of the precepts of loyalty are required; they constitute the very foundation of the *jus gentium.* Or, again, war of conquest is forbidden, because it prevents the state from watching over the welfare of individuals.

But how will the government fulfill its function? How will it aid the individual to attain his end,— which is above all a certain moral happiness, resulting from the *facultas contemplandi veritatem?*[5] The answer is this: By realizing the *unitas multitudinis,* a unity which is accidental and external, by realizing a *bonum commune,* which results from the harmonious and convergent activities expended by the citizen,—activities which the *De Regimine* is so careful to distinguish from the *unitas hominis* of each individual.[6]

[4] Regnum non propter regem, sed rex propter regnum. *De Regimine Principum,* III, c. 11.

[5] See Thomas Aquinas, *Comment in Ethic. Nicom.,* X, 11.

[6] Ipsa tamen hominis unitas per naturam causatur; multitudinis autem unitas quae pax dicitur, per regentis industriam est procuranda. *De Regimine Principum,* lib. I, cap. 15.

Government is charged with a threefold participation in the affairs of our common life.[7] First, it must establish (*instituere*) the common weal by guarding the peace within its bounds, sometimes referred to as *convenientia voluntatum*,[8] by inciting the citizens to lead a moral life, and by providing for a sufficient abundance (*sufficiens copia*) of the necessities of life. The public weal once established, the next duty is to conserve it. This is accomplished by assuring a recruitment of the agents of administration; by repressing disorder; by encouraging morality through a system of rewards and punishments; and by protecting the state against the attacks of enemies from without. Finally, the government is charged with a third mission, more vague, more elastic; to improve (*ut sit de promotione solicitus*), to rectify abuses, to make up for defects, to work for progress.

The *bonum commune* to be established and maintained by the government is based upon a splendid conception of solidarity: every good and virtuous act performed by the individual man is capable of benefitting the community,—the community in which he has membership, as a part of the whole. Hence it follows that, in the state, the individual good can be referred always to the common welfare: the scholar who studies and teaches, the monk who prays and preaches, these render service to the

[7] *De Regimine Principum*, lib. I, cap. 15.
[8] Thomas Aquinas, *In Ethic. Nicom.*, III, 8.

community as much as do the artisan and the farmer and the common laborer. Thomas Aquinas expressly teaches that every virtuous action (in the realm of nature or of grace) can enter into the constitution of general or legal justice (*justitia generalis vel legalis*); for virtue here adjusts, with an eye to the common welfare, the relations of order maintaining in the conduct of the various members of the community.[8a]

This conception assumes special significance,—a significance characteristic of the social order in the thirteenth century—when one reflects upon the Prince as *charged* with making effectual this virtue in the *justitia legalis*. It is he who possesses the virtue of justice by right of headship (*architectonice*), and in an eminent manner, whereas his

---

[8a] See *Summa Theol.*, 2a2ae, q. LVIII, art. 5, for the important text in this connection. "Manifestum est autem quod omnes qui sub communitate aliqua continentur, comparantur ad communitatem sicut partes ad totum; pars autem id quod est, totius est; unde et quodlibet bonum partis est ordinabile in bonum totius. Secundum hoc ergo bonum cujuslibet virtutis, sive ordinantis aliquem hominem ad seipsum, sive ordinantis ipsum ad aliquas alias personas singulares, est referibile ad bonum commune, ad quod ordinat justitia. Et secundum hoc actus omnium virtutum possunt ad justitiam pertinere, secundum quod ordinant hominem ad bonum commune. Et quantum ad hoc justitia dicitur virtus generalis. Et quia ad legem pertinet ordinare ad bonum commune, . . . inde est quod talis justitia praedicto modo generalis dicitur justitia legalis, quia scilicet per eam homo concordat legi ordinanti actus omnium virtutum in bonum commune."

subordinate possesses it only in administrative dependence and secondarily.[8b] The Prince is *custos justi,* the guardian of what is just; he is *justum animatum,* the personification of what is just.[8c] He is the peace-maker of society. By virtue of this title he is qualified to direct the activities of his subordinates, to bid men to pray or to battle or to build or to farm,—always for the greatest common good.[8d]

If, nevertheless, he who governs fails to be inspired with this sense of the public good and abandons himself to a selfish and capricious use of power, then he must be regarded as a tyrant.

Every treatise, written for the use of princes and future kings, exhibits a dread of the tyrant who allows his own personal advantage to override the good of the group. Dante reserves a special place in his hell for tyrants, by the side of brigands and assassins.

Each establishes an entire system of guarantees to preserve the state against tyranny, which is so opposed to its nature. Some of these guarantees are preventive. Thus, Thomas in the *De Regimine Principum,* would have the people,—for the

[8b] *Ibid.,* art. 6. "Et sic est (justitia legalis) in principe principaliter et quasi architectonice; in subditis autem secundario et quasi administrative."

[8c] *Ibid.,* art. 1, ad quintum.

[8d] The same principle was invoked by ecclesiastical authority in laying upon the Prince the *duty* of suppressing heresy. The *bonum commune,* as it was understood in the thirteenth century, required that man's end in the divine economy should be safeguarded and that therefore the Prince should rigorously check any error which might lead astray the members of the community.

thirteenth century, be it remembered, maintains the thesis of the *sovereign people*—at the moment of the choice of their rulers, inquire into their character, and find out whether they have a despotic temperament. "Look out for your king," he says (*providendum de rege*).[9] Some of these guarantees are intended to last throughout the period of their rule; for his power must be controlled and balanced by others,—wheels within wheels, as we shall show later. Finally, some of these guarantees are repressive. Resistance is not only permitted to unjust orders of the tyrant, but it is enjoined; and in extreme cases the people who have chosen can depose. While John of Salisbury considers tyrannicide as *licitum, aequum* and *justum*,[10] Thomas Aquinas expressly condemns tyrannicide. He desires that that people should do their best to endure an unjust ruler; but if the government becomes quite unendurable, he allows the right of deposing an unworthy ruler, which indeed is the necessary corollary of the power of choosing him.[11]

While it is clear that the philosophers of the thirteenth century were keenly sensitive to the pictures of tyrants, which they found in the *Politics* of Aristotle, it is no less clear that the public life of their own age afforded them actual illustrations of tyranny, which helped to provide an inspiration

---

[9] Lib. I, cap. 6. *Cf.* his *Comment Polit.* lib. III, lectio 14.
[10] *Polycraticus* III, 15.
[11] *De Regimine Princ.*, lib. I, cap. 6.

for their theory. Ptolemy of Lucques, who completed the *De Regimine Principium* begun by Thomas, poured contempt on the tyrants of the minor Italian republics of his day (*hodie in Italia*), who exploited the state for their own personal benefit. Perhaps he had in mind the *Podestas,* who were called from abroad to carry on the administration of the Italian republics, and who, once they had secured the position, thought only of advancing their own interests. Thomas Aquinas must surely have known cases of feudal tyrants, sovereigns who abused their power. The thirteenth century witnessed more than one royal deposition. It suffices to recall how the barons of John Lackland declared against him.

III

But their doctrine is self-consistent, no matter who is entrusted with authority. And this brings us to the third question, which is the most interesting of all. Where does sovereignty reside,—this sovereignty which has its origin in divine delegation and its raison d'être, its delimitation, in the social good?

While the jurists and canonists are occupied only with the Roman Empire, the existing monarchies, and the Papacy,[12] the philosophers take a more general view. The most striking is Thomas Aqui-

---

[12] *Cf.* Gierke, *op. cit.* (Maitland's transl.), pp. 30 and 70,—notes 131 and 174.

nas, who gave to the *droit social* of the thirteenth century a remarkable consistency,—which he imposed on his contemporaries and his successors. It was Thomas who also influenced his friend, William of Moerbeke, to translate into Latin the *Politics* of Aristotle.

To understand the political system of Thomas, we must distinguish two distinct aspects of the problem. On the one hand, *in any state,*—whatever its degree of perfection—there is the question of the seat of sovereignty. On the other hand, there is the question of this same sovereignty in the state which he believes to be *the most perfect.*

As regards the first question. In any state sovereignty arises from collectivity and belongs to *all the people,* that is to say, to the masses made up of individuals. Since it is the people who constitute the state, and it is for the good of all the citizens that sovereignty should be exercised, it is logical to conclude that God has entrusted to the collectivity itself the power of ruling and legislating. Thus the doctrine of the "sovereignty of the people" is not a modern discovery at all; it is in direct harmony with the leading idea of the scholastic political philosophy, that individuals are the only social realities, and that therefore, the state is not an entity outside of them. By a new link, then, this doctrine binds the *droit social* to metaphysics and ethics.

But the body of citizens is too numerous, too unformed, too fickle, to exercise by itself the power which has been assigned to it by divine decree. Accordingly, it in turn, delegates this power. Usually they commit it to a monarch; but not necessarily,—for the people may also delegate it to an aristocratic or to a republican form of government. If the people delegate it to a monarch—and that is the common mediaeval illustration—he represents the group and holds power for the group; *ordinare autem aliquid in bonum commune est vel totius multitudinis, vel alicujus gerentis vicem totius multitudinis.*[13]

The monarch, therefore, is only a vice-regent. This is so literally true that (as we have already seen in the *De Regimine Principum*) precautions were usually recommended, when a vice-regent was to be selected. Indeed, as Thomas says,[14] "among a free people who can make laws for themselves, the consent given popularly to certain practices, constantly made clear by custom, has more weight than the authority of the prince; for the latter holds the power of legislating only so far as he represents the will of the people." So, the power is transmitted, by this successive delegation from God to the people and from the people to the monarch. It is the entire collectivity which is the original subject of the power. The people possess it by a certain natural title, which nothing can destroy; but the

[13] *Summa. Theol.*, 1a2ae, q. XC, art. 3.
[14] *Ibid.*, q. XCVII, art. 3, *ad tertium*.

king holds it subject to the will of the people, which of course may change.

There is, then, at the source of the delegation made by the people to the king, a *contract;* in the less developed states this is a rudimentary or implicit will, but in states which have arrived at a high degree of organization the will is explicit. This will can give expression to itself, in a thousand different ways, each one of them sufficient to render legitimate the holding of power.

This mediaeval principle of the acquisition of power by *contract* is in admirable agreement with the metaphysical doctrine that the individual alone is a real substance. Since the state is not an entity, the will of a state is nothing but the result of the will of all its members; and the state cannot exist without the mutual trust of the members and those who are appointed to direct them. Again the principle is in admirable agreement with feudal society and feudal monarchy, which rests entirely upon the pact, *pactum;* upon the oath of fealty which is the religious guarantee of fidelity to the given word. Are not the pacts between kings and burgesses, barons and prelates, foundation principles of the institutions which envelop and assist in constructing the feudal monarchy? When one of the contracting parties breaks his agreement, the other at once withdraws his part in the bargain and resists. The history of the relations between the kings and their feudatories and towns is full of instances of such resistance.

In principle,—as we have said, the delegation of sovereignty by the people is of the same nature, whether it be made to a monarch, or to an aristocracy, or to a republic. In a monarchy, there is the advantage that the power is concentrated; and, as Thomas points out, the absence of diffusion is more efficacious (for both good and evil purposes) : *Virtus unitiva magis est efficax quam dispersa et divisa.*[15] But, he goes on to say, circumstances themselves must decide, at any given moment in the political life of a people, which is the best form of government; and this supplementary statement gives to his theory that elasticity which renders it adaptable to any set of conditions.

IV

Thomas himself, however, shows very marked preference for a composite form of government, which he considers the most perfect realization of this popular delegation,—and we have already considered that form in general. This mixed system is that in which the sovereignty belongs to the people, but at the same time it is combined with both an elective monarchy and also an oligarchy to curtail the exercise of power by the monarch. The general plan of his system is outlined from this classic text: "Whereas these (that is, the various

[15] *De Regimine Principum,* lib. I, cap. 3.

forms of government) differ in kind . . . nevertheless the first place is held by the "kingdom," where the power of government is vested in one, an "aristocracy," which signifies government by the best, where the power of government is vested in a few. Accordingly, the best form of government is in a state or *kingdom,* wherein *one* is given the power to preside over all; while under him are *others* having governing powers. And yet a government of this kind is shared *by all,* both because all are eligible to govern, and because the rulers are chosen by all. For this is the best form of polity, being partly kingdom, since there is one at the head of all; partly aristocracy, in so far as a number of persons are set in authority; partly democracy, i.e., government by the people, in so far as the rulers can be chosen from the people, and the people have the right to choose their rulers."[16]

In this passage, written about 1250, the following political principles are affirmed: universal suffrage, the right of the humblest citizen to be raised to the highest power, the consecration of personal worth and virtue, a representative and elective monarchy, and the right of the people to delegate, to those who are most worthy of it, that sacred gift of God called power.

This pregnant text contains in a condensed form,

[16] *Summa Theol.* 1a2ae, q. CV, art. 1. English translation (Dominicans), Part II (First Part), Third Number, p. 250, Benzinger, 1915, New York.

in *"latin lapidaire,"* a considerable number of problems, of which we shall consider only a few.

First, since the state must serve the good of the individual, it is necessary that those whom the popular will places at the head shall have intelligence, and sufficient moral integrity, to see and understand the public interest and to promote it. Thus, government by insight is necessary. Reason, which is given such a high place in the economy of individual life,[17] is also the sovereign guide in social life. The system of delegated power will be the more perfect in proportion as it sees to it that power shall be placed in the hands of the most deserving,—or, rather, the most virtuous, to use the mediaeval phrase. Again, men of action ought to be under the direction of men of insight; for, "in the direction of human affairs, excess arises from the fact that the man at the head really has no head. Those who excel in powers of understanding are natural leaders,"—*in regimine humano inordinatio provenit ex eo quod non propter intellectus praeeminentiam aliquis praeest.*[18]

This is why the most perfect form of delegation of power is the elective system; for as Thomas writes in his commentary on the Politics of Aristotle, *election is a work of reason,*[19] and the means

[17] See above ch. VIII, iii and iv.

[18] *Contra Gentiles,* lib. III, cap. 78. Illi qui intellectu praeeminent naturaliter dominantur.

[19] Electio per se est appetitus ratione determinatus *Com. in Politic.,* lib. III, lectio 14.

of choosing the most worthy. Such election applies to the monarch, and also to his ministers in the government, whom Thomas includes in his composite form of government without defining their functions.

Finally, Thomas lays down a condition for the exercise of popular election: it is necessary that the people be sufficiently informed on the issues at stake, and in consequence they must undergo a political education, an education in citizenship. Thus, in agreement with Augustine, he says: "If the people have a sense of moderation and responsibility, and are most careful guardians of the common weal, it is right to enact a law allowing such a people to choose their own magistrates for the government of the commonwealth. But if, as time goes on, the same people became so corrupt as to sell their votes, and entrust the government to scoundrels and criminals, then the right of appointing their public officials is properly forfeited by such a people, and the choice devolves upon a few good men."[20] We see here again, as always, how our fundamental principle comes into play: popular suffrage must contribute to the realization in the state of the good of all. If popular suffrage itself is detrimental, its exercise must be suspended.

[20] *Summa Theol.*, 1a2ae, q. XCVII, art. 1.

V

How does the sovereign power, whatever it be, carry out its functions? According to scholastic philosophy, the essential attribute, which enables a government to fulfil its mission, is the power *to establish laws*. To establish laws for others is, indeed, the most natural form of order.

The theory of human law, in the page of Thomas Aquinas, is intimately bound up with his psychology and ethics and metaphysics; and it forms part of an original whole which can be called briefly "the system of laws."[21] Human or positive law, *lex humana seu positiva,* has a twofold aspect; namely, the *jus gentium,* which belongs to all peoples alike, and the *jus civile,* civil law, which belongs properly to a single state as such. In either case, this human law is simply a derivative from natural law; and natural law in turn is only the application—to man as a natural creature—of the eternal decree of the uncreated wisdom, *lex aeterna*.

With regard to the question now before us, it will be sufficient to say that the law of nature, or natural human right, is that totality of regulations which rests upon the fundamental perfection of the human being; this does not change and cannot change, because it abides in the mutual relationship between the essence of God (the solitary support of all reality) and His creatures. Thomistic phi-

---

[21] *Summa Theol.,* 1a2ae, qq. XC-C.

losophy sums it all up in this formula: the natural law is a participation in the eternal law,—*lex naturalis est participatio quaedam legis aeternae*.[22] It follows, then, that each human individual bears in himself a totality of rights and of duties, which are the expression of his nature,—that is to say, of his status as a reasonable being. It also follows that the natural precepts of this law, the principles of social order, are the same for all men and for all time, and that to destroy them would mean the destruction of man himself. Positive, or human, law cannot violate them. For, as Thomas says, in so far as human law disagrees with the law of nature, it is no longer a law, but a *corruption* of the law;[23] it is placed outside the scope of human legislation.

The human law, indeed, draws its strength, its raison d'être, only from natural law,—of which it is the echo, so to speak, the lengthening out, the fulfilling. Direct applications, evident corollaries of the social nature of man, belong to the *jus gentium*, (that which is right for all nations) such as "justice in buying and selling and other similar things, without which social life would be impossible."[24]

But there are less obvious and more remote consequences of the natural law; and there are applications which *vary*, according to the concrete circumstances peculiar to each state. It rests with

[22] *Ibid.*, q. XCI, art. 2.
[23] *Ibid.*, q. XCV, art. 2.
[24] *Ibid.*

the government of particular groups, to determine these; and this is done under the form of positive law. For example, the natural law demands that the malefactor be punished; but it does not indicate the method or form of punishment,—whether he ought to be punished by fine or by prison or by death.²⁵ It is left to the wisdom of human law to set right the implications of natural law.

Thus, securely linked with the law of nature, all human law is bound up with reason, which is the basis of being human. "Human law is an ordinance of reason for the common good, made by him who has care of the community, and promulgated."²⁶

VI

To be sure, the state described by Thomas Aquinas is an ideal, or theoretical conception. As such of course it could not be realized in practice in any complete sense; for real societies are too complex to conform to any set or uniform scheme. But with this reservation, it seems fair to say that the great European states, which were all then in process of formation, attempted from their several angles to realize in fact some such system of "limited monarchy" as Thomas outlines. For example, the France of Louis IX, in which the transmission of power, resting upon the popular will, was modify-

---

²⁵ *Ibid.*

²⁶ Quaedam rationis ordinatio ad bonum commune et ab eo qui curam communitatis habet, promulgata. *Ibid.*, q. XC, art. 4.

ing the growing power of the king by a certain system of control, the England of the thirteenth century and a little later, was bringing its kings face to face with national parliaments; about the same time Spain also achieves its Cortes, a popular assembly raised up in the midst of the centralized government of Castile and Aragon.[27] Everywhere, the supreme prerogative of sovereignty lay in the exercise of the judicial power, which was nothing but the logical consequence of the power to give orders and to enforce them. Everywhere were manifest those efforts towards a more perfect consistency. But on the other hand, these efforts never attained to that form of administrative centralization which we have come to know in the modern state.

Then again it is important to note that the Thomistic doctrines applied to states and not to nations. The sentiment of love for fatherland, which appeared in the *Chanson de Roland*—where *la douce terre de France* is spoken of—found its place in the moral system of Thomas Aquinas. He speaks of the *pietas* which we owe to our natal soil,

[27] Concerning the historical origin of the divers political functions in Capetian France (the notion of the royal *officium*, the rôle of *justicier* played by the sovereign, the oath of fidelity from subjects, the importance of the elections and of the "sacre" and coronation, the *designatio* of the heir apparent before Louis VII), see Luchaire, *Histoire des institutions monarchiques sous les premiers capétiens* (987-1180), vol. I, Paris, 1891. *Cf.* Zeiller, *L'idée de l'Etat dans St. Thomas*, Paris, 1910.

—*in qua nati et nutriti sumus;* and he considers the citizen to be a debtor to his fatherland, *"debitor patriae."*[28]

But nation means more than state and fatherland. In our modern conception, a nation presupposes a strongly organized state,—with an accumulation of traditions behind it, with institutions, rights and feelings, with victories and sufferings, and with a certain type of mind (religious, moral, and artistic). These are its elements. The result is that the bond which unites the nation is above all psychical in character (intellectual and moral), rather than territorial or racial.

Now the European nations, thus defined, did not exist in the thirteenth century: *they were in process of formation.* The monarchical states were to become the nuclei of the nations of modern times. War was not then a contest between two nations, but a struggle between two members of a single family, or two kings, or two vassals, or between the vassal and the lord. It retained the character of a private feud; and the same is true of the quarrels between towns and between classes in the same town. Hence, in his philosophical doctrine of war, Thomas Aquinas insists that a war, to be just, must be declared by the legitimate authority.

It was just because the states of the thirteenth century were not formed into clearly defined nations, that they had more traits in common than

[28] *Summa Theol.*, 2a2ae, q. CXXII, art. 5; q. CI, art. 1.

those of today. But they were on the point of becoming diversified. The thirteenth century was like a central plateau, and the streams which flowed from it, cut their beds in different directions.

The Thomistic theory of the state represents the crystallization of the political experiences of the twelfth and thirteenth centuries; but it also represents conformity with the feudal and civil and canon law, which was making no little progress during this time. Consequently the three systems of legislation (feudal, civil, canon) are at one on so many important points, such as the divine origin of power, the subordination of the king to law, the king's character as servitor of justice, the force of custom, the intervention of the community in the delegation of power to the prince, and the participation of the people in government. In the same way natural law is for the legists and canonists an ideal to which positive (human) legislation must approach; and the prescription of the natural law must be adopted in so far as it is possible in existing circumstances.[29]

Finally, the thirteenth century theory of the state takes up and completes various philosophic doctrines which had found credit among former philosophers such as Manegold of Lautenbach, and

[29] *Cf.* Carlyle, *op. cit.* For the civilian lawyers, vol. II, pp. 27, 49, 75; for the canonists, *ibid.*, pp. 110, 145, *cf.* VIII, and p. 242; for the feudal lawyers, vol. III, pp. 32, 34, 44, 51, 100, 106, 116, 125, 137, 147, 162, and the conclusion.

John of Salisbury. But it has become a social philosophy, and it dresses all in a synthesis which is found neither among the feudal theorists nor among the legists, nor among the canonists, nor among the philosophers of the preceding centuries. It coordinates all, and attaches the doctrines which it establishes to a system of psychology, of morals, of logic, and of metaphysics. It is a kind of democracy, *conceived in moderation,* and based upon the pluralistic conception of the world and of life.

CHAPTER TWELVE

THE CONCEPTION OF HUMAN PROGRESS

i. The constant and the permanent. ii. Progress in science, in morals, in social and political justice, in civilization.

I

Is there a place in the scholasticism of the thirteenth century for a theory of progress? The question concerns not only the system of human laws; it is a general problem, and therefore, it must be solved according to general principles. Let us observe briefly how scholasticism succeeded in reconciling the constant and the variable, and in what degree it admits the possibility of change for the better.

We have already seen[1] what a capital rôle the stable and the permanent played in the thirteenth century conception of the world. Essences are unchangeable, and by them the natural species are fixed; they are imitations of the essence of God; and the degree of imitability does not change. From this it follows that what constitutes man, his *quiddity* as they then said, is everywhere and al-

[1] Ch. IX, iv.

ways the same. One is either a man or not a man. *Essentia non suscipit plus vel minus.* Similarly, the first principles of reason—that is to say, the judgments which express the fundamental relations of all being, the prerequisites of whatever reality may come into actual existence—are stable and permanent; their necessity and their universality are absolute. Take, for example, the principle of contradiction: "that which is cannot not be," or the principle of causality: *quidquid movetur ab alio movetur.* The scholastics referred to these principles as *per se notae,* knowable of themselves; for, merely by understanding the subject and predicate one can grasp the absolute necessity of the relation which unites them, independently of all experience, and in consequence independently of all existence. The first principles of mathematics, although less general in that they have to do only with quantity, express in the same way invariable relations.

Nor is it otherwise with the principles of moral and social order. That good must be done and wrong avoided, that the state is for the good of individuals, are principles necessary and fixed; and we have seen that there exist rights derived from nature, which no human legislation can violate. However, the necessity of these moral and social principles is of a different kind from that of mathematical propositions, and of the principles of reason. These moral principles imply a *condition;* namely, the existence of humanity in its actual state,—the fact of creation. The same also holds true concerning the principles of the natural sciences. Hence, such principles are not knowable by mere analysis and comparison of their subject and their predicate (*per se notae*); they manifestly rest on observation and on experience (*per aliud nota*).[2]

II

On the other hand, the world of limited existence involves change, and scholasticism studied with care the problem of change. The doctrine of act and potency,—the actuality and potentiality in each changing being—is nothing but their solution of this problem.[3] Change appears everywhere in the physical world. But change itself follows certain uniformities; it is dominated by finality. The unvarying return of the seasons, the movements of the planets, the cycle of physical and chemical laws, the recurrence of vital phenomena in plants and animals,—all of these exhibit the striking regularity which is inherent in the realm of change. In so far as one considers inorganic beings, the vegetable and animal world, this same recurrence admits of no exception. It is not only the species which are fixed; the activities exhibited by the most diverse

---

[2] On the scholastic distinction between judgments *per se nota* and *per aliud nota* (*aliud* here means observation and experience), see Mercier, *Logique,* Louvain, 1919, pp. 135 ff. *Cf.* Thomas Aquinas, *De anima,* II, 14.

[3] See above ch. IX, iii.

individuals beings do not vary. In regard to evolution, as we understand it today, the dynamic metaphysics of scholasticism neither includes nor excludes the change of one species into another. The problem did not present itself in the thirteenth century. Neither the theory of transformism nor the theory of mutation is irreconcilable with the scholastic theory of the world. Indeed, as we have seen above, a substance transforms itself always into another species of substance,—it does not matter how.

But human acts, are they bound by the same uniformities,—or, on the contrary, is human progress really possible? The question is the more interesting because the thirteenth century believed that it had realized a state of stable equilibrium, and because their extraordinary optimism lead them to believe that they had arrived at a state close to perfection. Accordingly it is necessary to explain how they conceived of humanity as having traversed the lower stages in order to arrive at this degree of perfection.

A precise formulation is furnished by their metaphysical psychology. Human nature is the same in all men, and whatever rests on this nature is stable and uniform. But the faculties,—the direct source of activities—differ from man to man, in power and in flexibility. The intelligence and the will are energetic in a greater or a less degree; they are susceptible of being perfected by education, and this perfecting itself is indefinite. The repetition of activities engenders permanent dispositions (*habitus*), which intensify effort. So it is that there is a place for progress in science. That which men have not been able to discover up to any given time, may some day be discovered by a genius more penetrating. Thomas Aquinas applies this to the geocentric hypothesis of which he foresees the possible supplanting.[4] Science, moreover, is regarded as a collective treasure, which is unceasingly increased by the contributions of succeeding generations.[5]

In the domain of morals and of social-justice, the place accorded to change (of course change for the better) is much more important. The concern here is not with the increase of moral or social judgments, as was the case with science; but real transformation, and adaptation, is involved, and the underlying reason for this is found in human liberty. Aside from the immutable principles (the point of departure and the standard of morality), scholasticism recognizes that there are applications of these principles more or less distinct, and more or less variable.[6] These principles govern the majority of cases, but they admit of exceptions. Reason has to weigh the value of all the circumstances which envelop a concrete and practical application of a moral law. The more numerous these circum-

[4] *Cf.* above, p. 113.
[5] *Cf.* above, pp. 139 ff.
[6] *Cf.* above, p. 259.

stances become, the greater is the elasticity of the law. The matter is well and clearly put by Thomas Aquinas[7] as follows: "As to the proper conclusions of the practical reason, neither is the truth or rectitude the same for all, nor, where it is the same, is it equally known by all. Thus it is right and true for all to act according to reason, and from this principle it follows as a proper conclusion, that goods entrusted to another should be restored to their owner. Now this is true for the majority of cases; but it may happen in a particular case that it would be injurious, and therefore unreasonable to restore goods held in trust; for instance, if they are claimed for the purpose of fighting against one's country. And this principle will be found to fail the more, according as we descend further into detail, e.g., if one were to say that goods held in trust should be restored with such and such a guarantee, or in such and such a way; because the greater the number of conditions added, the greater the number of ways in which the principle may fail, so that it be not right to restore or not to restore." The fundamental inclination towards good abides in the depths of human conscience; it can be darkened, *obtenebrari,* but not extinguished. In the worst men, human nature remains good and retains the indelible imprint of the eternal law.[8]

As for social truths and social laws, these are

[7] *Summa Theol.*, 1a2ae, q. XCIV, art. 4. Dominican trans., p. 48.
[8] *Ibid.*, q. XCVI, art. 6.

even more subject to the conditions of *tempora,* of *negotia,* of *personae* than are the laws of the moral individual.[9] They vary with them; they are not endowed with *infallibilities.*[10] Hence progress in human legislation is possible. It is certain that the system of limited monarchy, to which Thomas Aquinas gives his preference, constituted in his eyes a step forward from the primitive forms of government which he enumerates. In the following fine passage Thomas shows how law, as well as science, is capable of progress. "Thus there may be two causes for the just change of human law: one on the part of reason; the other on the part of man whose acts are regulated by law. The cause on the part of reason is that it seems natural to human reason to advance gradually from the imperfect to the perfect. Hence, in speculative sciences, we see that the teaching of the early philosophers was imperfect, and that it was afterwards perfected by those who succeeded them. So also in practical matters: for those who first endeavoured to discover something useful for the human community, not being able by themselves to take everything into consideration, set up certain institutions which were deficient in many ways; and these were changed by subsequent lawgivers who made institutions that might prove less frequently deficient in

[9] *Ibid.,* 1a2ae, q. XCVI, art. 1. *Cf.* the whole of q. XCVII ("De mutatione legum").

[10] *Ibid.,* q. XCI, art. 3, ad tertium.

respect of the common weal. On the part of man, whose acts are regulated by law, the law can be rightly changed on account of the changed condition of man, to whom different things are expedient according to the difference of his condition."[11]

Thus the Thomistic theory opens the way for progress in human legislation; and since legislation is the attribute of sovereignty, it opens the way likewise for progress in the government of states. But forthwith Thomas adds this counsel of wisdom: not without good reasons, should human law be changed. For, any change in the law is made at the expense of the power and majesty that reside in the legislative power,—*quando lex mutatur, diminuitur vis constructiva legis.*[12]

On the basis of Thomistic principles, it is therefore possible to justify a series of progressive measures. The thirteenth century could of course not envisage them; but they are in the logic of its system. For, whatever the government may be, it must look ever towards betterment (*ut sit de promotione solicitus*); it must put at the disposal of individuals the means of perfecting their personality. It must assure, for example, all that concerns education of the physical faculties, of the intelligence, and of the moral will; it must organize the conditions of production and of work.[13] A like

[11] *Ibid.*, q. XCVII, art. 1. Dominican trans., p. 77.
[12] *Ibid.*, q. XCVII, art. 2.
[13] *Cf.* above, p. 246.

mission belongs to the social authority, whatever may be the form of this authority. Following the fine and judicious distinction of Thomas, one must determine in varying circumstances, just what form of government is most propitious to the realization of its social mission.

Finally, like the state and the collective life, human civilization in its entirety is capable of progress; for it is the result of human activities which are always perfectible. Education, heredity, the influence of authority, can all act on the development of the artistic faculties, of scientific labors, of customs, of religious practice.

To sum up, then. Fixity of essences and essential relations; act and potency; perfectibility of faculties; liberty and adaptability of the collective life to circumstances and needs,—these are the principles by which scholasticism solved the problem of progress. They did so by answering in their way the ancient Greek query: How reconcile the fixed and the changing?

CHAPTER THIRTEEN

Philosophy and National Temperament in the Thirteenth Century

i. Scholastic philosophy reflected in the temperament of the peoples who created it. ii. Three main doctrines: the value of the individual; intellectualism; moderation. iii. Scholastic philosophy the product of Neo-Latin and Anglo-Celtic minds; Germanic contribution virtually negligible. iv. Latin Averroism in the thirteenth century. v. The lure of Neo-Platonism to the German. vi. The chief doctrines opposed to the scholastic tendencies: lack of clearness; inclination to pantheism; deductive method à outrance; absence of moderation.

I

Scholastic philosophy is the dominant philosophy of the thirteenth century. Such is the outstanding fact, the significance of which we have attempted to estimate by correlating it with the other factors of that civilization.

This philosophy is the result of a slow and progressive development, and it follows the general trend of western civilization. The doctrinal fermentation, rather slow in its beginning, becomes intensified in the eleventh and twelfth centuries, as the social and political structure is taking its feudal form; and it reaches its most fruitful period just as the distinctly mediaeval mode—of life and of thought and of feeling—is revealing itself clearly in every department of human activity. This great philosophical system reflects the unifying tendencies of the time; its influence is cosmopolitan; its optimism, its impersonality, and its religious tendencies place it in accord with the entire civilization; and its doctrines exert a profound influence on art and on literature and on social habits.

As scholastic philosophy is the work of western races, it is likewise an original product. In it the western peoples reproduce, to be sure, the problems of the Greek and the Oriental worlds. But the solutions of these problems are cast in a new mould, they are imbued with a new mentality. Herein lies the secret of the wonderful growth and expansion of the scholastic philosophy in the West.

Seeing that the peoples of the West were constantly preoccupied with it, there is little wonder that this philosophy should have played a part in moulding philosophical temperament; that it should have given them an intellectual bent, a specific turn of mind. We need not be surprised then to find,— in that unique period of history when the minds of the various European peoples were taking on their several casts,—the development of certain general characteristics, whose influence survived in philosophy after the thirteenth century, and even the whole Middle Ages.

Economic forms, political organization, structure of social classes, artistic culture,—these all disappear, or are transformed; indeed, by the end of the fourteenth century, these elements of the civilization have lost their distinctly mediaeval significance. But moral and philosophical temperaments endure, because they belong to the deeper lying emanations of human spirit. In the individual man, the bodily temperament, which depends upon physiological conditions, persists throughout his entire life. Similarly, in a group of individuals the mental temperament, which finds its support in common ideals, both intellectual and moral, survives in the race. Thus, the habits of honor and courtesy, under the combined influence of Church and feudal society, were transmitted through succeeding generations as staple realities,—which we find even today in our modern conscience. In like manner, the philosophical temperament of the thirteenth century,—I mean the setting in operation of certain methods and doctrines—entered into the modern epoch and even now directs our mode of thought. Indeed, scholastic philosophy set in operation three main doctrines,—which may also be called methods—which have become our common approach to problems and their solutions.

II

The first of these doctrines lays emphasis upon the worth of the individual, or person, as the only human reality. Scholastic philosophy, being a pluralistic conception of the world, makes of each man an autonomous agent, having a body and an intelligence and a will and a liberty all his own. Each human individual possesses abilities which give to him as a representative of the race a purely personal power of action; and this inequality of faculties explains the several capacities of various individuals for artistic or scientific or professional or public life. The human individual has a right to personal happiness and is called after death to enjoy personal blessedness. He is protected against the state, or the group, by a whole system of intangible rights.[1] Accordingly, the philosophy of the thirteenth century is opposed to everything that resembles the subjugation of one man to another. For the same reason, it exhibits a profound dislike for monism and pantheism; it was at great pains, and this cannot be too strongly emphasized, to eliminate every pantheistic tendency from its teaching. Indeed it developed a horror for any doctrine which fuses in one sole being some or all beings,—in particular, which makes all men parts or becomings of a great whole, of one Being, and which therefore suppresses their individuality.

This doctrine, that the individual alone is substantial reality, and alone has real value in the universe, is of course Aristotelian in origin. It is written on the first page of his *Metaphysics*, that

[1] *Cf.* chs. IX and X.

splendid book of common-sense which has nourished the thought of men for two thousand years. But with their special concern for the natural equality of human beings, the scholastics went much further than did Aristotle. While he stated that men are naturally unlike, and that nature made freemen of some and slaves of others, the scholastics regarded slavery and serfdom as *conventional*,—not as natural. And we may be sure that if this turn of thought—a turn toward enhanced value of the individual—had not been in accord with the deepest aspirations of the mediaeval civilization (in the peoples who were its supreme representatives), it would never have found entrance into their marrow, and into their blood. For, the western minds took only what suited them, —whether from Aristotle or Plato or Augustine or Avicenna or Averroes—and they took it because it suited them.

Nothing is more false than the judgment, which finds credit among so many historians, that one must await the Renaissance to see human personality appraised at its true worth. There are few philosophers who have accentuated the metaphysical, the psychological, the moral, and the social value of the individual so much as did the scholastics. And just as the thirteenth century is a century of striking personalities, it is also a century of discussions on all the problems which the question of personality raises.

There is a second doctrine which also involves the philosophical mentality, and which is closely connected with that which we have just exposited. This is intellectualism, or the royal rule of reason in man, and in all that concerns human life. It introduces the supremacy of reason into all departments of human activity.[2] Thomas Aquinas and Duns Scotus are its striking representatives; but it is also found though in a lesser degree, in all of the scholastic philosophers.

It is because the dominant philosophy of the thirteenth century was an intellectual philosophy, that it promoted a love of clearness and precision; that it struggled against the perplexing vagueness of Arabian mysticism; that it introduced into discussions an atmosphere of precision and exactness which exercised on the formation of the developing minds the most beneficent influence. It is to this mental discipline that the philosophical Latin of the masters owes its pliability,—and to the same source the modern languages are indebted for large portions of their vocabularies.[2a] We have already seen how this intellectualism and love of clarity are revealed in the most important forms of thirteenth century culture.[2b]

But, in addition to individualism and intellectualism, there is a third deep lying character which

[2] *Cf.* ch. VIII.
[2a] *Cf.* above, p. 176.
[2b] See ch. VII, v.

enters into the temperament of those who framed and developed scholastic philosophy. And this is their spirit of *moderation,*—a moderation revealed in considered choice. Their philosophy is the *via media* between the views of Plato and of Aristotle; it tempers the naturalism of the latter with the idealism of the former. Thus the equilibrium which appears in all the social forces of that age manifests itself in their dominant philosophy.

We have seen[3] how scholastic metaphysics is a dynamic philosophy; but its dynamic character is moderate,—because the form or the principle of any given perfection, that may reside in each being, unfolds in matter. It gives the corporeal world an evolutionary interpretation; but this is a mitigated evolution, since it does not apply to the essences themselves. Thus, for example, their conception of evolution combines efficient causality and finality; it furnishes a moderate realistic solution, by reconciling the individual nature of external realities with the abstract character of our corresponding concepts.[4]

Scholastic psychology is a moderate form of idealism, since abstract ideas arise in sense-perception,[5] and man is regarded as a unitary combination of both soul and body. Similarly, this moderation finds expression in their ethics, which explains the

[3] See ch. IX, iii and iv.
[4] See above, pp. 59 and 181.
[5] *Cf.* ch. VIII, i.

compatibility of duty with pleasure, and of variable moral laws with its unchangeable principles.[6] The same is true of their aesthetics, since the beautiful is at once subjective and objective. And again in their logic this same spirit appears, as they establish the right of both deduction and induction. This moderation appears also in their social philosophy; for sovereignty in the state belongs both to the people and to those who receive power, by delegation from the people.[7] Moderation is likewise found in their theory of progress and culture, which takes account of both that which is fixed in human nature and that which is changeable and perfectible.[8]

Thus, in all of its reflection scholasticism seeks the golden mean and avoids extremes; it delights in the solution that mediates between opposing views. For all these reasons it is a profoundly *human* philosophy,—that is, a philosophy which is fitted for beings bound by corporeal conditions and yet also participating in the spiritual realm.

The importance of personality, the supremacy of reason and of clear ideas, a sense of measure and of moderation in the doctrines which constitute it; these three characteristics of scholastic philosophy are in perfect accord with the western civilization of the thirteenth century.

[6] *Cf.* ch. XII, ii.
[7] *Cf.* ch. XII.
[8] *Cf.* ch. XI, iii.

III

And now we must consider a further fact—one of central importance. This civilization is above all the product of French influence; France is the centre from which it casts its light everywhere.[9] From this angle, it is interesting to note how the masters of scholastic philosophy, those who brought it to its full development and who affixed to it the imprint of their genius, were all *educated* in France, —whether French or Italian or English or Flemish, or Walloon. Thomas Aquinas and Bonaventure belong to great Italian families; Alexander of Hales, Duns Scotus, William of Occam, and many more, are Anglo-Celts; Gérard of Abbeville, William of Auvergne, William of Auxerre belong to France; Henry of Ghent, Siger of Courtrai are natives of Flanders; Godfrey of Fontaines is of the nobility of Liége. All of these masters met in Paris, where they resided and taught; and they are therefore French by education. Scholastic philosophy in the thirteenth century is even more a system of *Gallicae Sententiae* than it was in the time of Adélard of Bath.[10]

On the other hand, the rôle of the Germans is surprisingly negligible. The only personality of note that comes from beyond the Rhine is Swabian, Albert the Great, Count of Bollstadt. His contribution to scholastic philosophy is deserving of the

[9] See chs. II, ii; III, i; IV, ii, iii; V, iv.
[10] *Cf.* above, p. 41.

closest attention; but his services are of a very special kind. Albert the Great was an indefatigable compiler of texts, a tireless commentator, an observer of facts, an excellent encyclopedist; but he was not a profound philosopher.[11]

I do not mean, of course, that the Germans had no share in the philosophy of the thirteenth century; for they produced some men whose thought is of the greatest significance in respect to civilization. But their philosophy is not scholastic philosophy, as we have been at pains to outline it in these pages. Their system of thought contained seeds which were foreign to the scholastic genius; and therein are found the beginnings of their later deepest aspirations.

This contrast between the two types of mind is both striking and instructive. We may therefore profitably consider it more closely in concluding our study.

IV

What is this philosophy to which the Germans so generally gave preference? To understand the full significance of this question, it is necessary to consider the non-scholastic philosophies of the thirteenth century.

[11] *Cf.* Schneider, "Beiträge zur Psychologie Alberts des Grossen," Baümker's-*Beiträge,* IV, 5, 1903. Albert in *de animalibus* is fond of distinguishing the Germani and the Galli. *Cf.* H. J. Stadler, Albertus Magnus de animalibus L. XXVI. Baümker's-*Beiträge,* XV-XVI, 1916 and 1921. Incices, verbis Galli, Germania, Germani.

It should be stated at once that we must disregard the unusual; for our study is one of general tendencies. In that century, which was so rich in important personalities there were certain isolated but brilliant thinkers, who swept the philosophic sky in meteor-like fashion,—leaving little trace of real influence on their environment. Roger Bacon is perhaps the most fascinating of these men. But while he was far beyond his day in all matters touching mathematics and natural science, he fell just as far behind in his view of philosophy itself,— as mere apologetics in furthering religion. Thus he represents a twofold anachronism,—not only in science, but in philosophy as well! Hence, however interesting this personality of the thirteenth century may be, he remains none the less an exception, and deserves only a secondary place in our study.

Aside from scholastic philosophy, two principal currents of thought manifest themselves,—namely, latin Averroism and Neo-Platonism. These are all the more marked by the upheaval which they occasioned; nevertheless, in contrast with the great river of scholasticism, they are really mere rivulets. The first emerges suddenly; but it disappears gradually from view, in the fifteenth century,—like a stream which sinks into some subterranean channel. The second, on the other hand, arose slowly, but it widened its channel and deepened its current; and, as it did so, it carried with it the German genius. Let us consider each of these in turn.

Latin Averroism differs from scholastic philosophy as the Gothic cathedral differs from the Arabian mosque,—and not as the Cathedral of Amiens differs from that of Chartres. The conflict between the one and the other presents two distinct conceptions of the world and of life, two systems of metaphysics and of psychology.

The researches of Mandonnet have served to enrich our acquaintance with the origin and nature of these Averroistic doctrines.[12] That they appeared at Paris about 1256, and that between 1260 and 1270 they were the source of much disturbance to the Faculty of Arts of the University, are now clearly established facts. In the philosophic duel which then was waged between scholasticism and Latin Averroism, there appeared Thomas Aquinas as the champion of the former, and Siger of Brabant, a Fleming who championed the latter and gathered about him a small number of admiring followers. To combat the Averroistic doctrines, all the scholastics united in an alliance, both offensive and defensive,—including also such men as Roger Bacon.[13]

[12] See P. Mandonnet, "Siger de Brabant et l'Averroisme latin au XIIIme s." in *Les Philosophes Belges,* vol. VI (1911) and VII (1908), Louvain.

[13] Thomas Aquinas wrote a special treatise entitled *De unitate intellectus contra Averroistas.* Duns Scotus speaks of Averroes as *"maledictus ille Averroes"* (Oxon. IV, d. 43, q. 2, no. 5).

In this contest we may confine our attention to two principal doctrines, which the scholastics never tired of attacking,—namely, the theory of one single soul for all mankind, and the theory of the twofold truth. The former has to do with an important aspect of psychology, and it has significant bearings on religion; the latter involves the relation of philosophy and theology. We shall treat briefly of each.

This theory of the single intelligence in men teaches, that all human thoughts occur by virtue of a *single intelligence,* which belongs to the race,— and, as substance, remains in a state of isolation from the individual human beings. Our personal thoughts arise, when our individual sense perceptions and imaginations are illuminated by this single intelligence, by virtue of its momentary action in union with the sensitive soul (*anima sensibilis*) in each of us. Furthermore—and as a consequence of this—the soul of mankind is alone endowed with immortality, and the soul or form that is individual in each of us passes away at death. Men die; the soul of the race is immortal.

Such a doctrine runs counter to any deep sense of human personality, by minimizing the individual aspects of thinking and of religious experience, —and by eliminating personal immortality. The bitter struggle of the scholastics against this doctrine is therefore readily intelligible as a registering of their profound yearning for, and emphasis upon, the value of human personality. Traini's[14] portrayal of the defeat of Averroes (and the other productions inspired by Traini's great work) reflect also this same sense of personal worth embedded in the wider complex of that civilization, society at large, of which philosophy is a part.

The theory of the twofold truth[15] asserts, that a doctrine may be true in philosophy but false in theology, and conversely. This pragmatic doctrine enabled the harmonizing with Catholic dogma of ideas which were utterly foreign to its spirit and subversion of its teachings. Setting truth over against itself, it contravenes the principle of contradiction,—indispensable not only to the preservation of theology, but also to the principles of moral and social order. The deepest lying tendencies of that civilization and the fundamental doctrines of their logic and theology are alike incompatible with the theory of the twofold truth. It was just this incompatibility which lead to its formal condemnation in 1277 (as is clear from the beginning of that interesting document) ;[16] and the same is evident in the work of Thomas against the Averroists. Hence one can understand the intensity of the struggle which the doctrine aroused in the schools.

Latin Averroism is not a product of occidental thought, but an exotic importation. Its protagon-

[14] *Cf.* above, pp. 84 and 154.
[15] *Cf.* above, p. 165.
[16] Denifle-Chatelain, *Chartul. Univers. Paris.* Vol. I, p. 543.

ists proclaimed the philosophical infallibility of Averroes, and it was their constant concern to avoid betraying him. The motives which prompted this occidental affiliation with the oriental interpretation of Aristotelian naturalism remain a matter of conjecture. It may have been sincerity or conviction; or, it may have been the desire to justify the relaxation of faith and of morals, as Mandonnet believes. But, in any event, it is certain that Latin Averroism did not penetrate the mass of the intellectuals. At Paris it was the creed of a small group; and when the condemnation of 1277 checked the professional career of Siger of Brabant, its expansion was arrested,—though it did not entirely disappear. Indeed, at the court of Frederic II, King of The Sicilies, Averroism scored a local triumph. But that court reflected the spirit of the Orient far more than it did that of the Occident; Frederic II being an Oriental prince both in caste and in manners.

If Averroism did not penetrate the spirit of men of learning in the western world, still less did it penetrate into the channels of ordinary life.[17] Being, *as a whole,* alien to occidental civilization, it is necessary to seek elsewhere the influence of the Averroistic doctrines upon the civilization which we have studied. First of all, it kindled an atmosphere of conflict; and thus it obliged scholastic

[17] Alphandéry, "Y-a-t-il eu un Averroisme populaire aux XIII'° et XIV'° s.?" (*Revue de l'histoire des religions,* 1901, p. 394.)

philosophy to formulate its position with greater precision, and it united on fundamentals, those who otherwise were divided. Furthermore, a few detached theories of Averroism, by virtue of their inherent force, continued their influence,—an influence which increased during the centuries that followed. For instance, the doctrine of the twofold truth gradually undermined the Catholic faith; and certain Averroists of the fourteenth century lent their support to the legists, who were engaged in subordinating the Papacy to the State. Finally, certain elements of Averroism contributed to reinforce another current of ideas born in the thirteenth century, the Neo-Platonic current which we must now consider.

V

Occidental Neo-Platonism could no more compete in influence with the scholastic philosophy of the thirteenth century than could Latin Averroism. The doctrines of emanation and the vaporous mysticism of Proclus,—especially as contained in the *Liber de Causis*—were in direct opposition to the temper of scholasticism. But Neo-Platonism succeeded in alluring a group of German philosophers; and in view of its contribution to the tendencies which developed in Germany, especially during the fourteenth and fifteenth centuries, its study is of the greatest historical interest. It is not within the scope of the present work to examine in detail the

Neo-Platonic movement of the thirteenth century, which would involve a separate study; we shall therefore touch upon it only, and give in outline certain general results.

The first translators of Neo-Platonic works—such as Robert Grosseteste, Alfredus Anglicus, and William of Moerbeke—had no sympathy with Neo-Platonism, other than the special fondness which every translator of that age felt for the work which he translated. And the same may be said of Albert the Great as commentator, for, in commentating Aristotle and Neo-Platonic writings, respectively, he inclines toward each in turn.

But in the second half of the thirteenth century a group of German philosophers turn deliberatively to certain Neo-Platonic theses. These men are contemporaries of, or immediate successors to, Albert the Great; and several of them, like Albert himself, are dignitaries of the Dominican order in Germany. I refer to Ulric of Strasburg, the immediate disciple of Albert, to the Silesian Witelo, to Thierry of Freiburg (in Germany), to Berthold of Mosburg, perhaps a disciple of Albert, and to Meister Eckhart, the most celebrated of all. These thinkers succeed in coordinating the whole of their doctrines, in organic unity, on the basis of Neo-Platonic thought. In different degrees, their works combine the emanational view of reality, the tendency to make knowledge arise in the soul independent of the external world, and the mystic impulse toward the infinite.

VI

Now, if we confine our enquiry to Thierry of Freiburg and Meister Eckhart—the striking personalities of the group—it is very remarkable that these men (whose works are now published or well known)[18] part deliberately with the scholastic philosophy,—the philosophy which dominates the minds of Neo-Latins and the Anglo-Celts, and with which the German thinkers are thoroughly familiar. Thus, Thierry of Freiburg says expressly, that he wished to separate himself from those who taught the common philosophy,—from the *communiter loquentes*—and he boasts of it.[19] The same sense of

[18] I here give the works of these men. The bibliography, at the end of these lectures, may be consulted for details. Ulric of Strasburg is the author of a treatise entitled *De Summo Bono*, of which brief fragments have been published (*cf.* Ueberweg-Baumgartner, *op. cit.*, p. 462). Witelo wrote a work on *Optics* (*De Perspectiva*), and he is probably the author of the treatise *De Intelligentiis*. The works of Thierry of Freiburg have been published by Krebs. Berthold of Mosburg wrote a commentary on the *Elementa Theologica* of Proclus. According to Dyroff ("Ueber Heinrich und Dietrich von Freiburg," *Philos. Jhrb.*, 1915, pp. 55-63), the Henry of Freiburg ("de Uriberch"),—who probably belonged to the same family as Thierry of Freiburg, and lived at the same time—translated into German verse the mystical and Neo-Platonic discourses of Thierry of Freiburg. The German works of Eckhart have been published by Pfeiffer (1857), and fragments of his Latin works by Denifle (*Archiv f. Litt. u. Kirchengesch. d. Mittelalt.*, 1886).

[19] See above, *Sententia communis*, p. 83. *Cf.* E. Krebs, "Meister

difference appears in Eckhart, who says concerning some of his own doctrines: *primo aspectu monstruosa, dubia aut falsa apparebunt, secus autem si sollerter et studiosius pertractantur.*[20] Both of these thinkers take over certain characteristics and tendencies which are diametrically opposed to the tendency of thought of the Neo-Latins and the Anglo-Celts, which we have pointed out.

The first character is a lack of clearness in thought and of precision in language. Although he uses the fixed terminology of the scholastics, the celebrated Eckhart is an obscure thinker,—"Ein unklarer Denker" said Denifle,[21] his best historian and himself a German. To the clear ideas and precise expressions of scholastic philosophy, Neo-Platonic Germans oppose ambiguous theories and misleading comparisons. Their thoughts do not seek the clear light, and they are satisfied with approximations. Their imaginations delight in analogies, notably in the comparison of emanation with radiation or flowing, by which they represent creation as a stream of water which flows from the divine source and as a light which shines forth from the luminous hearth of the Divinity. Thierry speaks of the creative act by which God produces Intelligences, as an *ebullitio,* an interior transfusion

Dietrich, s. Leben, s. Werke, s. Wissenschaft," Baümker's-*Beiträge*, V, 5-6, 1906, pp. 150, 151.

[20] Denifle, *Meister Eckharts lateinische Schriften*, p. 535.

[21] *Edit.*, Denifle, p. 459.

by which His nature, sovereignly blessed and fertile, pours itself out.[22]

This brings us to a second characteristic, very much more important, in which the philosophy of the Germans of the thirteenth century is opposed to scholastic philosophy. This is the leaning towards pantheism, which unites men with God even to the point of fusion; the carrying of the soul for commerce with the Divinity, a mystic communion so intimate that every distinction between God and the soul disappears. In the whole group of German thinkers of the thirteenth century it is Eckhart who shows this tendency most strongly, and it is also he who exerts the greatest influence upon the German mind. He boldly teaches that the *existence* of God is also the very *existence* of creatures.[23] In this he differs totally with the scholastic philosophy, which gives to each person (as to each individual being) not only his own *essence*, but an *existence* distinct from the existence of every other being, and also from that of God.[24] He thus maintains a fusion of God and His creatures, since the same single existence envelops them both. One understands, therefore, how he can say that God is like an infinite sphere, whose centre is everywhere

---

[22] *Edit.*, Krebs, pp. 129 and 133.

[23] Ens tantum unum et Deus est. Extra primam causam nichil est; quod enim est extra causam primam, deum scilicet, est extra esse, quia deus est esse. *Edit.*, Denifle, p. 549.

[24] See above, pp. 195, 218.

and whose circumference is nowhere,[25] and that every creature has a lasting hunger and thirst for God: *qui edunt me adhuc esuriunt*. The animals. he writes, cease to nourish their young as soon as these have their fill; but beings are insatiable of God, for they exist in Him.[26]

On the basis of this metaphysics, Eckhart elaborates a mysticism wherein the soul contracts a union with God which would bridge the gulf between infinite and finite. The description which he makes of this mystic union makes one tremble. That which God loves in us is Himself, His very own existence; the soul is the sanctuary of God where He finds Himself! But God does not enter into the sanctuary unless the soul is prepared, it must have renounced everything,—not only all external things, but also its very self, its knowledge, its will, its feelings, its strivings, its personality. In short, God enters in only if the soul is in a state of absolute renunciation, of complete passivity, (*abgeschiedenheit*).[27] And then the miracle takes place; God discloses the unity and the infinity of His nature. The soul is transported into the silent desert where there is neither effort, nor doubt, nor faith: where, in order to know, there is no further need of images, of similitudes, of interpretation, of writing, or of dogma. God is found in me; He is not

[25] *Ibid.*, p. 571.
[26] *Ibid.*, p. 582.
[27] *Edit.*, Pfeiffer, pp. 650 ff.

complete without my soul.²⁸ As I am immanent in the being of God, He accomplishes all His works by me. God is made man in order that man may become God. This is the mystic deification; it is the return of man into the infinite, and with man the return into God of all creation, the ἐπιστρόφη of Proclus.²⁹

It is indeed difficult to clear such a doctrine of the charge of pantheism,—however Eckhart may protest against such interpretation of his doctrine. But here again, as in another connection,³⁰ we must bear in mind that the intention of a man rests with his conscience; it has nothing to do with his doctrine as expressed,—which is what it is.

Thierry of Freiburg writes against the pantheism of the *Liber de Causis* and the *Elementa Theologica* of Proclus. But he shares that deductive method *à outrance*, which was borrowed from Neo-Platonism, in common with Eckhart and Ulric of Strasburg and Witelo and the whole German group. This leads us to a further characteristic of the trend of thought which we are studying: the

²⁸ *Ibid.*, pp. 382, 458, *passim.*

²⁹ In contrast with the above, the truth of Henry Adams' statement appears, when he says of the mystics of St. Victor in the twelfth century: "The French mystics showed in their mysticism the same French reasonableness; the sense of measure, of logic, of science; the allegiance to form; the transparency of thought, which the French mind has always shown on its surface like a shell of nacre." *Op. cit.*, p. 304.

³⁰ See above, p. 167.

philosophy of the Germans in the thirteenth century lacks the moderation and equilibrium which is so beautiful a triumph of scholastic philosophy. In proof of this one example will suffice. Thus, scholastic method starts with facts, with observation of the senses and the testimony of consciousness, in order to discover the rôle of general notions and the operation of principles or laws. It is only after this work of analysis that it authorizes its deduction of all reality as dependent on God.[31] The German Neo-Platonism of the thirteenth century takes the opposite course. It does not begin with facts. It begins with the notion of God, or even with that of being in general, and traces out the emanation of all, step by step. Here again Eckhart represents best the spirit of the group. No person takes more delight than he in the majestic tranquillity and impenetrable mystery of the Divinity; in the obscure and fathomless abyss of its reality; in the effusion of the soul, passive and stripped of self, in that ocean of reality. Eckhart does not pause, as does Bonaventure, to mark the lower stages of the journey of the soul to God; his thought leaps to God Himself, towards the Being which alone is of interest to him. Thus, in the speculation of Eckhart we have the prototype of that strain of metaphysics which hurls speculation with dizzy speed into the abyss, without imposing on itself the restraint of actual experience.

[31] *Cf.* Ch. IX, vii.

This lack of moderation, which affects the philosophical method of the Germans, affects also each of their metaphysical, psychological, and moral doctrines. Moreover, it is extended by Eckhart to the facts of religious experience and the interpretation of dogma. His scorn for the external act, his exaggeration of the internal aspect of religious experience, the small place which he gives to the authority of Scripture,—all of this prepares the way for the Reformation, to be sure; but it stands in great contrast with the dogmatic and mystical and moral theology of Thomas of Aquin.

To sum up. Endowment of the personal worth of the individual with metaphysical support; devotion to clear ideas and their correct expression; moderation in doctrine and observance of a just mean between extremes; the combination of experience and deduction,—these are the characteristics, or, if you will, the tendencies, of the scholastic philosophy as it was elaborated by Neo-Latins and Anglo-Celts. But, in the Neo-Platonic group of German thinkers in the thirteenth century, all of this is replaced by very different characteristics,—fascination for monism and pantheism; mystic communion of the soul with Deity; craving for extreme deduction; predilection for the study of Being, and of its descending steps; aversion to clarified intellectualism; delight in examples and metaphors, which are misleading and equivocal; and above all the want of balanced equilibrium, in exaggerating certain aspects and doctrines regardless of all else.

CHAPTER FOURTEEN

Epilogue

i. Influence of thirteenth century philosophical systems on later thought in the West. ii. Pedagogical value of scholasticism for the history of modern philosophy.

I

The unifying ideas of the thirteenth century had disappeared by the middle of the fourteenth century. As the European states advanced in stability, the spirit of nationalism became increasingly diversified. The University of Paris lost its cosmopolitan character, as a centre of learning, and became simply a national institution. Furthermore, the authority of the Popes declined in the domain of politics. Thus, in the quickened and complicating course of events, certain specific characteristics of the mediaeval civilization passed out of existence.

But the philosophical systems of the Middle Ages had left their imprint on the western minds. The contrasts between the philosophers of Neo-Latin and Anglo-Celtic extraction, on the one hand, and the philosophers within the Germanic group, on the other hand, survived the thirteenth century. Descartes and Locke are much more indebted to scholasticism than is commonly supposed;[1] and the Germans have good reason for regarding Meister Eckhart as the first philosopher in their line.

This takes us back, then to our point of departure. For, it justifies our view of the thirteenth century as the watershed of European genius in its diverging flow.

II

If our reflections in these lectures have been correct, the study of the philosophic systems of the Middle Ages, and of scholasticism in particular, must take on new meaning and value for all those who prize the western mode of thought.

Even as the study of Greek and Latin classics is an indispensable preliminary to our literary culture; and as the study of antique statuary and mediaeval architecture and the painting of the Renaissance possesses inestimable power in forming the minds of our future sculptors, architects, and painters, and conditions the very flight of originality,—just so the study of modern philosophy must lean not alone upon Greek philosophy, but equally on

[1] For recent works on the indebtedness of later thinkers to mediaeval thought, see, for example: E. Gilson, *La liberté chez Descartes et la théologie*, Paris, 1913. E. Krakowski, *Les Sources mediévales de la philosophie de Locke*, Paris, 1915—P. Ramsay, *Les doctrines mediévales chez Jean Donne, le poète-métaphysicien d'Angleterre*, Oxford, 1916.

the conceptions of the world and of life which formed the temperaments of our very own ancestors. We are closer to them than we are to the Greeks; and, in the light of history, the study of their philosophy appears as a necessary stage in our philosophical education.[2] Thus, it seems contrary to all reason to ignore that age, as has hitherto been done all too often. We must really "traverse the scholastic philosophy of the Middle Ages," if we are to criticize or to go beyond it.

[2] My friend and colleague, Professor Horace C. Longwell of Princeton University has worked out these ideas in detail, independently and some years ago; he intends to publish the paper.

SELECTED BIBLIOGRAPHY

ADAMS, H. Mont St. Michel and Chartres, Boston, 1913.
ALTAMIRA, R. Historia de España y de la civilisacion española, tom. I, Madrid, 1913.
ASHLEY, W. J. An Introduction to English Economic History and Theory, Part I, (The Middle Ages), London, 1906.
BAEUMKER-BEITRAGE. Beiträge zur Geschichte der Philosophie des Mittelalters, Münster, 1891 ff.
BAEUMKER, C. Witelo. Ein Philosoph und Naturforscher des XIII'ten Jahrhunderts, Baümker-Beiträge, Bd. III, Heft 2, Münster, 1908.
——————. Die Christliche Philosophie des Mittelalters, Leipzig, 1913 (in Die Kultur der Gegenwart, Teil I, Abt. v, 2'te Ausg., Teubner).
——————. Der Platonismus im Mittelalter. Königl. Akad. d. Wissenschaften, München, 1916, pp. 49.
BARKER, E. Unity in the Middle Ages, Oxford, 1915, See Marvin, F. S.
BAUR, L. Dominicus Gundissalinus, De Divisione Philosophiae, Baümker-Beiträge, Bd. IV, H. 2-3, Münster, 1903.
BEDIER, J. Les légendes épiques. Recherches sur la formation des Chansons de Geste, Paris, 1909-13.
BERLIERE, DOM. L'ordre monastique des origines au XII° s. Paris, 1921.
BRANTS, V. Les théories économiques aux XIII° et XIV° Siècles, Louvain, 1895.
BREHIER, L. L'art chrétien. Son développement iconographique des origines à nos jours, Paris, 1918.
BRYCE, J. The Holy Roman Empire, London, 1904.

BUDINSZKY. Die Universität Paris und die Fremden an derselben im Mittelalter, Berlin, 1876.

CARLYLE, A. J. and R. W. A History of Mediaeval Political Theory in the West, Vol. II (The Political Theory of the Roman Lawyers and the Canonists from the Xth to the XIIIth Century), New York, 1909; Vol. III (Political Theory from the Xth to the XIIIth Century), New York, 1916.

CARLYLE, A. J. Progress in the Middle Ages, Oxford, 1916, See Marvin, F. S.

CLERVAL, A. Les écoles de Chartres au moyen âge du V'e au XVI'e s., Chartres, 1895 (Mémoires de la Société Archéologique d' Eure et Loir, XI).

CRAM, R. A. The substance of Gothic, Boston, 1915.

DANTE, A. De Monarchia, edited with translation and notes by A. Henry, Boston, 1904.

—————. The Divine Comedy, English translation by H. Johnson, New Haven, Yale University Press, 1916.

DENIFLE, H. (and CHATELAIN). Chartularium Universitatis Parisiensis, Vol. I-II, Paris, 1889-1891.

DENIFLE, H. Die Universitäten des Mittelalters bis 1400, Berlin, 1885.

—————. Meister Eckehart's Lateinische Schriften (in Archiv für Litteratur und Kirchengeschichte des Mittelalters, 1886).

DE POORTER, M. Le traité Eruditio regum et principum de Guibert de Tournai, in Les Philosophes Belges, Louvain, Tome IX, 1914.

DE WULF, M. Histoire de la philosophie médiévale, 4'e ed., Louvain, 1912.

—————. History of Mediaeval Philosophy, English translation by P. Coffey (from 2'nd French ed.) as 3rd edition of the above, London, Longmans, 1909.

—————. Le traité des formes de Gilles de Lessines, Louvain, 1901.

De Wulf, M. Etudes sur la vie les oeuvres, et l'influence de Godefroid de Fontaines, Louvain, 1904.
———. Etudes sur Henri de Gand, Bruxelles, 1895.
———. Scholasticism Old and New, English translation by P. Coffey, Dublin, 1907.
———. Histoire de la philosophie en Belgique, Louvain, 1910.
———. Mediaeval Philosophy, illustrated from the System of Thomas Aquinas, Harvard University Press, 1922.
Duhem, P. Le système du monde. Histoire des doctrines cosmologiques de Platon à Copernic, Vol. II-IV, Paris, 1914-'16.
Enlart, C. Manuel d' archéologie française depuis les temps mérovingiens jusqu' á la renaisssance, Vol. I-III, Paris, 1902-16.
Figgis, J. N. The divine Right of Kings, Cambridge, 1914. (First three Chapters.)
Geyer, B. Abaelards unedierte philosophische Werke, Baümker-Beiträge, Bd. XXI, H. 1, Münster, 1919.
———. Die Stellung Abaelards in der Universalienfrage nach neuen handschriftlichen Texten, Baümker-Beiträge, Supplementband, pp. 101-127, Münster, 1913.
von Gierke, O. Die Staats-und Korporationslehre des Altertums und des Mittelalters und ihre Aufnahme in Deutschland. (Bd. III of Das Deutsche Genossenschaft), Berlin, 1881.
———. Political Theories of the Middle Ages, English translation by F. W. Maitland, Cambridge, 1900 (Part of preceding work).
Gillet, L. Histoire artistique des ordres mendiants, Paris, 1912.
Gilson, E. La liberté chez Descartes et la théologie, Paris, Alcan, 1913.
———. Le Thomisme. Introduction au système de Thomas d'Aquin, Strasbourg, 1920.

GRABMANN, M. Die Geschichte der scholastischen Methode (nach den gedruckten und ungedruckten Quellen dargestellt), Bd. I-II, Freiburg Br., 1909-11.

—————. Forschungen über die lateinischen Aristoteles übersetzungen des XIII. Jahrhunderts, Baümker-Beiträge, Bd. XVII, H. 5-6, Münster, 1916.

HAUVETTE. Dante. Introduction à l'étude de la Divine Comédie, Paris, 1911.

HARRISON, F. The Meaning of History, Ch. V (A Survey of the Thirteenth Century), New York, 1904.

HAVET. Lettres de Gerbert, 983-997. Paris, 1889.

HENRICUS GANDAVENSIS. Summa Theologica, Art. I-IV.

JANET, P. Histoire de la science politique dans ses rapports avec la morale, tom. I, Paris, 1887.

JENKS, E. Law and politics in the Middle Ages. London, 1913.

JOHANNES SARESBURIENSIS. Polycraticus, ed. Webb, 2 vol., Oxford, 1909.

KREBS, E. Meister Dietrich (Theodoricus Teutonicus de Vriberg), sein Leben, seine Werke, seine Wissenschaft, Baümker-Beiträge, Bd. V, H. 5-6, Münster, 1906.

—————. Le traité de ente et essentia de Thierry de Fribourg, in Revue Néo-Scolastique de Philosophie, 1911, pp. 519-536.

KURTH, G. Les origines de la civilisation moderne. Bruxelles, 1903.

LAMPRECHT, K. Deutsche Geschichte, Bde II-III, Berlin, 1892-3.

LANGLOIS, C. La vie en France au moyen âge d'après quelques moralistes du temps.

—————. La société française au XIII'e s. d'après dix romans d'aventure.

—————. La connaissance de la nature et du monde au moyen âge d'après quelques écrits français á l'usage des laics, Paris, 1911.

LEMAIRE, R. La logique de l'art gothique. Revue Néoscolastique de Philosophie XVII, p. 234.

LUCHAIRE, A. Histoire des institutions monarchiques de la France sous les premiers Capétiens (987-1180), tom. I, Paris, 1891.

—————. Louis VII, Philippe-Auguste, Louis VIII, tom. III, Histoire de France, Paris, Lavisse, 1902.

MAITRE, L. Les écoles épiscopales et monacales de l'occident depuis Charlemagne jusqu' á Philippe-Auguste, Paris, 1866.

MALE, E. L'art religieux du XIII'e s. en France, Etude sur l'iconographie du moyen âge et sur ses sources d' inspiration, Paris, 1910.

—————. L'art allemand et l'art français du moyen âge, Paris, 1917.

MANDONNET, P. Siger de Brabant et l'averroisme latin au XIIIme siècle, in Les Philosophes Belges, Louvain, Tome VI (Etude critique), 1911, tome VII (Textes inédites), 1908.

MARVIN, F. S. The Living Past. A Sketch of Western Progress. Oxford, 1913.

—————. The Unity of Western Civilization, Essays edited by, Ch. IV (Unity in the Middle Ages) by E. Barker, Oxford, 1915.

—————. Progress and History, Essays edited by, Ch. IV (Progress in the Middle Ages) by A. J. Carlyle, Oxford, 1916.

MICHAEL, Geschichte des deutschen Volkes seit dem XIII'ten Jahrhundert bis zum Ausgang des Mittelalters, Bd. II, Freiburg Br., 1899.

PAETOW, L. J. The Battle of the Seven Arts, a French Poem by Henri d'Andéli, Berkeley, University of California Press, 1914.

PFEIFFER, F. Deutsche Mystiker des vierzehnten Jahrhunderts. Meister Eckhart. Bd. II, Leipzig, 1857.

PICAVET, F. Essais sur l'histoire générale et comparée des théologies et des philosophies médiévales, Paris, 1913.

POOLE, R. L. Illustrations of the History of Mediaeval Thought and Learning, London, 2d ed. 1920.

RASHDALL, H. The Universities of Europe in the Middle Ages, Vol. I-III, Oxford, 1895.

REYNAUD, L. Les origines de l'influence française en Allemagne. Etude sur l'histoire comparée de la civilisation en France et en Allemagne pendant la période precourtoise (950-1150). Tome I (L'offensive politique et sociale de la France), Paris, 1913.

ROCQUAIN. La papauté au moyen âge, Paris, 1881.

——. La cour de Rome et l'esprit de réforme avant Luther. Tome I (La théocratie, apogée du pouvoir pontifical), Paris, 1893.

ROUSSELOT, P. L'intellectualisme de Saint Thomas, Paris, 1908.

SAINTSBURY, G. Periods of European Literature, Vol. II (The Flourishing of Romance and the Rise of Allegory), London, 1897.

SANDYS, J. S. English Scholars of Paris and Franciscans of Oxford, in The Cambridge History of English Literature, Vol. I, Cambridge.

SMITH, A. L. Church and State in the Middle Ages, Oxford, 1913.

STEINHAUSEN, Geschichte der deutschen Kultur, Bd. I, Leipzig, 1913.

TAYLOR, H. O. The Mediaeval Mind, 2 vol., 3'rd ed., New York, 1919.

THOMAS AQUINAS. Summa Theologica, English translation by Fathers of the English Dominican Province, London, 1911 ff. See especially Pars I'a, QQ. 75-90 (Theory of Knowledge); Pars I'a 2'ae, QQ. 1-25 (Ethics); and QQ. 90-97 (Law); Pars 2'a 2'ae, QQ. 57-61 (Justice).

Thomas Aquinas. Summa contra Gentiles. Partly translated by S. Rickaby under the title: of God and His Creatures, London, 1905.
———. Commentaria in Ethicorum lib. 10.
———. Commentaria in Politicorum lib.
———. De anima; de regimine principum; de unitate intellectus contra averroistas.
Thurot, C. De l'organisation de l'enseignement dans l'université de Paris, Paris, 1850.
Traill. Social England. A record of the progress of the people. Vol. I-II. London, 1901.
Tribbechovius, A. De doctoribus scolasticis et corrupta per eos divinarum humanarumque rerum scientia, Jena, 1719.
Troeltsch, E. Die Sociallehren der christlichen Kirchen und Gruppen. Tubingen 1912. Ch. II, Der mittelalterliche Katholicismus.
Truc, G. Le retour à la scolastique, Paris, 1920.
Ueberweg-Baumgartner. Grundriss der Geschichte der Philosophie II. Die mittlere oder die patristische und scholastische Zeit, 10'te Aufg, Berlin, 1915.
Vacandard, E. Vie de St. Bernard, Abbé de Clairvaux, 2 vol., 3'e ed., Paris, 1902.
Walsh, J. The Thirteenth Greatest of Centuries, New York, 1912.
Webb, C. J. Studies in the History of Natural Theology, Oxford, 1915.
Wicksteed, Ph. H. The Reactions between Dogma and Philosophy illustrated from the works of S. Thomas Aquinas, London, 1920.
Zeiller, L'idée de l'Etat dans St. Thomas d'Aquin, Paris, 1910.

BY THE SAME AUTHOR

Histoire de la Philosophie scolastique dans les Pays-Bas et la Principauté de Liége (Louvain, et Alcan, Paris, 1895). Mém. couronné par l'Académie de Belgique, 404 p. Epuisé.

**Etudes sur Henri de Gand* (Louvain, et Alcan, Paris, 1895). Extrait du précédent. Prix: 2.50 fr.

**Le traité des formes de Gilles de Lessines.* (Texte inédit et étude.) 1901. xvi, 122, 108 p., gr. in-jésus, édit. de luxe.

Introduction à la philosophie néo-scolastique. 1904. xvi, 350 pages. Epuisé.

Scholasticism old and new. Translated by P. Corey, (Dublin, 1907), 328 pages.

**Etude sur la vie, les oeuvres et l'influence de Godefroid de Fontaines* (Mémoire couronné par l'Académie de Belgique). 1904.

**Les quatre premiers quodlibets de G. de Fontaines* (en collaborat. avec A. Pelzer). 364 pages, grand in-jésus. Edit. de luxe.

**Histoire de la Philosophie en Belgique.* (Louvain, et Alcan, Paris, 1910) xii, 378 p., 18 gravures hors texte.

**Histoire de la Philosophie médiévale* (Louvain, 1912).

**Les Quodlibets V-VII de Godefroid de Fontaines.* (Textes inédits). En collaboration avec J. Hoffmans). (Louvain, 1914).

**L'oeuvre d'art et la Beauté;* Conférences philosophiques faites à Poitiers (Louvain, 1920).

Mediaeval Philosophy illustrated from the System of Thomas Aquinas (Harvard University Press, 1922).

* For books so marked apply at Institut de Philosophie, 1 rue des flamands, Louvain, Belgium.

INDEX OF NAMES*

Abaelard, 1, 32, 40, 44, 48, 52, 53; Glossulae super Porphyrium, 58, 59; apologetic method of, 162; autobiography of, 140; and Heloise, 35; on revelation, 164; on universals, 58-59.
Absalon of St. Victor, 52.
Accursius, 107.
Adam of St. Victor, 35.
Adams, Henry, 35, 104, 210, 295.
Adelard of Bath, 40, 41, 47, 57, 142, 282.
Agricola, 7.
Alan of Lille, 40, 52, 142, 174.
Alberic of Rheims, 45.
Albert the Great, 1, 73, 76, 173, 283, 290.
Alcher of Clairvaux, 143.
Alexander III (Rolando Bandinelli), 44, 121.
Alexander of Hales, 1, 64, 73, 76, 82, 109, 130, 166, 282.
Alexander Neckham, 42.
Alfarabi, 79.
Alfred Anglicus (of Sereschel), 73, 289.
Alphandéry, P., 288.
Alphonso, X, 101.
Altamira, R., 102.
Anselm of Canterbury, 1, 3, 44, 48, 52, 141, 164.
Anselm of Laon, 40, 85.
Ampère, 137.
Antolin, 41.
Antoninus of Florence, 122.
Aristotle, 2, 11, 97 sq., 128, 141, 153 sq., 181, 212, 280, de Anima, 78; Metaphysics, 78, 139; Organon, 45, 47, 70; Physics, 78; Politics, 220 sq., 249, 251, 256; actuality and potentiality, 200 sq., astronomy, 112; and city state, 227 sq., definition of good, 224, divisions of philosophy, in, 91; on slavery, 278; on state and society, 227 sqq., substance, 196.
Augustine (St.), 11, 141, 251, 278; De Civitate Dei, 115, sq., 126; Confessions, 140; on society, 227.
Augustus, 127.
Averroes, 79, 84, 139, 278, 288.
Avicebron, 79, 195.
Avicenna, 79, 174, 278.

Bacon, Francis, 3.
Bacon, Roger, 1, 64, 73, 77, 83, 129; Opus Majus, 139; apologetics of, 164, 284; astrology of, 113; and Averroism, 285, character of, 78, and natural science, 284.
Baker, E., 104.
Baümker's-Beiträge, 58, 128, 184, 189, 222, 283, 292.
Baldus, 232.
Bandinelli Rolando, see Alexander III.
Barker, E., 237.
Bartholomeus Anglicus, 106.
Baur, L., 96, 128.
Baumgartner, M., 150.
Bede the Venerable, 141.
Benedict (St.), 24 sq., 147.

* I want to express my thanks to my pupil, Mr. J. L. Zimmerman, who made this index.

INDEX OF NAMES

Bernard of Auvergne, 74.
Bernard of Chartres, 45.
Bernard (St.), 31, 35.
Berthold of Mosburg, 290 sq.
Binder, 155.
Boethius, 57, 78, 99.
Boethius the Dacian, 73.
Bonaventure, 1, 64, 73, 82 sq., 109, 129 sq., 282, 296.
Bourget, Paul, 232.
Bradwardine, Thomas, 174.
Bréhier, L., 49.
Brunetière, 176.
Brunschvigg, 140.
Buridan, John, 186.
Burleigh, Walter, 73.
Busse, 155.

Caesar of Heisterbach, 156.
Can Grande della Scala, 158.
Carlyle, A. J., 56, 263.
Catherine of Pisa, 154.
Cavalcante, Guido, 174.
Chambon, F., 161.
Charlemagne, 22, 117, 119, 121 sq.
Chatelain (see Denifle-Chatelain).
Chaucer, 37, 174.
Cicero, 47, 146.
Clerval, 47.
Comte, Auguste, 98, 127.
Constantine of Carthage, 44.

Dante, 114, 121 sq.; Divine Comedy, 9, 105 sq., 137, 166, 175, 190; Epistolae, 158; Inferno, 94; Paradiso, 190; de Monarchia, 115 sqq., 129, 146, 174, 227 sq., 232, 242; on Aristotle, 97; on beauty, 94; and Can Grande della Scala, 158; on the divisions of philosophy, 129; on peace, 119; principle of parsimony in, 110; theory of the state of, 115 sqq., 227, 232, 248; on tyranny, 248; on war, 228.
d'Andéli, Henri, 174.
Denifle, 65, 161, 182, 291 sq.
Denifle-Chatelain, 67, 169, 287.

de Meung, Jean, 190.
De Poorter, A., 222.
Descartes, 11, 154, 198, 299.
Dionysius the Areopagite, 77.
Dominic, (St.), 74
Donatus, 46, 93.
Dover, Richard, 42.
Duhem, P., 113.
Duns Scotus, 1, 73, 82 sq., 109 sq., 129 sq., 144, 282, 285. Grammatica Speculativa, 93; on freedom, 184; the good and martyrdom, 185; intuition in, 183; on philosophy and theology, 164; principle of parsimony in, 110; avoids psychological determinism, 186.
Dyroff, A., 291.

Eckhart (Meister), 182, 290 sqq.; 293 sqq.; 296 sqq.
Edward I, 100, 102, 107, 157.
Eleanor of Aquitaine, 20.
Endres, J. A., 222.
Engelbert of Volkersdorf, 239.
Etienne of Tournai, 33.
Euclid, 47, 146.

Fénelon, 8.
Ferdinand III, 100, 102.
Ferdinand of Castile, 157.
Fra Angelico, 76.
Francis (St.), 9, 11, 64, 74 sq., 137.
Frederic Barbarossa, 103, 121.
Frederic II, 100, 103, 122, 157, 288.
Fulbert, 45.

Gauthier of Bruges, 73.
Gauthier of Mortagne, 45.
Gerard of Abbeville, 282.
Gerbert, 48.
Geyer, B., 58 sq.
Gierke, O. (von) 120, 231 sq., 239, 250.
Gilbert de la Porrée, 32, 41, 52 sq., 58 sq., 175, 182.
Gilbert of Tournai, 222.
Gilles of Lessines, 113.
Gilles of Rome, 73, 222.

INDEX OF NAMES

Gillet, 84.
Gilson, E., 299.
Giotto, 158.
Giuliani, G., 158.
Godfrey of Fontaines, 71 sqq., 96, 186, 282.
Goethe, 8 sq.
Gozzoli, 84.
Grabmann, M., 49, 51, 58, 79, 128, 163, 189, 221.
Gratian, 107, 223.
Gregory VII (Hildebrand) 16, 29, 121, 123.
Grosseteste, Robert, 74, 129, 151, 290.
Gui of Hainaut, Count, 129.
Gundissalinus, Dominicus, 96, 128, 143, 151.

Harrison, F., 101.
Haskins, C. H., 42, 79.
Heloise, 35.
Henry II, 20 sq., 132.
Henry IV, 29 sq., 121.
Henry Bate of Malines, 129.
Henry of Ghent, 73, 86, 130, 144, 152, 165 sq., 168, 282.
Herrad of Landsberg, 49.
Hobbes, 3.
Horace, 47.
Hugh of Cluny, 30.
Hugh II, of Lusignan, 221.
Hugh of Noyers, 32.
Hugo of St. Victor, 1, 40, 49, 52 sq., 127, 151, 162.
Hume, 136.
Huxley, 203.

Innocent III, 33, 44, 103, 121 sqq.
Innocent IV, 114, 119, 231.
Irnerius of Bologna, 47, 232.
Isaac of Stella, 42.
Isidore of Seville, 90, 141.

Jacopo de Voragine, 106.
James I (of Aragon) 107.
James of Viterbo, 73.
Janet, P., 125.

Johannes Andreae, 119 sq.
John of La Rochelle, 74.
John of Salisbury, 1, 42, 48, 52, 141, 238, 264; Metalogicus, 57; Polycraticus 59 sq., 220, 239, 249; state compared to human body, in, 240; on tyrannicide, 240.
John Scotus Eriugena, 1, 50.

Kant, 154.
Kilwardby, Robert, 73, 128.
Krakowski, 299.
Krebs, E., 293.

Lackland, John, 101, 250.
Lamprecht, 30, 37.
Lanfranc, 44.
Langlois, 72.
Leibnitz, 11, 202, 208, 210.
Lippi, Filippino, 84.
Little, A. G., 79.
Locke, 199, 299.
Louis VII, 20, 122, 132.
Louis IX, 35, 100 sqq., 222, 260.
Louis XIV, 127.
Luchaire, A., 20 sq., 33, 101, 157, 261.
Lully, Raymond, 64, 73, 130, 164.

Maitland, F. W., 120.
Mâle, E., 49, 132, 173, 191 sq.
Mandonnet, P., 79, 285, 288.
Manegold of Lautenbach, 220, 263.
Map, Walter, 42.
Marchesi, 79.
Marius Victorinus, 47.
Marvin, F. S., 238.
Mathew of Lorraine, 32.
Maurice of Sully, 33.
Mendenez y Pelayo, 79.
Mentellini, 106.
Mercier, D., 181, 267.
Michael Scot, 73, 128.
Michael of Corbeil, 51.
Migne, 26.
Mill, John Stuart, 150.
Minges, P., 184.
Montesquieu, 8.

Newton, 214.
Nicholas of Autrecourt, 136.
Nicholas of Oresmes, 113.
Nizolius, 7.

Odon of Tournai, 45.
Otloh of St. Emmeram, 43, 51.
Otto I, 29.
Otto III, 43.
Otto of Freising, 43.

Pascal, 140.
Peckham, John, 77.
Pelzer, A., 79, 110, 143.
Peter Damien, 51 sq.
Peter Lombard, 44, 52 sq.
Peter of Blois, 42, 51.
Peter of Capua, 44.
Peter of Corbeil, 33.
Peter of Poitiers, 163.
Peter of Spain, 73.
Peter of Tarantaise, 73.
Peter the Venerable, 26, 55, 58.
Petrus Petri, 147.
Pfeiffer, F., 291, 294.
Philip Augustus, 64, 100 sq., 107, 125, 132, 157.
Philip the Fair, 21.
Philo, 162.
Plato, 2, 11, 97 sq., 118, 141, 154, 211, 278, 280.
Plutarch, 239.
Poppo of Stavelot, 24.
Porphyry, 58.
Porter, A. K., 49.
Praepositinus of Cremona, 44.
Priscian, 47, 93.
Proclus, 78, 289, 291, 295.
Ptolemy of Lucques, 244, 250.

Quintilian, 47.

Rabelais, 155.
Radulfus Ardens, 127.
Ramsay, P., 299.
Rashdall, H., 65.
Raymond of Toledo, 81.
Remi of Auxerre, 47.
Reynaud, 24.

Rhabanus Maurus, 90.
Richard of Middleton, 73.
Richard of St. Victor, 40, 42.
Rivalta, Ercole, 174.
Robert of Sorbonne, 161.
Rocquain, 123 sq., 126.
Rose, 79.
Rudolph of Habsburg, 157.

Sandys, 42.
Savigny, 230.
Saintsbury, 37, 176.
Schneider, 283.
Seneca, 47.
Shakespeare, 176 sq.
Siger of Brabant, 1, 73, 129, 285, 288.
Siger of Courtrai, 93, 282.
Simon of Bucy, 72.
Simon of Montfort, 157.
Spencer, Herbert, 98, 127.
Stadler, H. J., 283.
Steinhausen, 37, 43.
Stephen Langton, 73.
Stephen of Tournai, 51.
Sylvester, II.

Taine, 97, 198.
Taylor, H. O., 171, 173.
Tennyson, 240.
Theodoric of Chartres, 41.
Thierry of Chartres, 45, 48.
Thierry of Freiburg, 1, 73, 290 sqq., 295.
Thomas Aquinas (St.), 1, 3, 64, 73, 81 sqq., 109, 114, 130, 144 sq., 155, 195, 210, 242, 256, 261, 272, sqq., 278, 282, 285, and passim. De Anima, 187, 267; De Coelo, 113; Contra Gentiles, 86, 110, 143, 166, 256; Ethica Nichom., 94, 193, 226, 234, 245 sq.; Metaphysica, 91, 139; Perihermeneias 182; In Politic. comm., 249, 256; de Regimine Principum, 221, 227 sq., 244 sqq., 248, 250, 252, 254; de unitate intellectus, 140, de veritate, 218; aesthetics of, 187 sq., artes liberales and artes mechan-

icae, 95; astronomy, 112 sq., 269; on authority, 142; and Meister Eckhart, 297; epistemology, 182 sqq., ethics, 93 sq., on eternity of the world, 169; God, 216 sqq., law in, 129, 236, 248 sqq., 243, 271 sq., and Leibnitz, 202; logic, 93; and Monte Cassino, 44; on music, 168; on order, 193; political philosophy, 93, 242 sqq., theory of progress, 266 sqq., 271 sq., psychology, 187 sq., and science, 86, 96, 187, social philosophy, 221 sqq., on sovereignty, 244, 249, 254; on the soul, 212; on substance, 204; theology and philosophy, 95, 152 sq., on war, 262; divisions of philosophy, 91; theory of justice, 247 sqq., on tyrannicide, 249.
Thorburn, W. M., 110.
Traini, 84, 154, 287.
Trajan, 239.
Tribbechovius, 155.

Ueberweg-Baumgartner, 150, 291.
Ulric of Strasburg, 73, 290 sq., 295.
Urban, II, 28.

Vacandart, 32.
Vacant, 79.

Vincent of Beauvais, 74, 90, 106.
Virgil, 47, 190.
Vives, L., 7.

Walter of Mortagne, 57.
Walter of St. Victor, 52.
William of Aquitaine, 24.
William of Auvergne, 64, 74, 82, 143, 282.
William of Auxerre, 74.
William of Champeaux, 40 sq., 45, 65.
William of Conches, 41.
William of Meliton, 73.
William of Mende, 106, 158, 190.
William of Moerbeke, 220, 251, 290.
William of Occam, 1, 3, 73, 110, 282.
William of St. Amour, 74.
William the Conqueror, 21.
Witelo, 74, 290 sq., 295.
Wolff, 91.
Wüstenfeld, F., 79.

Ximines, Rodriguez (Cardinal), 73, 81.

Zeiller, 261.
Zurbaran, 84.